Community Projects as Social Activism

Community Projects as Social Activism

From Direct Action to Direct Services

Benjamin Shepard
New York City College of Technology,
City University of New York

Foreword by Steve Burghardt

Los Angeles | London | New Delhi
Singapore | Washington DC

Los Angeles | London | New Delhi
Singapore | Washington DC

FOR INFORMATION:

SAGE Publications, Inc.
2455 Teller Road
Thousand Oaks, California 91320
E-mail: order@sagepub.com

SAGE Publications Ltd.
1 Oliver's Yard
55 City Road
London EC1Y 1SP
United Kingdom

SAGE Publications India Pvt. Ltd.
B 1/I 1 Mohan Cooperative Industrial Area
Mathura Road, New Delhi 110 044
India

SAGE Publications Asia-Pacific Pte. Ltd.
3 Church Street
#10-04 Samsung Hub
Singapore 049483

Acquisitions Editor: Kassie Graves
Digital Content Editor: Lauren Habib
Editorial Assistant: Carrie Baarns
Production Editor: Jane Haenel
Copy Editor: Kristin Bergstad
Typesetter: C&M Digitals (P) Ltd.
Proofreader: Rae-Ann Goodwin
Indexer: Michael Ferreira
Cover Designer: Anthony Paular
Marketing Manager: Shari Countryman

Printed in the United States of America

Library of Congress Cataloging-in-Publication Data

Shepard, Benjamin, 1969–

Community practice as social activism : from direct action to direct services / Benjamin Shepard, New York City College of Technology, City University of New York. — First Edition.

pages cm
Includes bibliographical references and index.

ISBN 978-1-4129-6426-5 (pbk.)

1. Social movements—United States. 2. Community-based social services—United States. 3. Political participation—United States. I. Title.

HM881.S53193 2014
361.8—dc23   2014004080

This book is printed on acid-free paper.

14 15 16 17 18 10 9 8 7 6 5 4 3 2 1

Brief Contents

Detailed Contents

Foreword

In a society with a dominant culture that prizes material comfort, celebrity and status through acquisition (*lux* coffee grinders, Manolo Blanick shoes, power), trying to understand why people do community organizing can be a puzzling task leading to a mix of disbelief and condescension. "Oh, you do *that?* How nice that someone does those things . . . " For some, it's cute to be a community organizer in your twenties—*how brave, how naïve!* By your thirties, you're immature—*isn't it time to get serious?* In your forties and fifties, you've got a character disorder. If you make it to your sixties, of course, you get to be cute all over again. *How brave, how demented!*

In reality, condescension is the precarious perch for the frightened and alone, those who underneath the fleeting pleasure of their latest purchase keep wondering why they're unfulfilled and—strangely, oddly, compellingly—unhappy. They might be better off if they paused in their search for the latest trend and took a gander inside the pages of Benjamin Shepard's *Community Projects as Social Activism: From Direct Action to Direct Services*. What Benjamin has done is special: He's provided a set of rich case studies—portraits—of organizers and why they do the uphill work of social justice organizing. It's the rare book that takes you inside campaigns that, while steeped in the pain and marginality of fighting oppression, locates the joy, happiness, and love of people finding common cause and common purpose together to make a better world. As you'll read here, people trade in friendship and support, not commodities and cash. They grow rich in the security of their joint purpose and the trust that others fighting the same fight will be there for them, too.

Read carefully, you see that social action has a therapeutic cleansing through the work itself. It takes people out of the world of self-involvement and replaces it with a self involved with lots of other "selves" in creating a more just world together. What a relief! Equally important, Shepard provides ample evidence of how social workers who organize can move from "case to cause" (when private troubles of individuals, whether AIDS, homelessness, or environmental degradation become public issues requiring collective action) and then back to "case" again, this time through better services that are framed within a social justice paradigm rather than in distinction from it.

After you finish Shepard's book, you may want to make your part of the world a better place: Join a social movement of your choice. Get involved with the collective and the communal. Dig in a community garden. Join a food bank. Show up at the next march against racism or homophobia. As Benjamin has done here, give added texture and provide voice as to what animates those who organize. It's not about stuff. It's not about status. It's about love.

Steve Burghardt
Silberman School of Social Work
Hunter College, City University of New York

Acknowledgments

Books are not written as much as they are the product of years of collective experience, collaboration, stories, conversations, and in this case engagements between friends and colleagues, organizers, activists, teachers, students, mentors, and others connecting worlds and community projects. Much of this story began when I was assigned to teach community projects at Cal State Long Beach. There, John Oliver engaged me in countless conversations about teaching organizing. Between these chats, class preparations, and class time with students, the ideas and experiences grew into a book proposal written for Kassie Graves at SAGE. The project would not have happened if not for Graves's patient support over the seven years from initial proposal through completion and polishing of the manuscript. Others, such as Steve Burkhart, offered constructive feedback and encouragement along the way. Ian Landau helped me transcribe and edit many of the raw interviews used as the basis for this story. And Peter Labella helped edit and polish the prose. The Honorable Judith Kaye deserves great thanks for connecting me with the Red Hook Community Court. Steve Duncombe, James Tracy, and Ron Hayduk offered constructive advice on ways to move the project forward. And Brennan Cavanaugh, Peter Meitzler, Allan Clear, and other activists and photographers offered me permissions to use their wonderful photographs.

Yet, there would not be a story of community projects as social activism if it were not for a generation of organizers who linked a theory of change with a model of practice. Countless activists sat for interviews before and during doctoral research. Their ideas form the basis for this research: Panama Alba, Mark Andersen, Greg Berman, Kate Barnhart, Jeane Bergman, Jay Blotcher, L. M. Bogad, Andrew Boyd, Brendon Cavanaugh, Arthur Brazier, David Crane, Bill DiPaula, Tim Doody, William Etundi, Donald Grove, Ron Hayduk, Jenny Heinz, Susan Howard, Keegan, Bob Kohler, Kate Crane, Bonfire Madigan, Steve Quester, Karen Ramspacher, Matthew Roth, Ginny Schubert, John Sellers, Eustacia Smith, David Solnit, Dean Spade, Starhawk, James Tracy, Andy Velez, Randy Wicker, L. J. Wood, Susan Wright. This book would not be possible without their support for these efforts. The research on AIDS, gardens, and public space activism would not have been possible without the support of community groups such as Time's Up!, Occupy, and ACT UP!

I would like to thank all the activists involved with these communities, including two of the youngest garden supporters in New York City, Dodi and Scarlett Shepard, both of whom have spent years and years of weekend afternoons taking part in garden work days, playing and hanging out in this public commons of our own imagination and creation.

The work was made possible by the generous support of a PSC-CUNY 38 University Committee on Research Award, as well as the support of research archives, including the ACT UP Oral History Project.

And finally, early pieces of the story were presented at annual conferences of the Association of Humanist Sociology, the Mid Atlantic Consortium of Human Services, and the National Organization of Human Services. Related journals, including *Humanity and Society, Working USA, Socialism and Democracy, Reflections: Narratives of Professional Helping, Interface Journal, Social Justice in Context,* as well as the Team Colors' book *In the Middle of a Whirlwind: Movement, Movements, and Contemporary Radical Currents in the United States,* and the Council for Standards in Human Services Education Monograph, *Best Practices in Human Services,* featured early excerpts. The author gratefully acknowledges the work of the editors and these books and journals and their permission to republish this material.

Over the years, this book's framework has become the basis for my community organizing classes. Thanks to the City University of New York Human Services Department faculty and students for supporting this work, while furthering the links between campus and community projects.

But most of all, thanks to Caroline for supporting me and the project through all the years and moves, ups and downs, ebbs and flows of history, time, coasts, social change, and date nights.

About the Author

By day, **Benjamin Shepard**, PhD, LMSW, works as an Associate Professor of Human Services at City Tech/CUNY. By night, he battles to keep New York from becoming a giant shopping mall. To this end, he has done organizing work with the AIDS Coalition to Unleash Power (ACT UP), SexPanic!, Reclaim the Streets, Time's UP Environmental Organization, the Clandestine Rebel Clown Army, Absurd Response, CitiWide Harm Reduction, Housing Works, More Gardens Coalition, Right of Way, Public Space Party, and Occupy Wall Street.

He is also the author/editor of five other books: *White Nights and Ascending Shadows: An Oral History of the San Francisco AIDS Epidemic* (1997), *From ACT UP to the WTO: Urban Protest and Community Building in the Era of Globalization* (2002), *Queer Political Performance and Protest* (2009), *The Beach Beneath the Streets: Contesting New York City's Public Spaces* (with Gregory Smithsimon, 2011), and *Play, Creativity, and Social Movements: If I Can't Dance, It's Not My Revolution* (2011).

In 2010, he was named to the Playboy Honor Role as one of 20 professors "who are reinventing the classroom."

A social worker, he has worked in AIDS services/activism for two decades, joining ACT UP Golden Gate in the early 1990s, opening two congregate facilities for people living with HIV/AIDS, serving as deputy director for a syringe exchange program, all while remaining active in efforts to bridge the gap between direct action and direct services. Today, he remains involved in organizing efforts around transportation, HIV/AIDS, labor, public spaces, and environmental policy.

Trained at the University of Chicago School of Social Services Administration, the City University of New York Graduate Center, and the William Alanson White Institute of Psychiatry, Psychoanalysis, and Psychology as well as through collaboration with some of the most powerful organizers and movements of this era, Shepard combines these experiences to frame *Community Projects as Social Activism*.

Part I

Theory, Contexts, and Understandings

On Community Practice

Community Projects as Social Activism is a book about the need for—and the ways to achieve—social organization for a better life. Our world grows ever more populous, new media platforms espouse their ability to connect us socially, and yet many (or most) of us feel a sense of isolation—that we alone are enmeshed in our problems and overcoming them rests only on our own shoulders. The focus of this book is the creation of community, through social organizing in the everyday experience of life. This serves not only to improve our own chances for individual fulfillment and happiness, but is also a way to improve the lives of our communities, and ultimately our world.

Some argue that organizing is about labor movements and material ends—but this is a narrow view. For many, organizing is also about shifting the mechanisms of everyday life, challenging the regimes of the normal. Efforts as diverse as planting a garden, cooking a meal, singing, surfing, or riding bikes together can be seen as forms of social organizing. Each helps us break out of isolation, while cementing new kinds of social relations based on care and affect, rather than work. These approaches

Community gardens, such the El Jardin del Paraiso in the Lower East Side of Manhattan, are ideal spaces for community projects and practices. Neighborhood members converged in the garden for a memorial for legendary gardener Michael Shenker in the fall of 2010. Working with the More Gardens Coalition, Shenker helped fashion the organizing framework advanced throughout this book.

Source: Photo by Brennan Cavanaugh

to community building serve as a tonic for a world of people bowling alone, a place where alienating social relations, management, and social controls often dominate (Ollman, 1977; Putnam, 2000). Community organizing, as we will see, encompasses a very broad range of possibilities. Inviting friends over for a dinner party, meeting with a group in a church basement, organizing a group bike-ride, an all-women's surf afternoon at a local beach, or a walk in the park with friends—each of these endeavors involves some form of community organizing (CO). Adding in a commitment to improving the world around us—mixing community projects and social organizing— we can take a more active approach to our lives, striking a blow against the despair and isolation that can overwhelm us. Rather than wait for the government to address our problems and inevitably feeling let down, working together in community helps us feel more connected and proactive, while at the same time helping others.

Let me cite a personal example. Recently I participated in the "Occupy Sandy" relief efforts after Superstorm Sandy hit the East Coast. Occupy Sandy organized relief hubs all over the city, with neighbors offering each other food, assistance, and mutual aid. "We must take care of each other or die" was one slogan of the movement. "Mutual Aid, Not Charity" was another. People all over the city took part in the relief efforts, bringing food, offering sweat equity. My group, Time's UP!, brought bicycles to help transport food and supplies from one part of the city to the other when the subways and roads broke down. Before one of our relief rides, we joked, groaned, moaned, hooked trailers up to our bikes and set out for Clinton Avenue where Occupy Sandy collaborated with the Church of St. Luke and St. Matthew. Riding over, we were greeted by people on the street and welcomed warmly as we arrived to pick up more supplies. Signs all over the church highlighted the importance of mutual aid and of gestures of concern. However limited these gestures

A well-organized Occupy Sandy relief station.

Source: Photo by author

might be, they speak to a greater point: There is very little point in letting what we cannot do prevent us from doing what we can. The mutual aid of Occupy Sandy points to a model of practice based on affect and care, not just contracted services.

Helping to break down barriers of isolation by creating a more community-based activism has other benefits as well. Those who live in isolation from community have less reason to stop themselves from doing shameful things. Shortly after the storm there was another crisis, the shooting rampage at Sandy Hook Elementary School in Connecticut. A great hue and cry arose in the aftermath of the tragedy, with some arguing for stricter gun control, while others felt that the issue was a failure of the mental health system.

This author at an Occupy Sandy relief distribution center at Beach 21 inside of St. Camillus Parish shortly after the storm.

Source: Photo provided with permission by Barbara Ross

Ideally, effective community practice can help engender systematic change that draws from many different possibilities. At its best, CO is a way to understand social work practice as an approach to coping with social issues large and small. After all, most social work takes shape through basic steps involving (1) engagement, (2) assessment, (3) intervention, and (4) evaluation. This includes forms of micro practice such as addressing the basic needs of individuals, mezzo practice when leadership skills are developed, and macro practice when used to organize communities and groups. All are needed to create change on small scales and large. Integrating each level represents a dynamic form of practice (Alerman, Collin, & Jewell, 2011). The subtitle of this book, *From Direct Action to Direct Services*, speaks to this aspiration. It emphasizes the importance of a do-it-yourself approach liberated from bureaucratic restrictions.

In the years before a community organizer was elected president of the United States, countless observers suggested that community organizing was a method whose best days were behind it (Sites, 2003). Yet for many people, such organizing remains a vital tool, a means to gain power and effect social change. "Organize— don't agonize" helps explain the work of activists across the country. Sadly, many histories and teaching texts frame the practice as if it were a relic of the past, highlighting mostly male leaders and past victories as if they were somehow not a part of a larger, more continuous story of organizing in which our struggles are connected and continuous (Alinsky, 1969; Chambers, 2003; Davids, 2007; Netting, Kettner, & McMurtry, 2004). Many deny the possibility that current organizers can create their own successful forms of engagement (Sites, 2003, p. 105). Others under emphasize current struggles (Reisch & Andrews, 2002). Yet, to a great degree, community organizing remains a vital resource for those with little other access to social and political power. Over the last century, activists have helped articulate an approach to organizing to create power and generate alternative solutions to myriad problems. *Community Projects as Social Activism* is written as a tribute to those who have kept the field alive so it can remain vital. It is also a short, informal history of approaches to organizing throughout our recent past. I am particularly interested in sharing the stories of organizers and their campaigns. I have witnessed many of the stories addressed in this book firsthand.

This book considers not only the *outcome* of community projects, but also the *process:* organizing, critical thinking, and community practice. To do so, we will first look at the theoretical framework of practice in Part I. We will outline a working model for social action used by practitioners. Part II will focus on models of application, and in Part III we will examine the intersection of theory and practice. Throughout the entire book, I will draw heavily on case studies of community groups that illustrate the themes outlined in the book. In addition, these case studies serve as best-practice models in community organization: highlighting the line from protest to program, from direct action to direct services, borrowing from historic and contemporary examples of practice.

I am profoundly committed to the work of the groups and individuals featured throughout the pages to follow. I have worked, played, committed civil disobedience, achieved wins, lost a fight or two, and built community with many of the groups discussed in the case examples. Faced with an ongoing cultural narrative that suggests community organizing is a relic of the past, my experiences with these groups informs my view that there is always room for organizers if they are open and ready to organize.

Most of the stories found in the text are borne of these experiences. The narratives were compiled from a purposeful sample of life story interviews with New York activists (Patton, 2001). Each describes a mobilization aimed at creating and preserving spaces for regular people, offering multiple perspectives of community life and organizing. Much of the work is based on primary research, including extensive long interviews (McCracken, 1988). The narratives are compiled following extended case methodology (Yin, 1994). Because they are primarily supported by recollections of the social actors involved, they are narratives. Quotations without footnotes or references come from these original interviews of activists reflecting on their practice.

A Framework for Action

What characterizes this activism is the willingness to connect a series of well-honed practices with a flexible framework for organizing designed to create wins and sustain campaigns. Throughout the examples to follow, a seven-stage model for moving an organizing campaign forward is delineated. The model is as follows:

- Begin with a clear issue, goal, and task
- Research extensively on the issue and its effects
- Adopt and maintain a coherent approach to communicating your goal
- Mobilize around the issue
- Take direct action to move the issue forward
- Use legal advocacy, for short- and long-term goals
- Use sustainability strategies, including play, to keep things fresh

In total, this framework offers the outline for a strategy of articulating a goal, achieving power, and building a workable alternative model. Each of these steps is highlighted through working case narratives, incorporating the words and stories of the organizers themselves. Here, the focus is on both lived experiences and stories, highlighting best practices in community organizing.

Sara Schulman, a veteran of the Lesbian Avengers and the AIDS Coalition to Unleash Power (ACT UP) describes her approach to organizing (Shepard, 2002a). "I've always been interested in political movements that have concrete political goals, that have issues for campaigns, that mobilize people, that create countercultures— that stuff has attracted me," she explains, describing her own activism. "The theory is not complex. You have to have an idea that is winnable. You have to have a campaign that is viable. And you have to follow every step of it. It's quite easy." Yet, Schulman cautions, "If your goal is not winnable then you are in trouble. And if you don't have an idea of how to reach [your goal], you'll never reach it. It sounds simple, but it's very hard to get people to follow it." While many movements face a struggle to bridge a gap between political wanderlust and an effective approach to create change, there are any number of current struggles that work from the ethos Schulman describes. In this way, community organizing remains a vital approach to fashioning alternative approaches to problems, framed around solutions and new possibilities.

It is easy to become overwhelmed by the sheer number of problems, large and small, thrown at regular people in this period of late capitalism. A friend is kicked out of her apartment, so a group of friends scrambles to help her find a new place. A short-term problem is solved, yet the larger issue of homelessness, displacement, and foreclosure remains. While organizers hope to do more than manage poverty while leaving current oppressive structures in place, we cannot overlook everyday injustices. Rather, organizing has long been recognized as a way of addressing such challenges. As the process takes shape, many find themselves split about where to begin. Some push to address the bleeding, while others take more systematic approaches, challenging a system that allows people to be poor and without housing. Others push to handle both simultaneously. Each approach, from direct action to direct services, has value.

Addressing endemic inequalities, community psychologist Bill Oswald turns to the metaphor of a three-legged stool. Each leg represents an approach for intervention. The first—*remediation*—involves fixing what is immediately broken, while *amelioration* addresses root causes, and *capacity building* strengthens networks of people. This approach marks a shift from managing poverty to challenging the conditions that create the harm (Totten, 2008).

Throughout the cases to follow, we consider examples of groups organizing for power, building networks of support, fashioning alternative models, and sustaining themselves through mutual aid and care. Rather than pine for changes in an uncertain future, this book points to practical approaches to invention already shaping community building, organizing, and policy formation. Hopefully, the organizing stories found here open up spaces for more questions and opportunities for reflection. Which best practices can be expanded and which have become outmoded? Which are appropriate to a given situation? What works and how can we get involved and do it? In between theory and practice, such questions point to a flexible user friendly application of knowledge to action in community organization.

Community Practice: Theory and the "Real" World

In his *Thesis on Feuerbach* in 1845, Karl Marx argued, "Philosophers have only interpreted the world, in various ways; the point, however, is to change it." It is one thing to analyze the world; it is another to improve the conditions of people's lives. Yet how do we do this? Many look to a theory and practice of change to get started. Others argue we need to pay attention to the world around us, looking at what is actually going on and respond from there. This book works from both vantage points, considering peoples' lives and experiences, as well as broader social forces and theories (Freire, 2000; Moch, 2009). Here, effective social change activism is thought to involve "reflection in action" in which theory and practice intersect. With community practice, theory is thought to be the application of knowledge to action, as a "kind of self-creating action, unifying theory and praxis" to borrow Martin Jay's (1973, p. 4) words.

In this way, organizers connect both critique and action, creating a feedback loop for reflection, and a synthesis of the lessons of action (Henderson, 2007). Such practice connects social theory with activism "to create pressure from the bottom up to promote social change," notes social welfare scholar Sanford Schram (2002, pp. 1–2). Countless activists have built similar approaches to engaged scholarship, melding activist theory and practice (Duncombe, 2007; Sen, 2003). Frances Fox Piven and Richard Cloward are probably the most famous practitioners of this brand of research (Schram, 2002, p. 2). Their work helps demonstrate that scholarship can shape policies and programs that both energize social movements and extend beyond service provision. This theoretically informed "praxis for the poor" "holds that the ultimate truth of things cannot be known in advance, that theory cannot dictate practice." Rather, "knowledge arises within the context of struggle and is therefore historically and contextually contingent, and that the relationship of theory to practice is ultimately dialogical: theory takes ongoing struggle as its premise and works to help create the capacity for critical reflection within it" (Schram, 2002, p. 3). Through community practice, social action functions as a "lived theory" of everyday life (Duncombe, 2003). Here practitioners ask questions, assess problems, act, and reflect on their action.

A few words about the term *community practice* are instructive. Paul Henderson (2007, p. 4) describes this practice "as including all those processes that are about stimulating, engaging, and achieving 'active community.'" This practice simultaneously embraces and extends beyond community organizing. "[I]t includes work with a community focus undertaken by people other than community workers, and it embraces the development and implementation of community policies" (p. 4). Those involved include "community workers" as well as "members and activists in self-managed community groups and organizations" working for "social change in their neighborhoods or communities or identity or interest" (pp. 4–5). Anyone and everyone can participate in community practice. After all, democracy is not a spectator sport. Community practice invites people into this game of democratic living (Banks, 2003).

Throughout the chapters to follow, we trace the struggles of communities in their efforts to challenge neighborhood threats with solutions and strategies and well as coordinated campaigns. Some involve individual needs; others, larger social struggles. Many are somewhere in between. In studying community practice, eventually everyone hears the story of the child walking on the beach who sees a group of baby turtles washed up on the shore. Each is struggling for its life. So the child starts throwing turtles back into the water. Her friend asks why is she doing this? "It does not matter," her friend insists. "Well, to them it matters a lot," the child retorts. Even the smallest gestures can have enormous impacts on people's lives. They are implicitly connected to broader social forces. Through advocacy for individuals, friends, and families, small-scale battles inform and give a shape to larger community struggles and movements for social change (Reisch, 1987). They give life and narrative contours to large, sometimes abstract social forces.

Over the long term, then, community practitioners hope to do more than put out fires or throw turtles back into the ocean. This was the case with New York political scientist Ron Hayduk.

"Social work was a natural in terms of being an advocate for your clients," he explains. "I did my work in Times Square at Covenant House. The first kids that I was working with were kids from all the neighborhoods in the city who were pushed out of their houses, only to become homeless. There's a lot of poor people in this city, mostly people of color, who were just like, 'You know it's OK, you're 16, and we need that extra room that you're living in for the newborn. Can you go get a job?' Or the kids are just tired of it and just want to get the f*** out, and they're checking out the city."

Working with runaway youth in Times Square, Hayduk gradually became aware of their lives and struggles. "So it was a great lesson for me to go hang out with them and learn about New York City, learn about their lives," he recalled.

Listening to their stories, Hayduk began to look at the connections between individual and neighborhood-level needs and a bigger picture of displaced youth in a global city; doing so, he crossed a Rubicon from case management to advocacy and organizing. While many social workers have walked away from such anti-poverty work (Cloward & Epstein, 1967; Specht & Courtney, 1994), there is a long tradition of social workers who've grappled with the structural dimensions of poverty and social and economic inequality (Bailey & Brake, 1975; Brake & Bailey,1980; Ferguson & Woodard, 2009; Galper, 1980; Lens & Gibelman, 2000; Mullaly, 1993; Wagner, 2009).

Many of these social workers work with hard-to-reach populations who share a number of similar features. (1) Many are poor and becoming poorer; (2) they tend to have endured debilitating emotional hardships; and (3) the larger world of services tends to consider them invisible, pushing them away. Over and over, "ignorance, stigma, and misinformation collide with dominant ideologies to suggest they deserve to be poor" (Guy, 2004).

Hayduk was one of these social workers. He started to think about the sources of the problems—from the fundamental lack of affordable housing to abuse and neglect—that make the kids homeless. "I realized those personal problems are part of bigger forces that are at work," he mused. "Behind every person who's in need there's a person right behind them that's in need. It's like how do you stop the bleeding?" Coping with one crisis after another, he started to feel like he was simply "stopping the bleeding . . . putting on Band Aids" on problems with deep roots. "Someone's in pain, someone's hurting, that's primary. You never want to lose sight of that, you don't want to stop doing that." Gradually, Hayduk started thinking about larger systems. "If you really want to try to help solve that problem, I came to the conclusion that you needed to do more advocacy."

Drifting from direct services to mobilizing and organizing, Hayduk linked service provision with support for large-scale efforts aimed at creating change. "One of the really important things is connecting what looks like service or caring work to issues of justice and pursuing more fundamental change," notes Washington, D.C., based organizer Mark Anderson in an interview with this writer. "The great challenge is that the kind of revolutionary folks, if you will, look at service work as just charity, and not really challenging the system." Yet, there are those who suggest smart advocacy can do just that (Lens & Gibelman, 2000).

"A way must be found to meet clients' day-to-day needs as well as to change the circumstances that currently reinforce inequality, injustice, poverty and lack of access," argue the authors of the Building Movement Project Report, "Social Service and Social Change" (BMP, 2006, p. 5). They suggest social workers would be well advised to recognize that human service organizations can be spaces for creating change. After all, these organizations have daily contact with those in need, forming a core constituency. Much of the services infrastructure is positioned to support advocacy. Yet, "[t]he people directly affected by these issues—those who use social services to help meet their basic needs—must play an active part in crafting solutions to the problems they face" (p. 6).

Hayduk was profoundly influenced by this line of thinking. Over the next few years, Hayduk moved away from direct services toward a career in government and advocacy. He also started organizing in the Lower East Side, his own New York City neighborhood, with the Lower East Side Collective (LESC). Throughout this book, we will look at the stories of many of the organizers in the Lower East Side Collective as well as other community groups, many of whom work out of informal organizational settings. We will examine how problems that first took shape on the neighborhood level ripple through city, state, national, and transnational boundaries. A subprime mortgage crisis in Florida can spur a global recession. As the world becomes more and more interconnected, neighborhoods increasingly reflect global dynamics.

While this book considers the interconnection between local and global forces, it recognizes the impact of major political and economic transformations tends to be felt first in neighborhoods. The ways community organizations respond can reveal the possibilities for a future global city that is more open, egalitarian, safe, just, and joyous. This is not to suggest that there are not economic and environmental threats on the horizon—of course there are. But the ways communities respond in the face of these challenges suggests there is still a role for individual agency, as well as community organization (Team Colors, 2010). Neighborhoods and their members sometimes manage to thrive as organizers fight displacement, support immigrants, run soup kitchens, build syringe exchanges, create legal protections, plant gardens, and ride bikes through streets in examples of what healthy neighborhoods can be.

This work describes how a number of distinct groups and movements have struggled against social and economic threats to build effective coalitions and caring communities, and to create wins. We will examine models of social action in historic campaigns, such as those carried out by the Woodlawn Organization, the Young Lords, and the Black Panthers, as well as newer direct action groups including ACT UP, Housing Works, VOCAL, Time's Up!, the Sylvia Rivera Law Project, the Lower East Side Collective, and Occupy. These new groups reveal the continuity in organizing practice extending from the earliest days of the Settlement House movement through the rise of the National Welfare Rights Organization, women's liberation, ACT UP, global justice, and harm reduction movements.

Take Ilyse Hogue, the president of NARAL—a key organization devoted to the protection of reproductive rights. I first met Hogue in high school in Dallas, Texas, where she revealed a passion for fun, skiing, and socializing. In college at Vassar, she was the first person I ever met who used the term, "Think Globally, Act Locally." After school she bummed around the country, skied, went backpacking, and landed in Austin, Texas, where she worked as a waitress. This may seem like an inauspicious beginning to her career as an advocate, but this "hanging around" process is not uncommon. Many of the best advocates stumble into the work when history offers a challenge. At least this was the case with Hogue. "Something started to happen there that perked my interest. . . . [T]here was a developer who wanted to build a huge development on a patch of land that sat right on top of our aquifer," she recalls. "It didn't seem like rocket science that you actually don't want to build something with industrial metal and toxins on top of drinking water. I thought, 'I'm only 21, and I understand that? Why don't these people get this?'" (Bravo, 2007).

So Hogue got involved in the organizing effort to halt the process. Hogue and company did everything organizers are supposed to do to influence the political process in a democratic contest. They collected signatures, lobbied, put the initiative up for a vote on a local ballot, knocked on doors, passed out flyers, and organized to make sure the initiative passed by a hefty margin: 75%.

On the very next day, however, Hogue and company woke up to find their effort was for naught. "[T]he company that wanted to build had gone to the state legislature to get them to pass a law to undercut the local ordinance that would protect our water," recalled Hogue (Bravo, 2007). So she did some research, finding out the company was part of a corporation called Freeport-McMoRan, one of the largest mining and manufacturing companies making copper strip, cadmium copper, copper wire, and bars in the world. "When I did a little digging, I realized that aside from threatening our water supply in Austin, Texas, they had essentially done that in Indonesia, and the Philippines and pretty much all over the world" (Bravo, 2007). Coming out of this experience, Hogue drew a stark conclusion. "I started to understand that there was a system at play that needs to change" (Bravo, 2007). It was not long before Hogue started working for Greenpeace and Rainforest Action Network. There she served as a program director, organizing their Global Finance Campaign, "which created pressure on Wall Street executives to think about where their investments were going, and put environmental and human rights greens on their investments" (Bravo, 2007). She was in Seattle at the World Trade Organization protests in 1999 and helped elect President Obama nine years later. Hogue is one of many who have connected their neighborhood-based organizing with broad-based movements for social change.

Hogue's is one of countless stories of a new cohort of engaged organizers. Take Tim Doody, a New York environmental activist originally from Pittsburgh, Pennsylvania. "I dropped out of college, started driving a cab. I was just a completely naïve White kid from the suburbs, a Mormon," recalled Doody, describing his beginnings as an activist. "The day that I was given a driving test, I had to go around the city, me and another fellow from Nigeria. Everywhere I went, everyone was glued to these TV screens, because it was the day the OJ Simpson verdict was announced. . . . There was a ton of racial tension." The other cab driver had been involved with a case of police brutality and was nervous he would not get a job. "Shortly thereafter, there was an incident involving the murder of an unarmed Black man in Pittsburgh. . . . The only reason this case got any press was he was the cousin of a Pittsburgh Steeler. He was pulled over in a white part of town, [where] they were claiming that he was driving erratically. Subsequently, he was busted for being a Black person driving a Mercedes Benz in a white neighborhood. Five White officers held him, one on each arm, each leg and his head and proceeded to beat him to death with clubs. He was unarmed."

Tim Doody raising a banner at Washington Square Park.

Source: Photo by Rainforests of New York, with permission of Tim Doody

The event was an awakening for Doody. "I started doing police brutality demonstrations, and I started asking the other Black male drivers driving Yellow Cabs if they had any run-ins with the police involving brutality. They all had stories of brutality or trumped-up charges. My perspective went from thinking 'these people did something wrong and the cops acted overzealously,' to 'there is a widespread epidemic here.'"

Through stories such as these by and others featured throughout this text, we see how people move from isolated incidents, toward recognition of larger trends, critical thinking, and efforts to create something better within their own communities, through their own distinct models of lived theory, their own activist praxis.

While globalization from above is often seen as a monolithic, irresistible force, those craving an authentic democracy are looking for approaches to agency. Community involvement allows regular people to exercise influence upon forces that often seem inevitable. Today, activists continue to identify issues, assess needs, research and provide data, raise their voices, and pressure targets to create change. By studying their stories, we see just what effective urban-based activism can look and feel like—and how to gain the skills in order to make it our own.

Activism in a Changing World

Looking Back to Move Forward

I n the beginning of Chapter 1, we took a brief look at the present state of the world as a way to suggest the deep need for social activism. We spoke of the disparity of wealth and resources, of the isolation and alienation that seem to overwhelm our own sense of agency. How did we get here?

The Assault on the Poor

To understand the need for social activism in our contemporary world, it is informative to consider some of the recent history that has brought us to this place. In 1964, Herbert Marcuse alluded to a merging of mass media, corporate power, and the blurring of social welfare into militarization. The ingredients of this merger—corporatism, concentration of wealth, increased state police powers—are familiar enough. Over the final decades of the 20th century, the policy landscape in the United States shifted from an emphasis on public welfare and prevention toward policing (Davey, 1995). A recent example of this long-term trend is the prioritization of "law and order" over human needs during Hurricane Katrina.

Much of this shift in social policy can be traced to the backlash against the social activism of the 1960s. By 1968, years of racial unrest had created fertile ground for a political shift. By linking crime and race, President Richard Nixon mobilized an anti-crime coalition. Its aim was to justify an ongoing expansion of federal authority under the guise of the War on Drugs, which thrived at the expense of other public services.

With each election cycle, politicians fanned the flames of the danger of social outsiders, as fear over urban public spaces diverted attention away from the real problems, and urban spaces became battlegrounds (Hall, Critcher, Jefferson, Clarke, Roberts, et al. 1978).

By the 1990s, "three strikes," "get tough," and "broken windows" policing strategies found favor across the country (Shichor, 1997). By 2000, well over 6 million American citizens were incarcerated, on parole or probation, or under other forms of police supervision (Morone, 2003).

The economic crisis of the 1970s resulted in policy decisions that furthered the shift away from human need. Most of these decisions amounted to an assault on services for the poor. Critical geographer David Harvey (2010) suggests a few of these include (a) a well-choreographed attack on the labor movement and the gains of workers, (b) a global concentration of corporate power, with resources moving from the middle to the top tier of income distribution, (c) an attack on the environment and on environmental protections born out of the movements from the early 1970s, and (d) new forms of primitive accumulation, "primitive globalization" (Sites, 2003). This includes heightened reliance on "accumulation by dispossession" vis-à-vis foreclosure. Here, the poor are displaced from homes and communities, from Brazil to New Orleans, Chicago to Brooklyn. The subprime housing market in the United States, which meant huge losses of assets for African American populations, was only the latest expression of this long-term trend, born of predatory banking practices dating back decades (Wilder, 2001).

Final ingredients of this assault on the poor include the growth of debt levels that were a disincentive to creating viable government-supported, safety net provisions to keep poor people from falling through the cracks. Reagan's first budget director David Stockman famously noted that the budget deficit would be Reagan's perverse gift to future administrations, strapping them with debt preventing them from creating programs that would limit the damage of the administration's assault on the gains of social movements (Harvey, 2010).

A critical perspective on these socio-economic trends as well as the movements that challenge them informs the practice of community organizing. Groups around the world have wrestled with how to cope with what looks like an imbalanced, uneven economic system. Over and over, activists have argued that "another world is possible."

Social activism challenges the narrative that austerity must be used to bludgeon the public sector (Panayotakis, 2011). While it is clear that neighborhoods and community groups face immense problems in the era of corporate globalization (Moody, 2007), it is also the case that the very process of impoverishment and dislocation has simultaneously inspired a series of creative responses and modes of activist engagement. Responding to the challenges of corporate globalization, regular people worldwide have helped spur social change, organized as "[h]orizontally networked as opposed to hierarchically commanded systems of coordination between autonomously organized and self-governing collectives" aimed at creating solutions to these challenges (Harvey, 2010). Increasingly, those involved have turned to organizing, in large and small ways.

Organizing for Social Justice

Such gestures of opposition take any number of forms. In New York City, for example, the battle was over baked goods. A city ordinance was enacted that made bake sales— a tool for parents to aid their chronically underfunded schools—illegal. Why? Because home baked goods might include unregulated amounts of sugar. Instead of homemade goods, the city favored regulated junk food where content was clearly labeled! Faced with this absurd logic, the parents responded. "I love my mom's oatmeal cookies!!!" and "No Dorito's, No Pop-Tarts!" read the signs in front of city hall a few weeks later as parents and their children staged a "bake off" demonstrating their recently deemed "dangerous" cookies for all to see (C. Lee, 2010). These forms of ridicule—"weapons of the weak"—help inject a feeling of agency and power into often oppressive mechanisms of everyday life (Scott, 1985). Faced with a message that their work was not of value, these communities responded in a thoughtful and compelling fashion, using humor and fun to make their point.

The stories of community mobilization that follow represent counter-narratives that highlight ways to challenge globally linked, local inequalities. Each represents an effective form of community mobilization in the era of corporate globalization. Fisher (1994) suggests that while contemporary activism may not be as glamorous as the "golden era" of U.S. activism, it is perhaps smarter and often more effective. The stories, which run throughout this text, confirm this outlook.

These narratives offer images of how regular people—people like me, and more importantly, people like *you*—can stake a claim and build healthy communities, affordable housing, and community spaces. *Community Projects as Social Activism* highlights a few of the sparks that propel this activism.

It should be understood that confronting the problems of the world is an enormous and daunting task. This book—and its emphasis on building from the community outward—aims to reframe the task. A key component is sustainability. If we do not enjoy ourselves in our work, it is hard to keep going. Guilt is a terrible motivating factor for social work, and it is ultimately counterproductive. Recognizing this, Harold Weissman (1990) looked to the energizing, revitalizing dimensions of *play* for organizing and community building. The values of play for community practice are many. "A good tactic is one your people enjoy," Saul Alinsky (1969) asserts in his classic book *Rules for Radicals*. Tim Doody and others throughout this text concur. It helps us get away from the paternalistic guilt-ridden models, and instead move toward a different, more vital form of engagement. The pleasure of authentic community engagement and collaboration represents a vital dimension of community practice. It helps us beat back alienation, while supporting social connection. The term *social action* conjures up this spirit of connection between self and others.

Social action also refers to a historic framework for community organizing. In "Approaches to Community Intervention," social work scholar Jack Rothman (1995) suggests that purposeful community change work can be broken down into three distinct categories: urban, rural, and international, which are then divided into three additional categories of practice: locality development, social planning/policy, and social action. "Social action presented a special challenge," argued Rothman. "Professional fields are typically conservative and eschew any taint of militancy—and that was especially true in the wake of the conformity—drenched decade of the 1950s, when any connection with radicalism was viewed with supreme suspicion" (p. 27). In an effort to legitimize a framework for direct action—based community practice, Rothman looked to the historic term *social action* (see Fitch, 1940). The concept "did not exist in professional schools at the time" (Rothman, 1995, p. 27). Yet, it helps create a space for discussions of direct action–based practice, including thinking about prefigurative politics in which organizers aspire to create the world they hope to create within their organizing, building a new world within a shell of the old This politics takes shape through direct action and various forms of civil disobedience. Rothman's schema is useful in many ways, although it fails to speak to the emotional realities of such forms of practice, particularly the need for communities to stay engaged over the long term. We will address this point throughout the chapters that follow. With its emphasis on sustainability, the framework running through this book addresses the emotional and practical needs of practitioners as well as movements. If practitioners are to stay involved and engaged, they must find forms of nourishment in the work. "People must get their needs met or they book," explains movement scholar Eric Rofes (Shepard, 2009, p. 184–185). "[M]ost people who sustain themselves as organizers need to have fun and need to get social, cultural, and pleasure needs met through organizing" (pp. 184–185).

Many of the groups discussed bridge the gap between direct action and direct services to create approaches that represent a radical departure from the conventional wisdom, which holds that activist organizations cannot also provide services. Yet, organizers have come to realize that they must build innovative organizations in order to address community needs, particularly with financial support for nonprofits retracting. As gaps in the social safety net expand, many look to mutual aid models of mutual support to survive and thrive. Such a strategy keeps campaigns and community building moving forward, in the face of even stiff opposition.

In the United States, only a small portion of this new organizing comes from social workers. Still, community organizing is enjoying a pulsing resurgence, propelled by new frameworks for participation and citizen engagement. These new frameworks emphasize creating open spaces for dialogue, creativity, experimentation, community, direct democracy, services, and action. The lessons of this work for social workers and organizers are many. In this space, social workers collaborate with social movements and community practices in a range of fields from housing to AIDS services. Through such collaboration, the field is forced to grapple with the merits of radical versus reform-minded models of practice.

Community Projects as Social Activism considers a few of these dilemmas, particularly in relation to social movement organization and the challenges of moving from community projects to organization and organizational development. Today, many reject the path toward formal organizational development, prioritizing mutual aid and friendship networks, rather than toward the "nonprofit industrial complex." There is good reason for this—in the years since the 1960s, many organizers have worked with virtually no support from the federal government. The money that is available involves ever more stipulations and bureaucratic nightmares from foundations. Despite facing a better-funded opposition and numerous setbacks, these activists have continued to broker deals and compromises that make cities more livable. Today, local community organizers continue to compile research, provide data, preach, scream, pressure targets, and use direct action to communicate their messages to the multiple policy bodies necessary to create change—as well as to the broader public.

So then, considering the challenges presented within the post-welfare neoliberal city, we must ask ourselves: How do we organize to have an impact? How do we actually support efforts instead of hindering efforts already taking place on the ground? How do we support self-determination among community partners, while addressing assumptions about culture and community and grappling with the lessons of colonialism and paternalism?

To do so, a new generation of providers has come to look to antiauthoritarian models of care and connection. Through the stories told by organizers themselves, we will see how different constituencies connect to different projects, services, and spaces, highlighting new ways of living. Here, people begin to see their own power and trust their own narratives, matching effort with fun, seeing how that effort simultaneously heals and engages. Culture, humor, and storytelling are infused within a bottom-up organizing process that brings regular people into the process of community.

Between markets and government there has to be space for civil society. Yet, today this space is being marketed, and transformed into a commodified version of citizenship, as everything from water to government is being privatized and sold to the highest bidder. The fact remains: You cannot commodify happiness. You cannot heal through a commodity. In a world with far too much alienation and isolation, the stakes could not be higher; the need for community connection could not be greater. Hence, the imperative of social organizing.

Social organizing typically takes shape as a recipe for social change built around solidarity, joy, and a jigger of justice among other ingredients in a campaign for social change. It suggests solutions can be found among networks of friends, rather than formal organizational solutions. Through social activism regular people demonstrate that efforts to combat alienation are valid forms of social intervention in and of themselves. And, in doing so, they connect organizing with an abundant experience in social connection.

"A politics of play that is engaging . . . is not just generative, it grows," explains William Etundi. Through such expressions, social actors connect individual experiences with broader social forces, linking social ties with learning, organizing, and even activism. In this way, we can embrace efforts aimed at play and creativity that support freedom of the body and imagination. Freed from limitations that separate people and movements, the body and the mind find space to participate in a broad range of actions for social change, large and small (Adorno, Frenkel-Brunswik, Levinson, & Sanford, 1964/1993; Reich, 1980). Here pleasure is seen as an important part of social change (B. Ehrenreich, 2007). With connection between desire and movements, citizens reconnect with personal hopes, passions, and authentic community practices.

Today, the field of organizing is in constant flux, with practitioners experimenting with innovations to cope with a range of threats, challenges, and exponential complications. In many ways, then, the point of social activism is to challenge mechanisms that control the social body, countering social controls with gestures of freedom, fueled by the social imagination. Doing so, we come to value social connection among people across communities, borders, and ways of thinking. Conceptually, this understanding finds its expression in a highly humanistic approach to social organizing (Dolgan & Chayko, 2010). Flexible rather than ideological, it integrates a range of perspectives; yet more than anything else, it recognizes that organizing involves core elements of human kindness (Stebner, 1997).

In this way, the process counts as well as outcome. This is not to suggest the practice of social organizing privileges process at the expense of outcomes; it does not. "The attention we apply to how we practice does not imply a substitution of process over content," argues social welfare scholar Steve Burghardt (1982, p. 3). "Economic relationships are paramount factors that affect us in our work, determining the type of choices we face daily. However, the primacy of objective conditions does not make subjective, interpersonal conditions irrelevant" (p. 3).

Getting Started—Playfully

Social organizing links personal needs with attention to political issues that are often intimately interconnected with social and cultural forces. It includes a diversity of approaches, integrating both resource mobilization and contemporary ludic frameworks (Duncombe, 2007; McAdam, McCarthy, Zald, & Mayer, 1988). For those involved, pleasure really does count. Social organizing is practiced with an implicit understanding that that there is nothing wrong with people occasionally just enjoying themselves. This is where pleasure comes in. It is important to remember that there is always more to play than simple diversion. It opens new ways of looking at the world. It is a free activity, involving hearts and heads, stories, moving back and forth between reality and fantasy, experiment and frivolity. Such activity helps us experiment with alternative perspectives on social reality; it is also fun. Without a space for engaging creative energies, many find it difficult to cope with life's challenges (Wenner, 2009). Such practices provide energy. Batteries recharged, actors are ready to re-engage, "to get from the outside world whatever is needed for self-preservation" (Lantos, 1943). Play inspires innovation in any number of ways (Weissman, 1990), helping actors convey a message by creating situations (Bogad, 2003, 2005; Reed, 2005). And it engenders fun.

Yet it is not a substitute for a larger more coherent organizing strategy. Rather it is one of many tools in the activist's toolbox. Such a framework for social change typically includes a clear and well-articulated proposal, research and analysis of the problem, media, legal strategies, and an element of surprise, combined with a jigger of play to sustain things. In this way, play is but a complement to a larger organizing campaign. It helps keep people engaged. It keeps ideas flowing, civil society pulsing. It's an easy point of entry to activism. Most important, it is simply one of any number of ingredients within a gumbo of methods understood as social activism. It offers important flavor.

Through social activism, pleasure links with activism, as social actors bridge friends and networks within the common cause of organizing for social change. Sometimes the process involves recreational activities, such as Anarchist Cricket, gardening, or rides with the Puyallup Daffodil Three-Wheeler Club. In other cases, such as the Critical Mass group bike rides, such activities alter the rules of the game of urban life, challenging the ways cities understand themselves. Unlike more formal organizing, everyone is allowed to be a leader, taking part in the mass of bodies. It involves skills and knowledge, as well as a strengths-based approach to living (Saleeby, 1996).

Such activism promotes inclusion of multiple voices, many of which are often omitted from contemporary social discourse. Yet, the metaphor is one of a party, rather than a duty-bound effort (Duncombe, 2007). Recall Cher's tongue-in-cheek soliloquy before her class in the 1995 film, *Clueless*, based on Jane Austin's *Emma*:

Without leaders or a planned route, Critical Mass, seen here in Bike Summer 2003 in New York, serves a moving community.

Source: Photograph by Peter Meitzler © 2003–2014

> So, like right now for example. The Haitians need to come to America. But some people are all, "What about the strain on our resources?" Well it's like when I had this garden party for my father's birthday, right? I put R.S.V. P. 'cause it was a sit-down dinner. But some people came that did not R.S.V.P. I had to haul ass to the kitchen, redistribute the food, and squish in extra place settings. But by the end of the day it was, like, the more the merrier. And so if the government could just get to the kitchen, rearrange some things, we could certainly party with the Haitians. And in conclusion may I please remind you that it does not say R.S.V.P. on the Statue of Liberty. Thank you very much. (Heckerling, 1995)

It most certainly does not say RSVP on the Statue of Liberty. As she completes her exposition, Cher bows to a classroom full of applause.

The point of social activism is to break down the lines between policy and practice, work and play, insider and outsider, so more people are able to participate with social and collective processes of authentic democratic living. By inviting everyone, social organizers participate in a profoundly inclusive experiment in living. An alternative to being alone or struggling with isolation (Putnam, 2000), social activism is akin to holding a party. It invites us all to participate. Such gatherings are a cornerstone of contemporary activism (Duncombe, 2007).

As the stories we have heard and will hear suggest, there are many ways to come to social activism. With the idea that there is a certain amount of fear to stepping off the sidewalk into a more activist life, let's start by planning something simpler and more attainable—a street party.

French Philosopher Henri Lefebvre (2003) argues that we all have a right to the city. Living in the post-welfare neoliberal city, it is easy to forget this. One way to remind yourself is through a self-styled, do-it-yourself street party. After all, a good revolution should feel like a carnival. Conversely, the biggest mistake a social change activist can make is to become boring. A street party is usually anything but. Countless groups have improvised with different models of party as protest. In particular, international public space groups, such as Reclaim the Streets (RTS) and Time's UP!, helped experiment with this basic recipe for a street party as a model of social protest. Created by Reclaim the Streets (n.d.), the following offers some of the ingredients of a street party as a model for community building:

Don't overplan it. Much like jazz, a street party is an interactive improvisation among organizers and those on the street. Yet, to be done well, this improvisation takes shape within a framework. Throw in a little music, righteous indignation, put on dancing shoes, and mix. A recipe for social activism is anything but linear, with a lot of room for variations—indeed, not all steps are always needed, some occur in a different order, and some are carried out simultaneously. The following is based on the widely emulated recipe born from Reclaim the Street (n.d), a British public space group, with groups around the world.

Step 1: Have a Clear Goal

The goal here is straightforward: to bring the community together by sharing communal public space in an outpouring of music, dance, refreshments, and conversation. Some components might well include the following:

Imagination: This is a vital ingredient of any recipe for change. Before you can create anything you need to be able to dream it. Daydreaming big is a good way to start.

A raison d'être (a reason to be there): "Public Space for the People!" was Reclaim the Streets' line. Celebrating non-polluting transportation, that's why Time's Up! does what it does. As the civil rights movement showed us, when music and songs are connected with a cause, cultural resistance gains in urgency and potency. Here, organizers connect their party with a cause for change.

Get together with your crew: As Margaret Mead reminds us, all it takes is a few people to change the world. Invite friends to brainstorm about what you would like to accomplish—a bit of fun, to highlight a campaign, ideally a combination thereof. Successful street parties have long connected dancing bodies with social movements. Some events are carefully planned, while others, like the events of June 1969 igniting the gay liberation movement, grew organically out of a street riot near the Stonewall Inn. So, get together, plan, and dream.

Date: The first step for any action is a solid date and time. This lets you start to publicize and plan for an action that is actually going to happen.

Step 2: Research Extensively on the Issue and Its Effects

In most cases this would mean to listen closely to the voice of the community. What are their issues? What is the most effective case to be made for their advocacy? For our street party, for which the primary goal may be to engender the kind of community spirit necessary for future action, the issues may be simpler:

Permit or no permit: Many suggest that the First Amendment itself is their permit. Others think it is a good idea to obtain permission. Some argue the process invites surveillance. A party maintains its subversive dynamic when it retains its liberatory character.

Location: Given a theme, the next step is to establish a location or multiple locations for your action. Some actions are suited for one particular location. Be it a canyon or the back of a supermarket or the lobby of a bank, a street party needs a solid starting point. But more than one location is useful if the blue meanies decide to shut down a given space. The more mobility and flexibility the better.

Holding the streets and the space: Once you have a location, establish a plan for holding it. Reclaim the Streets used to use tripods; Time's Up! uses bikes and bodies. Whatever your scheme, establish a plan. Keep your head and remember what you are doing. "At the center of non-violence stands the principle of love," Martin Luther King Jr. reminds us.

Step 3: Adopt and Maintain a Coherent Approach to Communicating Your Goal

A media team: Being ready to take photos, video, and publicize the event helps get the word out. Until you figure out a way to communicate your goals to the public, no one will know this is not just any street fair: It is a festival connected with social change.

Theme: It may be useful to connect your street party with a theme or concept. It could be a color, or a campaign—such as saving the community gardens.

Step 4: Mobilize

With planning largely completed, now is the time to make sure your activities meet the goals you have set:

Visual Arts: Once a theme and location are established, connect them with visual arts and propaganda. How will you use visual arts to transform the location of the street party? A well-selected banner or perhaps grass or chairs can transform a street corner into a living room or even a community garden. Invite musicians, artists, street performers, dancers, anyone who help turn the street into a space for new ways of conceptualizing the relationship between the individual and public space. Connect the visuals with the message of the party. Art is part of getting the ideas out there.

Communications: With visual propaganda in mind, pull together a small crew of word-smiths to media gurus to draft a press release. Feel free to poll the group for sound bites, but let only two or three people draft the press release, answering the who, what, when, and why of your action. Send the press release out to media outlets, through blogs, Internet list serves, social media, and reporters. Print a few to have at the event itself, along with a "What are we doing here today" flyer explaining the rationale for the action in connection with the campaign it is supporting. Unless it has the capacity to speak out beyond its base, a street party loses its capacity to shift social discourse or connect bodies with movements. You may also want to draft a broadside or pamphlet connecting your actions with larger ideas. Publicize this event in the streets, pubs, and play spaces.

Mobility and flexibility: Make sure your party has the capability to be mobile. Bringing a sound system in a shopping cart or sound bike is useful. The more bikes, the better—this will help keep the party mobile and flexible.

Step 5: Take Direct Action to Achieve the Goal

Music: Lots of music, both live and recorded. This involves a few decisions about technology. There are multiple options. Sometimes an old-school drumbeat works as well as a rave anthem or iPod. The choice of music to play on it is vital.

Sound: An effective street party needs a **sturdy** sound system. Boom boxes, car stereos, amplifiers, drums, or other live instruments—any or all of these can work. The medium is part of the message.

A generous heap of **friends and strangers, fun, and fellowship add spice to a street party for social change**. Social movement success is very much dependent upon the kindness of strangers. A useful mix of both keeps the recipe fresh.

Party! You've done the planning; now enjoy the fruits of your labor. Enjoy connecting with friends, making new ones, and shaking in ways you usually do not shake. Dance with someone you do not know. And when the police arrive, move on unless you plan to get arrested. Here's where planned mobility comes in. If you do plan on getting arrested—not advisable though not always avoidable—establish a support team to collect the names of those arrested. Make sure the team is there when arrestees are liberated. Hold a legal meeting the following week. But if an event remains mobile, there is no reason to face arrests. Just keep on moving.

Step 6: Organize Legal Support

It is vital to understand the legal implications of what you are planning to do, and where you are planning to do it. After all, our style of peaceable assembly is quite often their style of disorderly conduct. For actions such as this, make sure a jail support team is on hand, ready to help get people out of jail or at least support them through the process in the event of arrests. Still, know your rights.

> **The U.S. Constitution is your tool, use it wisely and well:** "Congress shall make no law respecting an establishment of religion, or prohibiting . . . or abridging the freedom of speech, or of the press; or the right of the people peaceably to assemble, and to petition the Government for a redress of grievances."

> If people have a right to maintain a hand-grenade launcher in their backyard on Second Amendment claims, then you have a right to dance on First Amendment grounds. Bring a copy to remind any public officials who may arrive that you are guaranteed a right to speak out or dance in public. Avoid a confrontation, if possible.

Step 7: Use Sustainability Strategies to Keep the Campaigns Alive

In this example, the goal may have been to simply engage the community and open it up for future ideas.

> **Plan another street party:** Keep on fighting for the right to party. Evaluate the action and plan for another one. We all have a right to the city. What better way to express one's "Pursuit of Happiness"? And if that will not do, there are other ways to get out and make one's point. The ingredients for a street party can easily be altered to create a street carnival, a Critical Mass, riot, or even a street rally (Reclaim the Streets, n.d.).

Again, this is simply one way to start, an entrée into a world of engagement with one's surrounding community to start to take back some ownership of our social world. In the next chapter, you will learn of another.

Learning From Community Projects

While the social activism we discussed in the previous chapter is a vital aspect of organizing, it is but one of a wide range of practices. Each organizer comes into the practice in a different way. The following offers a narrative of my journey to it. Throughout, I reflect on my teaching, experiences as a student and practitioner, and the ways these experiences inform my approaches to teaching the subject.

For years now, I have taught community organizing and community projects. The goal for these classes is to establish the grounding for the budding practitioner's subsequent social justice work. No class or community project or even understanding of the concept of justice is the same; rather, everyone comes to these classes in their own ways, from their own perspectives. Yet, in each class, I hope for students to connect their lives with some notion of community and civic engagement. Students are invited to view their experience and story in relation to larger injustices as well as solutions and possibilities. Sometimes awareness begins with something as small as a gripe about tuition increases at the school or a car accident; in other cases, it follows a friend or family member getting sick with HIV/AIDS or cancer, the callousness of the medical system, racial profiling, or an immigration policy gone wrong. Through such thinking, many students come to see and value something larger than their own individual self-interest. And many find themselves in the middle of a struggle to create change.

I was first assigned to teach Community Projects at California State University, Long Beach, and then at the City University of New York (CUNY). In teaching these courses, I have always asked students to consider the links between the history, theory, and current practice of both community organizing and agency-based practice. Before teaching, I spent well over a decade consumed within the practice in settings including

AIDS housing, harm reduction, syringe exchange, welfare rights, grassroots organizing, community gardening, and the like. I also tried to keep up with the literature in social work. In doing this, I was constantly reminded that what was written about practice rarely kept up with what was going on in the field. So much had happened since the 1960s as radical social work and community practice continued to shift and evolve across a range of issues, including immigration, labor abuses, deinstitutionalization, homelessness, environmental disaster, HIV/AIDS, anti-war activism, and struggles against neoliberalism. I attempted to address this shift in my writing, activism, and teaching, reflecting on these changes in each class.

Throughout the classes, students are charged to take on the complicated circumstances of urban poverty, organizing, and community development, as well as services provision. Here, students are given the opportunity to compare their hopes and desires with the realities on the mean streets. In doing so, students are charged to become reflective practitioners as described by Schon (1987). In order to deserve Schon's designation, students are asked to contemplate and study the basic tools of a field to the point where "knowing and action" become one gesture (p. 25). To get there, students are asked to connect the dynamic work taking place in neighborhoods and communities with their budding development as practitioners. This interplay between the streets and classroom in community practice infuses vitality into their ways of seeing.

Approaches to Community Engagement

Throughout each class, students are asked to consider a range of approaches to community engagement. I suggest the following approaches: let stories move them, build community, go get the seat of your pants dirty with real research, organize around strengths, connect with a model, and connect the dots of a struggle within their own stories. Let's take a closer look at these approaches.

Let Stories Move You

For community practice and organizing to be useful, many students develop a meaningful connection with their own communities. My first social work internship at the Chicago Area Project (CAP) in 1995–1996 had helped galvanize this point. As part of my orientation, I learned about organizers associated with the project dating back to the 1930s. The organization's founder, University of Chicago sociologist Clifford Shaw, collected oral histories of delinquent youth, documenting their stories to highlight the multiple dimensions of their worlds and the various impacts on their lives. The lesson from Shaw's work was that there is no need to remain detached when listening to these stories, especially if one listens carefully with an eye toward changing social conditions (C. Shaw, 1930). Reading these stories, I was spurred into participation.

By the second year of my time in Chicago, I followed Shaw's calling, interviewing many of the organizers who had worked with him starting in the 1930s. One of the first interviews for my oral history was with Billy Brown, a diminutive 86-year-old African American woman with short, curly brown hair and animated eyes. She explained what she had learned about neighborhood life from Clifford Shaw.

> I think Dr. Shaw felt that this was yours. This was my plot where I belong so I want to make it the nicest part of my life and the nicest part of my entity to live here. It was just like a castle, like a castle that belonged to you. And he felt that way about each person. Just wherever you went that was your home. If you were a part of it, you lived there. Its small neighborhoods, that's what it was, small neighborhoods. And he felt that you could organize wherever you went. And this organization could be your castle. (quoted in Shepard, 1997a)

A love for community was intimately connected with her story. Brown was not the only member of CAP to reflect on the group's neighborhood emphasis.

Another organizer with the group, Tony Sorrentino, recalled Clifford Shaw's understanding of community:

> Shaw's approach was, sure he wanted to bring about change in the community but he believed in the notion that the way you do that is by neighbor helping neighbor. And so that was his experience of growing up in a very small town in Indiana in the early days of industrialization. He would give us such examples, if somebody's farm or home burned down, the neighbors all automatically came together, they didn't apply for a grant or call in the government. They just did it themselves. Likewise, with the delinquent, he'd get out of line, they didn't call in juvenile court. They just handled it informally. (quoted in Shepard, 1997a)

Sorrentino organized around a notion of community as primary interaction; here community is understood in terms of people's interpersonal interactions with each other (Effrat, 1974). Community conceived of as primary interaction includes aspects of Toennies's explanation of Gemeinschaft, which "included the local community, [it] also went beyond it . . . it referred to social bonds, . . . characterized by emotional cohesion, depth, continuity, and fullness" (Effrat, 1974, p. 3). Clifford Shaw outlined his community organizing philosophy in a 1939 report to the board of trustees: "[CAP's] activities are regarded primarily as devices for enlisting the active participation of local residents in a constructive community enterprise, for creating and crystallizing neighborhood sentiment on behalf of the welfare of the children and the social and physical improvement of the community as a whole" (p. 4). The core lesson of this approach becomes that student organizers must respectfully engage those involved within the life of the community, cultivating their "active participation" just as Shaw had once done.

To tap into this "active participation" one has to have a solid grip on the conditions as well as the cultural terrain of the community. To develop such an understanding practitioners assess conditions in the social environment, finding out what the community wants and then acting on it in a respectful manner (J. Bennett, 1981). Without this needs assessment, community practice is flawed from the start.

Much of this process begins with listening and relationship building. "This is a basic community organizing principle: you can't go to a community and say, 'These are the things you should care about,'" notes Washington, D.C., based organizer Mark Anderson: "You gotta go to them and you gotta talk to them and get to know them and find out what they think. And from that place of building a relationship where you have some mutual respect and understanding, then there's actually a reason why they might listen to us, and we will probably discover that our vision of the revolution has been transformed by our encounter with them. If only we can be open to actually listening as well as speaking." There is a "revolutionary power of an open mind and a listening ear." Cultivate an empathic ear.

Build Community and Democracy in the Classroom and the Streets

My goal for each class has come to be threefold: to build a community among students, to connect the campus with the community outside it, and to help students develop their own sense of social justice and democratic political engagement. When I first sat in Irving Spergel's community organization and development class at the University of Chicago I was struck by his sense of connection with the community, its pulse, problems, strengths, and people. A scholar of gang life, he talked about the life of members of the gangs he worked with; he hired them to do research with him. He wrote stories about them. He brought organizers into the classroom, and helped us feel like a community as we conducted our research studies. He also helped us see where organizing fit into the larger picture of the social work. Early in the class, he invited Saul Alinksy's protégé Ed Chambers to talk about ACORN's approach to organizing. Harkening back to Alexis de Tocqueville, Chambers suggested U.S. democracy was dependent on three elements: the market, the government, and a civil society. In between the market and government, there had to be space for civil society. Without it, democracy would be in peril. Over the next two decades, this idea would become more and more influential to my writing, teaching, and activism. *Civil society was word for public space and community. Without it, democracy as we know it would be doomed. And it is up to all of us to keep it going.*

"Go get the seat of your pants dirty with real research" was the advice of Robert E. Park, a luminary of the Chicago school. His point, of course, was to get out and get into the action. The best way to find answers about community life is by participating in it. If you are studying the lives of dancers at a club, go dance with one of them. Don't stand on the sidelines with a clipboard. Go hang out and get to know what is going on (Bulmer, 1986). If you are interested in learning about those looking for work, don't just study the census or unemployment rolls, go talk with the unemployed as well as those looking to hire them. Talk to all the stakeholders, find out what they think is going on. Get out into the mix and try to learn from these experiences.

Organize Around Strengths

During this same period, I ran across the writings of John McKnight (McKnight, 1995; Kretzmann & McKnight, 1993). Find a community strength, McKnight implored community practitioners. Each community has one. Don't just look for what is wrong. That is too easy. It is the job of organizers to find community assets, from day one. Look at what pushes communities forward. What gets them to click. Map community resources and assets. In communities people know by stories, he advised (McKnight, 1987). Solutions to challenges faced in the community will be found within these stories, assets, forms of leadership, cultural capital, social networks, and the like.

For McKnight (1987) regenerating community begins by recognizing that the typical social policy map is broken into two dimensions, between institutions and people. He argues that this thinking is flawed: that there is no acknowledgment of a role for community involvement or associations. He warned that a deficit-based therapeutic model sees community in terms of pathology and illness in need of correction; this leads to fragmentation and rejection of local knowledge or expertise, shifting funding toward services as opposed to local leadership. Loretta Pyles (2009, p. 129) warns, "Communities have been invaded by and colonized by professionalized services that have disempowered citizens and interfered with ways people can engage one another." With little to no room for input, those impacted, the consumers, reject current models (Heller, McCoy, & Cunningham, 2004).

It does not have to be this way. Rather than depend on institutions, the policy map could be drawn around community associations as well as counter-power. This community of associations includes interdependence among bodies, recognition of fallibility, indigenous leadership, flexibility rather than institutional interests, rapid response to problems, relationships individualized, and citizenship expressed. Here, regular people find a voice to speak and create solutions on their own terms (McKnight, 1987).

In fact, many early social workers were opposed to community practice driven by community members. In many cases, "the experts," social workers and policy analysts, had no special insight into or solutions to neighborhood problems. The social work establishment worried about those without training counseling delinquents. Clifford Shaw saw an opportunity to create a new paradigm. To help stem the tide of delinquency, he organized local leaders who worked with kids who had gotten in trouble. This group negotiated to have neighborhood youth spend time with local mentors under supervision. However, social workers said that this was work that could only be done by licensed social workers. The result was unsurprising: the youths, who had formed a bond of trust with their neighborhood mentors, did not trust the social workers. Community ties to the people doing the work were lost. The point of the CAP community approach to delinquency was to appreciate the assets that all community leaders possess, not just their official credentials. The question for students of community projects would be, How do social workers collaborate with community efforts, instead of talking down to people?

The problem is not uncommon. "The social worker is compromised if she or he becomes convinced that she or he possesses a technical expertise that is more to be defended than is the work of other workers," notes Paolo Freire (Moch, 2009, p. 94).

"They come to the people of the slums not to help them rebel or to fight their way out of the muck," Saul Alinsky explained (Meyer, 1945, p. 1, cited in Homan, 2008, 2011).

Instead, far too much social work seems instead to preserve the status quo. "[T]hey are paid to carry out dehumanizing institutional policies of social control when what is really needed is social change," writes Robert Knickmeyer (1972, pp. 64–65). "[M]ost social work does not even reach the submerged masses. Social work is largely a middle class activity guided by a middle class psychology," argued Alinsky. "In the rare instances where it reaches the slum dwellers it seeks to get them adjusted to their environment so they will live in hell and like it" (Meyer, 1945, p. 1, cited in Homan, 2008, 2011).

Through community projects, social workers change the hat they wear so they can actually collaborate and respect community practices. "And get respect in the community by doing things the community wants, by joining with them and enduring, for a time at least, the mistrust," elaborated Frances Fox Piven. "You have to expect mistrust because it is well founded. But I think only in practice can social workers become credible partners with low income people. It's a long term process" (quoted in Shepard, 2008b, p. 11). Over the years, much of community practice would come to incorporate such a perspective (McKnight, 1995).

Probably the most useful way to start this process is to respect the strengths of a given community. Here organizers tap into the greatest assets in a neighborhood: its people, history, and culture. Different communities have different strengths. For some, they are cultural; for others these have more to do with social assets. Every community has them—whether they are individuals, groups, networks, or associations. The challenge for organizers is to find them. This is part of why cultural research is so important. Look for what works in a given community. Instead of the "needs driven dead end" employed by non-governmental organizations [NGOs], strengths-based approaches reject models that see people as problems or communities in terms of negative statistics (Kretzmann & McKnight, 1993). Instead, strengths-based organizers break down lines between expert and non-expert, suggesting there are other ways to conceive of community life; that people can still be seen as active agents, rather than as clients. "The alternative path, asset-based or capacity-focused community development, can lead toward the development of policies and activities based on the capacities, skills and assets of lower-income people," explains Loretta Pyles (2009, p. 129).

Wonderful things happen when regular people access their own power and seek to create change in their own communities, when local people find their voice, expression, and collective power. "The key to neighborhood regeneration is to locate all the available local assets to begin connecting them with one another in ways that multiply their power and effectiveness and then to begin harnessing those local institutions that are not yet available for local development purposes," notes Pyles (2009, p. 129). Much of this process takes shape through the capacities of people involved in the current moment, the agendas they create, and the networks of informal and formal ties and relationships they bring to bear on the issues at hand.

"One thing that I've learned through activism is that anybody can do this," mused Eustacia Smith, a housing provider and direct action organizer in New York City. "You don't have to have an education, you don't have to go to school—anybody can participate in activism. In pushing for people's rights, you don't have to have any particular skill, you can participate."

Smith's message speaks to a frame of social work–based organizing rather than professionalized models of practice. "I think that comes from a history of social workers starting out as being these people that create a lot of social change, but then at some point started struggling for becoming a profession and there was so much emphasis put into that," noted Eustacia Smith in a personal interview for this book, echoing a theme in the social work literature (Reeser & Epstein, 1990). "In terms of being a social work student I would encourage people to spend time working in community organizations for sure," argued Smith as a response to this trend. "So many people go to social work school and say, 'I want to be a therapist. I just want to be a therapist.' It's not what it's all about. At least it wasn't for me."

Connect With a Model

As I was finishing my master's degree at the University of Chicago, Irving Spergel convinced me that Clifford Shaw and the history of Chicago delinquency was a topic that had already been well mined. So I decided to look to other alternate subjects and movements. This challenge became much more feasible when I moved to New York. It was a matter of days before I had plugged into the local activist scene and become involved with organizing around public space. After a few years of activism and research, I entered the doctoral program at Hunter College School of Social Work, where I hoped to reflect on what has happened out in the field. For my dissertation research, I collected the stories of organizers, asking them to reflect on their own practice. Listening to their many stories was one of the most joyous endeavors I have ever undertaken. One garden activist counseled that activists involved in the movement recognized the utility of connecting multiple methods, from direct action to legal strategies, mobilization with street theatrics and art, as part of their citywide organizing campaign to save the gardens. You may not win if you have only a rally, another cautioned, but if you connect it with lobbying, direct action, research, mobilization, and media work, that perfect storm of actions may create power and change, he explained. As I listened, I realized that many organizers see their work as part of a coherent organizational model. We can't be guaranteed success in every campaign, another organizer cautioned, but we certainly court failure if we do nothing. So it is useful to fight back, with a coherent organizing strategy that includes a clear position statement about what one wants to see happen with a given issue, research around this issue, mobilization of allies, coherent direct action, and media and legal strategies as well as a jigger of fun to sustain the campaign (see Shepard, 2011b).

Connect the Dots of a Struggle Within Your Own Story

I was drawn to my first demonstration with the AIDS Coalition to Unleash Power (ACT UP) after a close family friend suffered a long, painful period of mental and physical deterioration before succumbing to HIV/AIDS. On the ride to the action, I spoke with other AIDS activists about the experience. Many shared similar stories. After the action, I reflected on the ways our different stories interconnected. This experience of sharing stories became the inspiration for my first real research and activism (Shepard, 1997b). Hearing all these stories, I was compelled by take part myself (Shepard & Hayduk, 2002). This is part of the beauty of community projects; they allow us to be moved, to revel in an interconnection between stories, people, and communities. Martin Luther King Jr. (1963) long ago suggested our destinies are woven into a single garment of history. From this point of view, all of our lives are interconnected within a matrix of stories and gestures. The point of community projects is to explore connections between communities and stories. Students consistently report that their favorite part of the class is the class presentations, in which they share their findings and reflections on their projects. I have had students stand up and narrate their family histories as immigrants, connecting their stories with intricate gaps in immigration policy. Other students have talked about their experiences with losses to HIV/AIDS or their experiences with shifting conditions in neighborhoods. One group of students created a documentary film project, with interviews from an anti-war march. Others saw a lack of green space in a neighborhood and created a community garden. Many practitioners have come to describe an approach to learning by participating in community projects as service learning.

Community Projects and Service Learning

Each class in community projects involves a degree of service learning, engaging students in meaningful service that impacts the community. The goal is to cultivate ethical citizens with a reflective awareness of the interconnections between local practices and globalized systems. Here, students are sent out into the world to compare the theory they are learning in books with the realities of practice in the streets. The practice is rooted in the work of early 20th-century philosophers John Dewey and William James, as well as Hull House founder Jane Addams who famously linked social services with organizing and research with activism. In assumes that learning takes place when one develops "habits of mind," to borrow Dewey's words, to observe one's self in interaction with others in their community. This is an approach to citizenship in which regular people see their lives in a social context. Sociologist C. Wright Mills famously distinguishes between "personal troubles of milieu and the public issues of social structure." For Mills, "Troubles occur within the character of the individual and within the range of his immediate relations with others," while issues "transcend the local environments of the individual and . . . involve crises of institutional arrangements and larger structures" (Dolgan & Baker, 2010, p. 3). Through such thinking, service learning bridges modes of inquiry with community projects, emphasizing collaboration rather than paternalism. Students engage in dialogue with stakeholders, building their work around the expertise of those in the community, while reflecting on the process (Reason & Bradbury, 2001). And along the way, students tend to become not only better citizens, but stronger students (Ehrlich, 2000).

Part I
In Conclusion

This model begins with a dynamic view of community building that links education with action. It proposes that participation in civic culture can be a joyous endeavor. The world has changed, and so has education. This understanding can and should be reflected within the service learning environment. The challenge for researchers and students alike is to make sense of these shifting conditions of living and help contribute to solutions. Service learning is an ideal pedagogical approach with which to make sense of the myriad challenges faced by students and educators, citizens and their schools. The core point of community projects is to help students to connect their own lives and practice with stories of social justice. Here, just as students created a community garden, they create an experience in democratic living. Such social experimentation, innovation, and possibility go a long way. Mixing them together, organizers and practitioners draft their own chapter in a colorful history of practice. In doing so, they take their rightful place in the rich tradition of community practice.

Part II

Practice and Power

Introduction to Part II on Social Action and Power

Part II of this book will present a number of case studies and thoughts on building successful campaigns. First, I present an overview here in Chapter 4, and in subsequent chapters will elaborate on the 7-stage model for an organizing campaign that was introduced in Chapter 1. To recap, those stages are:

- Have a clear goal or task
- Research extensively on the issue and its effects
- Adopt and maintain a coherent approach to communicating your goal
- Mobilize
- Take direct action to achieve the goal
- Organize legal support
- Use sustainability strategies to keep campaigns alive

While not every campaign utilizes every stage, nor do they necessarily follow them in lock-step order, we will see that the general framework tends to inform the most successful campaigns. And virtually every successful campaign starts in approximately the same way. Perhaps the most important element of a direct action campaign, then, is its capacity to establish the affirmative, stating exactly what one wants to see happen. There is a power in stating what one wants and how to get it, rather than what one is against. *A clear goal, realistically attainable and clearly articulated, is the foundation for a successful campaign.*

CASE STUDY

"Set Jean Free!"

Jean Montrevil is a Haitian immigrant living in New York City. On the morning of December 30, 2009, at a routine check with Immigration and Customs Enforcement (ICE), Montrevil was detained for deportation to Haiti. This occurred despite the fact that Montrevil had been a legal immigrant in the United States since 1986, was the husband of a U.S. citizen, and the father of four children, each a U.S. citizen. The government's actions stemmed from a 20-year-old conviction, for which he had long since served his sentence. These actions became the latest flare-up in a generations-old controversy over the rightful role of immigrants and outsiders in U.S. life (Sen & Mamdouh, 2008).

What the ICE agents did not count on was how connected Montrevil was to his church and community in New York City. A longtime community activist, Montrevil is a leader in a variety of immigrant rights groups, including Families for Freedom, the NYC New Sanctuary Movement (NY NSC), and Detention Watch Network. In his fight for justice on behalf of all immigrants, Mr. Montrevil has gained the support of U.S. Reps. Jerrold Nadler and Nydia Velasquez, and New York State Senator Thomas K. Duane.

Jean Montrevil speaking outside the ICE detention center Varick Street, New York, NY, on January 26, 2010.

Source: Photograph by Mizue Aizeki; used with permission of the New Sanctuary Movement

On word of his detention, Montrevil's family and friends and immigration activists around the country immediately got the word out about what had happened by writing letters, leading sermons, and mobilizing supporters. In other words, they started organizing. The NYC New Sanctuary Coalition immediately called for an emergency vigil at 6 p.m. outside the Varick Street ICE Detention Center at Varick and Houston Streets, which ended with a procession to Judson Memorial Church for a service where they demanded that Mr. Montrevil be released and that ICE stop separating families and communities. Mr. Montrevil's wife and children as well as friends were present at the service. Inside a detention center far from home, Montrevil joined a hunger strike with other immigration detainees in York, Pennsylvania. "I am fasting side by side with nearly 60 other detainees to take a stand against this horrific deportation and detention system that is tearing families apart," Montrevil reported. Churches around New York helped get the word out about the situation. Clergy and politicians demanded Montrevil's immediate release and called for reform to the immigration laws, organizing an action. "Free Jean" became a battle-cry.

Throughout the week, the coalition speaking up about Montrevil expanded. Prominent clergy and elected officials called on the federal government to return him to his wife Janay and their children. "Jean represents all that is right about our nation and wrong with the deportation system," argued Rev. Bob Coleman of the historic Riverside Church and a leader of New York's New Sanctuary Movement. "He made a mistake. He paid his time. He represents a restored life. Who benefits by stripping him of his legal status?"

Montrevil entered the United States from Haiti in 1986 as a legal permanent resident. Following Montrevil's detention on December 30, 2009, hundreds of supporters across the country called David Venturella, Acting Director of ICE's Office of Detention and Removal Operations, urging Montrevil's release and the suspension of his deportation. "Contrary to the claims of ICE leadership that the agency will be transparent and accountable in its implementation of immigration laws, it has not responded to Montrevil or his attorney Joshua Bardavid," said Andrea Black, director of the *Detention Watch Network.* "There is no excuse for their silence."

"Jean has been nothing less than an inspiration. His work on behalf of immigrants being torn from their families across the country has been prophetic," explained the Reverend Donna Schaper of Judson Memorial Church, where Montrevil worships. "On Tuesday at 12:30 pm, I will join other people of faith at 201 Varick Street, the detention center in New York, and demand that ICE respond to us. We will no longer accept silence as an answer." She was not alone.

Members of the Judson Memorial Congregation, including Rev. Dr. Donna Schaper, rallying, getting arrested, singing, and collaborating with artists such as Dan Zanes to set Jean Free.

Source: Photographs by Mizue Aizeki; used with permission of the New Sanctuary Movement

January 5, 2010, at 12:30 pm, clergy and parishioners from Jean's church converged outside of New York's Varick Street Detention Center. Singer Dan Zanes was on hand to add a little cultural resistance to the mix. Singing the classic resistance folk song "We Shall Not Be Moved," elders blocked new detainees from entering the center, leading to the arrest of eight clergy. "I am being arrested because it is a moral outrage that our government would do this to such a great man and father," declared Rev. Schaper. "These immigration laws that destroy families contradict the values we should uphold as a society. They need to change now." Throughout the day, local television showed a loop of the members of the congregation speaking up about Montrevil's situation (Edroso, 2010; NY1, 2010).

And the campaign escalated. On January 14, the coalition held another rally, attended by elected representatives from the New York state legislature as well as other supporters. Many carried signs declaring, "Keep our Families Together." Rev. Michael Ellick, a pastor at Judson Memorial Church, stated, "It is outrageous that ICE is trying to tear this good man from his children at this holiday season. We will not rest until Jean is released and returned to his family and until immigration agents stop tearing our families and communities apart." The *New York Times* covered the direct action, propelling Montrevil's story into an international story of a church fighting an injustice with freedom songs and acts of civil disobedience harkening back to another era (Semple, 2010).

Within a week, the U.S. Department of Homeland Security dropped Montrevil off in front of Judson. The following Sunday he told his story. As he rose to speak, the congregation gave him a standing ovation. Rev. Ellick would later say the campaign was his first miracle at Judson. But the result was not a miracle. It was the result of a smart campaign.

In fact, much of the work of Montrevil and his supporters followed all seven stages of a well-coordinated organizing campaign.

- **Task Clearly Identified:** "Set Jean Free," "Keep Families Together"
- **Research Extensively on the Issue and Its Effects:** The church he belonged to and other interest groups he participated in throughout the community researched Jean's situation to help frame the action.
- **Coherent Approach to Communicating Goal:** "Team Jean" pursued a media strategy that used the direct action story to propel Jean's story from local news coverage onto the national stage.
- **Mobilize:** This began at the Judson Church with the news of Jean's arrest to the congregation, followed by multiple meetings bringing together multiple stakeholders.
- **Use Direct Action to Achieve the Goal:** This included the civil disobedience on January 5, 2010.
- **Organize Legal Support:** "Team Jean" developed a short- and a long-term legal strategy, linking Jean's immediate release to a reform of the immigration laws.
- **Use Sustainability and Cultural Strategies to Keep Campaigns Alive:** Include invoking Freedom Songs such as "We Shall Not Be Moved" to tie the specific issue to a larger one that engages the willingness to keep fighting even after the immediate goal of Jean's release was attained.

Direct action does tend to get results, yet none of the work would have been possible if Jean had not been part of an expansive community and network. Through such efforts regular people gain power, address their collective needs, and cope with problems. Many turn to organizing when formal political channels have dried up or offer little but closed doors. After all, organizing is about resistance; it is about a desire to create something better for one's life and community.

"There are those who are called social activists, who have been fighting all their lives for exploited people," explain the Zapatista Army of National Liberation. "[T]hey are the same ones who participated in the great strikes and workers' actions, in the great citizens' mobilizations, in the great campesino movements . . . and who even though some are old now, continue on without surrendering . . . and seeking justice" (Pyles, 2009, p. 43).

Most every progressive gain we have seen in the country—child labor laws, the New Deal, and even the Ryan White Care Act—springs from these sorts of social movements. Social work was born of the Settlement House Movement. Social workers have supported multiple movements from civil rights to antiapartheid. Still, the link between movements and services has never been easy. In the 1950s the field turned away from its links with social movements, breaking with the old left, associated with radicalism and communism (Reisch & Andrews, 2002). Many social workers walked away from social activism, or toward less radical forms of practice (Specht & Courtney, 1994).

Community practice offers any number of spaces for engagement. Our current environment, as we've discussed, offers ample opportunities and challenges. Public sector unions face constant threats, while funding for services continues to erode. Yet how should social services respond? Can social workers support mutual aid networks among those with whom we work? Are social workers willing to contribute to social movements as formal entities or to risk funding to fight oppression? Are social workers willing to support efforts outside of "professional practice"?

The Progressive Movement called for citizens to fight for the right to life, liberty, and the pursuit of happiness (J. Lewis, Daniels, & D'Andrea, 2011). Martin Luther King Jr. (1963) suggested that injustice anywhere is a threat to justice everywhere. The global justice movement reminded us that another world is possible, while Occupy helped us see the disparities in wealth between the 99% and the 1%. As a field that supports social justice, social work has long been poised to join social movements for progressive change (Tompson, 2002). Yet over and over, the field has favored professionalization and regulation of the poor, over support for social movements (Reeser & Epstein, 1990; Tompson, 2002). Yet, there are exceptions (Piven & Cloward, 1977) that point to a direction for social work advocacy. Since the days of the Progressive Movement, individual social workers have joined movements for social reform around issues related to poverty, labor, race, the vote, and social welfare provision. Social workers have been integral parts of many movements, including civil rights, women's rights, antiwar, antiapartheid, and LGBT (lesbian, gay, bisexual, transgender), to name just a few. They have supported others in countless ways. This is what community practice is all about.

The Changing Face of Social Movements and Social Work

Social movements have long served as a source of innovation for social work (Weissman, 1990). Social welfare scholar Robert Fisher (1994, p. 217) argues that five things characterize the new social movements.

1. Efforts are community based.

2. They transcend class rankings, boundaries, and borders of movements, crossing class lines to include previously excluded groups of social outsiders.

3. The ideological glue is democratic, antiauthoritarian, and bottom-up, not top-down. The leader is the group, not one person.

4. Struggles over culture and identity play a larger role than in previous class-based social movements, although this is gradually changing as many are turning away from identity-based social movements.

5. The focus is on community building, self-help, and mutual aid. In other words, the emphasis is on autonomy, not funding from the state.

Community practice builds on an eclectic range of perspectives from Marxist urbanism to today's social movements. Through this mix a form of practice takes shape, as "genuinely free, self-conscious, authentic activity as opposed to alienated labor demanded by capitalism" (Pyles, 2009, p. 30). Such activity is far more inviting than models of practice controlled by funding (Incite, 2007). Such practice views the world from the perspective of those displaced by storms, evicted from their homes, or dislocated by social policies and economic forces that favor privatization over all else (Pyles, 2009), as well as those organizing to create alternatives in their own communities (Carlson, 2008).

In the ebb and flow of social movements, community organizing keeps the process of social change moving forward in local communities. Here, people come together to act in their communities' interest. This organizing sheds light on the practices of governments and corporations; it also points to alternatives. Sometimes it generates social reforms. Other times it may spark community projects. It helps elect public officials and supports campaigns on the Left and the Right. It brings information about social issues to the general public, highlighting ways we can influence the process through methods including electoral politics, boycotts, picket lines, civil disobedience, and direct action. And perhaps most important, it helps those involved to realize their own power. Action equals life, AIDS activists declare. Organizers gain power through their individual and collective efforts (Homan, 2011).

Organizing efforts include wide cross sections of grassroots, faith-based, and community organization groups, supporting community-building efforts, using multiple methods. A few of these include direct services, self-help, education, advocacy, and direct action. From direct action to direct services, organizing involves steps including (1) forming a group, (2) providing self-help and mutual aid, (3) educating the members and the public about the issues, and (4) supporting efforts involving identifying problems and ways to do something about them as regular people come together to find solutions to common challenges (Homan, 2011).

Throughout this text, we explore ways organizers do their work. One of the most important qualities for any organizer is flexibility. Unfortunately, this element is often missing. Rather, many organizers tend to adhere to one method, ideologically fixating on a tactic at the expense of a larger strategy. As the old expression goes, theory is when you have ideas; ideology is when the ideas have you. When we are stuck in a rigid ideological stance, we observe reality selectively, seeing only what we want while ignoring those bits of information that fail to support our point of view; this phenomenon of neglecting bits of information that fail to fit into our perceptual schemas is sometimes described as selective observation. Here we omit pieces of data that are not in line with our own assumptions. Along the way, instead of thinking critically, we keep doing the same things over and over without evaluating our work or considering alternate perspectives.

This dynamic can be vexing when organizing groups. "Groupthink involves non-deliberate suppression of critical thoughts as a result of internalization of the group's norms," notes Irving Janis (1971, p. 44). The process takes place in any number of contexts. For example, organizer John Sellers (2004, p. 186) argues, "Marx's critique of capital is terrific, but I've always thought Weber was right that human beings can find some way to exclude and oppress one another without necessarily involving capital." To combat this phenomenon, many try to work with an eye toward outcomes and a respect for different approaches, preventing ideology from impeding goals (Duncombe, 2007).

Social movement scholar George Katsiaficas (2004) argues, "Diversity of tactics, organizations, and beliefs is one of the great strengths of autonomous social movements" (p. 8). Yet, not every organization takes such an approach. Those who have worked in groups or organizations that do not favor autonomous approaches know exactly how disempowering it is to work in a group that does not support diversity of approaches.

When one walks into a room and is told there is only one way to get to the bottom of creating change, this sense of disempowerment takes over. The best organizers favor more flexible approaches. Here methods are linked with circumstances. Rather than support one tactic above others, strategy is used to think about a coherent campaign and the steps needed to move it forward. Tactics are simply the tools used to serve this end. Sometimes those involved make use of an inside/outside strategy, with those at the negotiating table benefiting from the work of activists on the street, and vice versa. In others, organizers work from the streets or from the negotiating table.

Much of the process begins with a dialog in which different partners actually try to hear, understand, and respect each other as they organize around common goals. "I think that that's one of the great gifts of the kind of DIY direct action approach," explains Washington, D.C., based organizer Mark Andersen. The strength can only be harnessed when people actually listen to each other "when we are willing to engage in those leaps while continuing the conversation and basing them out of what we can learn from the larger community and not just simply following our own compass," notes Andersen. "So much of my approach is not about purity, it's not like there's one way or one approach or one lifestyle, it's much more about balance. There are values in all of these different approaches." This gives room for direct services as well as organizing and organizational innovation (Hasenfeld & Gidron, 2005; Minkoff, 2002).

Taking Power and Addressing Needs

At its core, organizing is an approach for those with little else to access power in order to address community needs. The question is, who has the power to influence decision makers to move? Here, action creates reaction. When his insurance company denied his claim for cancer treatment, ACT UP veteran Mark Milano (2009) sent an email to members of the AIDS Coalition to Unleash Power: "As some of you may know, in November of 2007, I was diagnosed with anal cancer and underwent radiation and chemotherapy treatment. Due to the fact that I also have AIDS, the chemotherapy nearly killed me. My CD4 count of 400 plummeted to 62 and I spent Christmas Eve in the Intensive Care Unit due to life-threatening neutropenia," wrote Milano. "In March of 2009 a follow-up PET scan found a mass in my right lung, which was removed and biopsied. It was confirmed that the cancer had metastasized to my lung, so adjuvant chemotherapy was recommended to destroy any microscopic cancer cells that may still be lingering in my body. Due to my immune suppression, my doctor and I decided to avoid chemo that is toxic to the bone marrow, and opted for the newer combination of Erbitux and Irinotecan. Unfortunately, while my insurance company, Aetna, has said it 'might' pay for the latter drug, reimbursement for Erbitux was flatly denied." In response, ACT UP New York planned an action with the Private Health Insurance Must Go coalition in front of Aetna's New York offices on September 29, 2009. "We're marching to Aetna, to demand that they provide the drug and to highlight the serious problems with private health insurance in this country," wrote Milano, inviting supporters to join him. The day before the action, Aetna changed course and honored Milano's claims. Yet the demonstration still went forward as planned. Members of ACT UP held a picket line and a handful of activists blocked the office doors of the building.

The march included signs as well as music. A saxophone player, from the Rude Mechanical Orchestra, played the Death Star theme from *Star Wars* in front of the anonymous Aetna offices, bringing a theatrical, campy quality to the otherwise serious action. Cultural components like this have long served as a resource in social movements. This is why songs such as "We Shall Not Be Moved" so appealed to activists during the civil rights years—and, as we learned, to those advocating for Jean Montrevil. Then as now, they serve as coping tools, humanizing the struggle, helping people feel strength and even joy in difficult moments. Such forms of culture bring a sense of power to a collective experience.

The actions on September 29, 2009, that took place in New York were part of a larger campaign coordinated by Mobilization for

A rally to support Mark Milano. Activists carry signs that declare "Health Care Is a Human Right."

Source: Photo by the author

Healthcare Now. More than 30 sit-ins took place at insurance companies around the United States, aimed at pushing the call for health care reform.

Mark Milano felt his insurer changed course only because of pressure from ACT UP. "These activists helped save my life," he later acknowledged. For members of ACT UP, action equals life; knowledge equals power. Through the group's organizing, they build a tradition of civil disobedience dating back to Gandhi and the civil rights movement.

As the Milano example demonstrates, part of the importance of organizing is to help influence others to change their mind (Gramsci, 1971). "Sufficient power focused on a sufficiently narrow point will produce a reaction that will lead to a change," notes Homan (2008, pp. 40–41). "Power is the capacity to move people in a desired direction to accomplish some desired end" (pp. 40–41).

Pyles (2009, p. 126) describes a number of types of power used in organizing, including legislative, consumer, legal, and disruptive forms of power. "By engaging in critical thinking and group dialogue," Pyles suggests, "organizers can identify the types of power for change that may lie behind their issue and then consider the power mechanisms that are feasible to pursue" (p. 126). From here, they can make use of existing sources of power, build it through organization, or support those involved in developing personal power as well as awareness of their own strengths (Saleeby, 1996). Wonderful things happen when those in a group actually respect the different kinds of strengths people bring into group organizing practice.

"This is where the creativity of the people you are working with, it's amazing how people come up with stuff," notes ACT UP veteran Andy Velez. "One of the great things and essential things to learn is: no matter who you are, you have something to contribute. Your exact experience, whether you've had schooling, haven't had it, no matter what you've done, if you're willing to do some work, who you are is going to be valuable, just out of your life experience."

In order to move on issues and influence policy, information is a tremendous resource. Through this command of the issues, organizers are able to persuade decision makers to change their minds. After all, organizing is about creating power to get what a community needs. To do so, organizers must be clear about what it is that they need and what is out there. Information is power.

While each of these case studies may seem impressive—or seem to involve the most extraordinary people—the fact remains that this kind of organizing is well within the reach of virtually everyone interested in helping effect social change. Further examination of the 7-step approach—your tool box, if you will—in subsequent chapters highlight a range of approaches most of you are already familiar with as organizers and leaders in your own communities. If they do not seem appropriate or useful, disregard them and remember you are the expert on your own community and its needs. Write your own chapter in the history of social change practice and teach it to others. What we are trying to build here is an approach to the intersection between theory and practice, in which organizers develop their own practice wisdom as reflective practitioners engaging in a dialogue about social change.

5

Identifying Issues

As the mobilization for Jean Montrevil highlights, the elements of a major campaign often include a clear "ask" born of an issue that galvanizes a group of people. "Set Jean Free," his supporters declared. The message was simple to convey, and through thoughtful repetition, stakeholders heard it. This chapter considers this first step of our schema: identifying an issue, setting clear goals for the changes that need to be made, and moving them forward. Some of the organizing involves storytelling and most of all getting to the bottom of a given issue. Examples from the Woodlawn Organization, ACT UP, and the Voices of Community Activists and Leaders (VOCAL) help illustrate the point.

Saul Alinski (1969) argued every campaign begins with an issue that pushes those impacted to organize. "I think that Saul Alinski and the Industrial Areas Foundation did a very, very excellent job of community organizing," noted Arthur Brazier, a Pentecostal Minister with the Apostolic Church of God and founder of the Woodlawn Organization, where he worked with Alinski. (For a historic account of these years, see Fish, 1973.) Noted for successfully organizing a campaign to push back the development of the University of Chicago in the Woodlawn neighborhood of Chicago, Brazier, who died in 2010, was recognized as one of the most effective organizers in history. For Brazier, organizing was about identifying issues, not enemies. "I think what you do is you identify a series of injustices. I never did look at the University of Chicago as enemy. I looked upon something that they were doing as something that was not beneficial to this community. And I didn't look upon slum landlords as enemies. I looked upon slum landlords as an injustice that had to be dealt with. As a Christian I do not want to identify anybody as an enemy. That creates a lot of animosity in your thinking." Rather, Brazier viewed issues as the glue, the passion that brings people together to move a campaign. "It's my view that organizing does not happen by snapping your fingers. People do not organize just for the sake of organizing. Unions do not organize just for the sake of organizing. You organize for a reason. The reason is you are trying to deal with some injustices that are happening. And you want to deal with that. You deal with that better if you organized as a group rather than trying to deal with it on an individual basis. I saw us opposing certain objectives to certain systems that I thought needed to be changed."

What needs to change? Brazier asked. What do we want see happen? What is in place to solve a problem? What needs to be proposed? What needs to be strengthened? What are the alternatives? Through such questions, organizing groups help identify what exactly it is that they want. ACT UP wanted "drugs into bodies." Their housing group argued that "housing works" for people with HIV/AIDS. They would later change their name to Housing Works and become a housing organization. The New York City AIDS Housing Network wanted "more housing and better housing." And the More Gardens! Coalition wanted more gardens. Each group effectively pushed for their given issue by clearly staking out a claim, declaring it to the world, and pushing it with a campaign.

The "Winnable Win"

Yet, what is an issue? How does it translate into a larger organizing campaign? Alinski argued that organizing groups must focus on achieving the **winnable win** around an issue, which moves a campaign forward. "I think that there are a lot of factors in play," notes Sean Berry, the Executive Director of the Voices of Community Activists and Leaders (VOCAL), describing how his membership organization chooses the issues it organizes around. "For us it's gotta be central to our work that we produce concrete wins," he noted echoing Alinski's claim. "There's tension between going for low hanging fruit and trying for incredibly audacious goals that cannot be realized in any meaningful timeframe for people. I just want to make sure that we are winning stuff and that we're going to start to build confidence in the organization. And then people will feel their power, even if it's just an incremental victory."

VOCAL is a grassroots membership organization in New York state building power among low-income people who are living with and affected by HIV/AIDS drug use and incarceration. They work to create healthy and just communities. The group accomplishes this through community organizing, leadership development, participatory research, public education, and direct action. For VOCAL, issues have to have a direct impact on the lives of their constituency, homeless people with HIV, with the drug users who help form the leadership of the group. In this respect, the issues chosen by groups, such as VOCAL, which provide services and involves consumers in organizing efforts, must be immediate, specific, recognizable, winnable, and help motivate people to act. The group has involved itself in successful campaigns to cap rents for people with HIV and to make sure police no longer arrest those attending syringe exchange programs. Over and over, the group has known and shown what it is they wanted and been able to explain why it offers a workable alternative solution.

Moving from anguish to problem solving when faced with the ongoing challenges, groups such as VOCAL begin issue identification through a few basic steps, including:

- Identifying a problem
- Organizing to turn a problem into an issue
- Developing a strategy that involves the skills of the group for winning and moving forward

In this way, organizing involves conceptualizing a problem, focusing on it, framing an action, and linking it to broader movement goals (Homan, 2008).

"Issue identification entails making critical choices and setting priorities balancing what is most prescient with what is most feasible," notes Loretta Pyles (2009, p. 116). "Ideally constituents are the driving force behind any organizing campaign, and this includes the practice of issue identification. The Zapatismo philosophy of *madar obedeciendo*, 'leading by obeying,' reflects a belief in direct accountability to the people, a kind of horizontal representation" (p. 116). To choose an issue, organizers pay close attention to the voices of people on the ground. "This may be achieved by gathering stories through individual conversations or focus groups," notes Pyles (2009, p. 117).

A campaign around a well-chosen issue can have powerful ramifications. It should result in a real improvement in people's lives. It should give people a sense of their own power—and alter the relations of power in their community. It ought to be considered worthwhile, winnable, and both widely and deeply felt. It should be easy to understand. And importantly, it ought to have a clear target to focus on that will be instrumental in actually institutionalizing the changes desired.

CASE STUDY

Jim Eigo and the ACT UP Treatment and Data Committee

The case study of ACT UP's Treatment and Data Committee highlights the utility of working around a clear issue—in this case, the delay in getting drugs approved that would help AIDS patients survive. With that in mind, the group made use of research, getting to the bottom of information, laws, resources, and mechanisms of drug approval policy (S. Epstein, 1996). Jim Eigo, a member of the AIDS activist group ACT UP, and one of the first to be arrested during AIDS-related civil disobedience in the United States, recalls one of many occasions when ACT UP members advanced an alternative policy, supported by research and a coherent organizing campaign (Shepard & Hayduk, 2002).

Initially, ACT UP's Treatment and Data Committee applied its work to local issues by identifying hospitals that received federal research funds for AIDS research and targeting them. In February 1988, Eigo (2002) wrote a critique of AIDS research at New York University (NYU). "We delivered copies to NYU's AIDS researchers. One suggestion of our (fairly primitive) critique was that the federal AIDS research effort should initiate 'parallel trials.' We advocated parallel trials

Jim Eigo, an AIDS activist for over a quarter of a century, carries a sign at a summer 2013 ACT UP protest outside the offices of the New York Department of Health.

Source: Photo by the author

which would enroll anyone with HIV who had no available treatment options," he recalled. Eigo's Treatment and Data group would eventually send their critique to Dr. Anthony Fauci, head of the National Institutes of Health. "In a few weeks, in a speech in New York, Dr. Fauci was using several phrases that seemed lifted from ACT UP's critique. But one he rephrased: 'parallel trials' had become 'parallel track'" (Eigo, 2002, p. 181). Thanks to ACT UP, a top leader of the U.S. government response to the AIDS crisis was echoing the language of AIDS activists in making AIDS policy. The key to the group's success lay in their focus on articulating well-researched, practical strategies for AIDS issues. Rejecting complicated language, the group laid out steps for what was needed to be done to fix the drug approval process, to get drugs into those who needed them (S. Epstein, 1996).

On April 30, 1989, Iris Long, Mark Harrington, and Jim Eigo addressed Dr. Louis Lasagna's National Committee to Review Procedures for the Approval of New Cancer and AIDS Drugs. Eigo recalled, "The committee was looking into why it was taking so long for drugs to gain approval in the US." The room was full of National Cancer Institute people; many would later embrace the ACT UP stance. "It was a landmark day, the first national hearing in a medical setting of the ACT UP critique," noted Eigo.

"I'm Jim Eigo from the Treatment & Data Committee of ACT UP, the AIDS Coalition to Unleash Power, the oldest and largest AIDS activist organization, based in New York City, the epidemic's epicenter," Eigo began "An Activist Analysis of Drug Regulation" by explaining, "ACT UP likes to call itself 'a diverse, non-partisan group united in anger and committed to direct action to end the AIDS crisis.' Lately, about 400 of us meet every Monday evening. Since its beginnings in March, 1987, one goal of ACT UP has been to see that promising drugs against AIDS and its related infections and cancers are made available to everyone who needs them as soon as possible." Eigo continued: "Members of the Treatment & Data Committee, one of several of ACT UP's very active committees, subcommittees and affinity groups, monitor the local and federal drug research and regulatory establishments, meet with health officials and advise ACT UP's general membership on actions it can take to advance its treatment goals."

Throughout his speech, Eigo framed his critique by situating activist knowledge and experience as an important support for scientific knowledge. "AIDS activists have long been vocal in their criticisms of Food & Drug Administration, the government's drug approval agency. By the fall of 1988, several years into the epidemic, FDA began to meet with community organizations and even granted small concessions. On October 11, 1988, ACT UP, along with thousands of members from several AIDS activist organizations from around the country, demonstrated at FDA headquarters in Rockville, Maryland, a protest against that agency's mismanagement of the drug approval process over the course of the AIDS epidemic." ACT UP stormed the building, charging they knew there was more the FDA could be doing. The group would ask, "What are the problems with drug regulation in this country? What changes might eliminate the problems?"

"Before I inventory some of the specific problems with FDA," Eigo explained, "I'd like to try to clear up one common misunderstanding about what AIDS activists want from the FDA. We are not ignorant of the effects of AIDS and its associated infections." Throughout his speech, Eigo highlighted the lived experience of AIDS activists as sources of knowledge. "Too many of us and our friends and our lovers have or have had the disease for that to be the case," Eigo continued, cautioning that the group was not against regulation. "What we are against is ineffective regulation. An FDA that can deny approval of a drug that is widely recognized as useful against an AIDS-related condition until regulatory niceties have been fulfilled is obstructionist. . . . AIDS activists want drug regulation that protects us, informs us, permits us and our physicians to make treatment decisions about safe therapeutic agents, and gives us, the affected community, a voice in the AIDS drug regulation process. . . . AIDS activists view FDA as a consumer protection agency and believe that the best way to protect consumers . . . is to keep them alive. FDA, which at this time passively protects consumers from potential bad drugs, must become active to meet a crisis. FDA must retool itself to speed promising therapies to people. . . . [M]ore than money, coping with the AIDS crisis will require an FDA with a new mission. It must strive to make drug trials humane. FDA must realize that, for a large segment of the U.S. population, the experimental medicine that it regulates, which includes clinical trials, has become healthcare. And healthcare is a human right."

"The average drug in the U.S. takes 7 years to gain marketing approval. In light of the human facts of AIDS, this is unacceptable," noted Eigo. "ACT UP has pressed FDA to cut the time for drug approval."

"In fall of 1988, FDA announced expedited approval procedures for drugs for AIDS and other diseases," Eigo noted.

"FDA must recognize that in the communities most affected by AIDS there exists a reservoir of experience and that FDA can best draw on that experience . . . [through] a dialogue with a AIDS service, advocacy and activist groups. . . . Therefore, ACT UP urges FDA to expand all its relevant committees to include people with HIV infection." After members of ACT UP testified, organized, and at one point actually engaged in waves of civil disobedience at their doorstep, many in the FDA would begrudgingly acknowledge this critique to be accurate (S. Epstein, 1996).

Over the years, the FDA moved on the proposals, such as expedited approval for HIV/AIDS drugs, that Eigo called for. A large part of the group's influence stemmed from its capacity to articulate a fundamental issue that it cared about—the need to get drugs into bodies in a much more timely way than thought possible—and to push this issue with its strength as a worldwide grassroots organization. Much of this mobilization occurred through skirmishes at local sites: at hospitals, schools, boards of education, and even department stores—anywhere the homophobia, sex phobia, racism, and sexism that helps AIDS spread reared its head. Most of all, the story of the ACT UP Treatment and Data Committee is an example of a group of organizers who connected their issue to a body of knowledge about a problem, and a push to create an alternative program (S. Epstein, 1996). The work was supported by substantive activist research, which gave the group credibility. This issue research is the subject of the next chapter.

Research
as Action

O nce your issue is identified and goals are set, it is time to do some detective work in the community. A few basic questions begin the process: What is the scope of the issue? Whom does it impact? What is it doing to the community? What can be done about it—and what should? Without a basic handle on a few of these questions, it is difficult to imagine a campaign moving forward. Often, there is either very little or far too much information. Yet, turning a problem into an issue starts with a breakthrough in social knowledge or awareness.

This transformation can happen in many different ways. Take Psychologist Ken Clark. In the 1940s and 1950s, he was trying to conduct research on the social impact of segregated schools by speaking with the people most affected—the school children themselves. But young children can be very hard to get reliable information from—so Clark had an idea. He approached the school children who attended these segregated schools to gauge their reactions to dolls—dolls that were either White or Black. Black youth responded negatively to images of Black dolls, describing White dolls as the "nice" ones. Other children broke down and cried. The work highlighted the deep and vexing impacts of racism on even small children, highlighting the point that "separate but equal" schools were anything but. Moved by Clark's findings, NAACP counsel Thurgood Marshall brought Clark's report on the impacts of school segregation to the U.S. Supreme Court to make the case against the practice. Judges with the Court would later concede that these data had a heavy influence on the landmark *Brown v. the Board of Education* decision that doomed the deeply flawed "separate but equal" doctrine (Clark, 1963).

Clark is certainly not alone in using research to make a case for change. In multiple areas, from sexuality research to public health, researchers connected with movements have looked to data to make sense of and explain complex social phenomena. After all, the presentation of effective research is often highly persuasive in influencing public sentiment about an issue. With the multiplicity of research strategies available to organizers and students of community projects, what is the best way to proceed? Much of the work of building a claim around an idea begins with a solid understanding of the legal, political, clinical, social, economic, historical, and cultural dimensions of an issue. A little flexibility is an imperative.

In the following pages, we explore the uses of participant action research (PAR) methods and their applications to community projects, as well as case examples from environmentalism, harm reduction, sexual freedom, and social movement ethnography.

Participatory Action Research

In participatory action research (PAR), social actors get out in the community to ask questions, collect information, and strive to make sense of data in order to inform interventions. This framework is shaped through an interplay between observation, identification of a condition, research on that issue, trial and error, and claim refinement. Rejecting positivism, PAR acknowledges that all people have a perspective worth considering and understanding. Those most affected by the problem to be studied should take the lead in asking questions about what should be done about the problems. Rather than a top-down, traditional research approach in which researchers drive their own research agenda, PAR posits multiple stakeholders who ask questions, compile data, and set out to use the research they have compiled to address pertinent challenges faced by the community. PAR is a collaborative effort, "related to the emergence of a holistic, pluralist and egalitarian worldview which accept[s] human beings as the creators of their own reality through participation, experience, imagination, intuition, thinking and action" (Van Rooyen & Gray 1995, p. 88).

Action steps for PAR include identifying the problem or condition, establishing a plan of action to remedy the problem, implementing the plan, assessing the results, sharing them with the stakeholders, and using what was learned to guide further action (Homan, 2011, pp. 128–129). Let's see how that might work in practice.

Throughout the 1990s, as the spread of HIV continued to torment those in particularly high-risk populations, an interesting although seemingly counterintuitive claim emerged: passing out syringes to drug users would reduce the spread of HIV without increasing the use of drugs (Des Jarlais et al., 1996). Politicians and many citizens blanched at that idea. When study after study corroborated those findings, do-it-yourself (DIY)-inspired syringe exchange programs helped propel innovative health programs in communities from coast to coast. Syringe exchange advocates collaborated with scholars in public health to make the case. As HIV/AIDS intersected with issues of public health, advocates helped identify the scope of problems and barriers including obstacles to federal approval of AIDS drugs, housing, syringe exchange, and the need for low-threshold programming accessible for hard-to-reach populations.

The harm reduction movement offers a telling example of the use of participatory action research (PAR). Harm reduction policies are public health initiatives intended to mitigate the consequences of human behavior (such as drug use and prostitution, among others). These policies are often controversial, with outcry over their efficacy as well as moral indignation over what appears to be tolerance of lifestyles that some find immoral. Over and over organizers collaborated with researchers, such as Don Des Jarlais and colleagues (1996), demonstrating the point of PAR that "all human beings can and should contribute to the development of knowledge" (Van Rooyen & Gray (1995, p. 88). Researchers and activists discussed what data were needed to help make the case for this radical public health intervention. The intervention grew through collaboration between those with different forms of expertise, breaking down strict lines between expert and lay knowledge (Grineski, 2006). "[PAR] is essentially a reaction against the control of knowledge by the elite few. It also assumes that knowledge and the creation of knowledge is potentially empowering for those involved" (Van Rooyen & Gray, 1995, p. 88).

As the positive results of harm reduction became known, and for the most part accepted, the movement grew to encompass the issues of health care and housing. Here, activists argued that long-term housing is cheaper than leaving people unstably housed and in and out of emergency rooms. Housing, they argued, equals health and helps in HIV prevention (Aidala & Lee, 2000; Schubert & Hombs, 1995). AIDS policy advocates had long fought those who harbored a moralistic interpretation of the AIDS crisis (Crimp, 2002). Their interventions would have to be smart and supported by evidence. So, harm reductionists took research findings about conditions, protested, and used them to create best practices in advocacy and service delivery for homeless, chemically dependent people with HIV/AIDS. Much of the movement was born of the idea that knowledge = power. It was highly compatible with PAR methods, which "place a high value on the knowledge and experience of people, particularly those people whose knowledge and experience has been suppressed or dominated by the controllers of science and knowledge" (Van Rooyen & Gray, 1995, p. 88).

PAR links social research with questions about social change. There is a long tradition of such research. Jane Addams and Frances Fox Piven used it to support their advocacy around social services, as did Ken Clark with school desegregation and ACT UP with access to medications, clean syringes, and housing. The results changed lives.

In order to bring the tools of PAR into education as well as organizing, practitioners are forced to grapple with a few core questions. Who is posing the research questions: the researchers or those in the community, and to what end? What is the outcome of the research: publication or social change?

Issues of power undergird questions about who manages the project and how the partners work to meet their own mutual goals. "Research can be a tool for reinforcing the status quo as much as a tool for change," note Shdaimah, Corey, Stahl, and Schram (2011, p. 1). All too often, those who are thought to be good at research are less effective at "taking on substantive issues in their chosen field and vice versa" (p. 3). PAR acknowledges that there are other routes toward the production of knowledge beyond academic and professional research. Through collaborative models of inquiry, social researchers expand their efforts to meet community goals by answering pertinent questions, compiling data, and getting to the bottom of problems identified by those in the community. Favoring dialog rather than top-down inquiry, this model builds a "healthier relationship in working with the community" (p. 11).

Discussions of collaborative research between researchers and community members can sometimes open into a conversation about the nature of social work. While social workers sometimes do support health and personal freedom, the field's inattention to community needs sometimes inadvertently furthers injustice, policing, and social stigma. Yet, there is a way out if social workers are willing to do the work of truly collaborating with community members as partners in their struggles. Collaborative research changes not only social work, but research. "Opening up research to input at all phases is radical because it challenges hierarchies of control and privilege," note Shdaimah et al. (2011). "[I]t wisely seeks to learn from the people studied in ways that can empower them to obtain the changes they seek" (p. 179). In this way, PAR is useful for knowledge production as well as intervention, reminding us of what social services is about at its best (p. 179).

Much of the collaborative process begins when the community practitioner gets out of the classroom, off the Internet, and into the streets to ask questions. What is going on out there and who is the community, Randy Stoecker (2005, p. 46) wonders in his study on action research, suggesting that these should be some of the first questions researchers ask. It is rarely the institutions or the funders, although you may find pieces of community in the hospital waiting rooms, central booking at the police station, or in the streets. Here, one will find, are the people coping with the situation at hand. The question is, Why are they there? How many of them are there? And what got them there? Is the population involved connected geographically or by interest? What commonalities do they share? "Trying to study community is like trying to eat jello with your fingers," muses sociologist Marcia Effrat (1974, p. 1). "You can get hold of some but there is always more slipping away from you." Some communities are more open than others. Some are expansive; others very restrictive. What is going on out in the streets? And what do those who have been there for a while, the stakeholders, think is going on? Do younger people have different views than the elders? Do issues break by race or gender? Where do those impacted hang out—on the street corners or the 12-step meetings? Who are friends with whom? Do they go to church or spend their Sundays in leather on Folsom Street in San Francisco? Everyone worships at different altars. It is useful to know who they are and what their rituals mean to those in the community (Kahn, 1970).

To get to the bottom of an issue, community projects expand from a simple framework for researching an issue. Different schools take different approaches, but most involve the same questions. A few words on one example of this framework are instructive.

Community Analysis Framework

At the Cal State Long Beach Department of Social Work, every student is required to take a yearlong sequence on community projects. Each student group identifies a project topic, involving a problem, topic, population, and/or community. Their task is to work as partners with community members to identify problems and needs in their communities. Students are charged to take an assets-based rather than a deficits-based approach, focusing on the community's strengths and aspirations (McKnight, 1987; Saleeby, 1996). If the blind population at a program wants to put on a fashion show, find out what can be done to help support this. Along the way, students are asked to make sense of their experience as researchers and community members, while identifying the best methods for answering questions. Those considering the scope or conditions use surveys, while those looking for the meaning of experience use ethnographic approaches. Yet, most everyone is asked to "get the seat of their pants dirty with research," as Park and Burgess implored students of urban ethnography at the University of Chicago (Bulmer, 1986).

When studying a community issue, the initial process often moves from systematic observation to case notes and ethnographic field notes. How many police cars are parked in bike lanes and why are they sitting there, a cyclist might ask (see Shepard & Smithsimon, 2011). After observing a problem such as this, researchers start to identify the conditions of a problem, highlighting multiple dimensions including assets and barriers within the community, forming hunches and asking other community members: Am I on the right track? What's the history of the problem? Out of these questions, advocates start thinking in terms of claim refinement, asking, What has worked in addressing this issue in the past? How was it defined? Does this definition address the problem? How does this definition inform our approach to intervention? What is the most logical step toward action? And is a different approach to necessary? What else is being done? The process begins with a question, a research plan to seek answers, and a willingness to engage in fact finding—seeking answers, checking challenges, hunches, and acting on them. Along the way, students are asked to identify signs and symbols in the community, considering cultural meanings, as well as strengths and stressors.

Throughout the process, those involved reflect and report back, thinking reflexively about themselves as researchers and participating observers. After all, as Harry Stack Sullivan (1954) used to say, there is no neutral participation. Through this process, students observe themselves in the community as they develop skills as reflective practitioners. "Research, action, reflection . . . action is the middle term . . . between moments of hard reflection," Saul Alinski's protégé Ed Chambers (2003, p. 15) suggests. This reflection on organizing in action helps keep organizers and researchers honest about their work.

Sometimes the process just begins with hanging out, chatting, participating in community events, and observing (Bulmer, 1986). While doing so, it is useful to maintain an eye toward social dynamics, while observing the social phenomena. The world can be a research site. People can stumble upon questions for research at the grocery store, a bodega, a club, providing case management sessions, in the waiting room, going to the bathroom in a public university, or waiting in a line (Cohler, 2004). The point is to maintain an eye toward observation, taking field notes and thinking.

As one identifies a condition for inquiry, it is useful to start identifying specific elements of a given issue in terms of need, population, and geography. From here, community practitioners fill in the pieces of a community analysis framework:

1. Identify participants and name the population: How many are there? What's the scope? What are the organizational conditions of the community?

2. Geography: Where does the population reside? Where does the problem take shape? Does it take place in private spaces or SRO hotel rooms (Feldman, 1998; Netting, Kettner, & McMurtry, 2004)?

3. Identify community assets, strengths, and resources (McKnight, 1995).

4. Review the literature on the condition, problem, need, or opportunity: Explore relevant theoretical and research literature, including key historical events (Netting, Kettner, & McMurtry, 2004, p. 100).

5. Interview key informants: Seek to understand concepts and issues related to the problem. Seek diverse perspectives. Explore past experiences with the target population and problem. Select factors that help explain the underlying causes.

6. Identify important historical events and compile data: Then discuss what appear to be the major factors that help in understanding the problem. Select factors that help in understanding the target population. Identify political and contextual factors, the interests, concerns, and worries of the key decision makers, gatekeepers, and stakeholders. Specify potential barriers and obstacles one may encounter attempting to implement this change effort. Consider potential allies that would be supportive of this change effort and why they would want to assist in this effort.

7. Perform a causal analysis: What are the characteristics of the target population? Consider personal, socioeconomic, ethnic, gender, and other demographic factors in your analysis. What characteristics of the service providers might be contributing to the existence of the problem or need? Analyze causal factors outside the system that may be contributing to the persistence of the problem or that may be difficult to control, such as cultural factors, legal barriers, disabilities, poverty rates, and so forth.

8. Data analysis and presentation: Use relevant sources of data, including the census, government statistics, research articles, reports, secondary data sources, key informant interviews, participant observation, and more.

9. Develop a working hypothesis of etiology about the problem. Identify potential solutions and strategies to address the identified problem: What seems the most feasible and takes into consideration the identified concerns and barriers, costs issues, target population issues, and community concerns.

10. Establish basic criteria for solution(s): Consider and evaluate alternative solutions and the advantages and disadvantages of each potential solution.

11. Identify what is in place to solve the problem: Does it need to be improved or limited or does something else need to be put in place? Is a proposed solution or alternative consistent with community needs?

Social Settlements and Community Projects

Community practitioners have long engaged in the practice of studying their communities with an eye toward social change. Social work pioneer and Settlement House Movement founder Jane Addams (1910) first framed the practice of social work as a part of the Chicago social science research tradition (Deegan, 1990; Elshtain, 2001).

A brief review of her work provides an understanding of the links between research and community projects. After a visit to Samuel Barnett and Henrietta Barnett's reform-modeled Toynbee Hall in London, Addams helped found the settlement house in Chicago in 1889. There she brought in immigrants to live and adjust to their new lives in the United States. Anticipating Maslow's "Hierarchy of Needs," the movement first provided food and shelter and then higher-order needs, including work, organization, and participation in democratic living. Noting that many of the children who lived in Hull House were involved in sweat-shop labor, Addams started asking more questions of Hull House residents, collaborating with them to collect data about the scope of the problem. She also sent residents out into the community to figure out what was going on. "Hearing more and more stories, she approached the Illinois State Bureau of Labor and suggested they investigate the issue of child labor in a more systematic way" (Pyles, 2009, p. 125). The bureau put together a report that called for significant labor reforms. With data confirming widespread child labor abuses, Addams started mobilizing, connecting the settlement and labor movements. Together the intersecting movements educated and informed supporters of reform, while pushing for policy changes. The state of Illinois passed strict child labor laws regulating sanitary conditions in factories while establishing minimal age limits for those working in them (Pyles, 2009).

Just as Jane Addams looked to the residents of Hull House to outline and establish questions about child labor, PAR suggests those impacted by the problem should be most involved in the ongoing challenge of generating questions and supporting research efforts about their lives and the challenges they face. With PAR, the process of asking questions and creating solutions is taken out of the province of researchers and placed in the hands of the people who are then challenged to generate questions and solutions about their own lives. Such thinking supports research whose aim is not just social knowledge, but social justice. Here community-based expertise transforms approaches to knowledge, emphasizing information generated from firsthand experience and life in the community (Pyles, 2009).

CASE STUDY

David Crane and the "We Can't Breathe" Campaign

Participatory action researchers make use of multiple models of knowledge production. "Environmental knowledge and how it is acquired and deployed are important features of local environmental politics in the U.S.," notes Sara Grineski (2006, p. 25). As groups organize campaigns, they look to countless forms of data, sometimes collecting information about companies, patterns of discrimination, or city policing. Some methods involve policy research; others quantitative survey methods, or a basic accounting of costs and benefits. An example helps describe the process.

Like Jim Eigo and ACT UP's travails through the bureaucracy of the U.S. drug approval process, the struggle to make sense of environmental policy and regulations in New York offers any number of challenges. In the late 1990s and early 2000s, David Crane, a veteran of ACT UP, involved himself with the Lower East Side Collective "We Can't Breath" campaign to rid New York City of buses that illegally polluted its streets and harmed neighborhoods. The LESC struggle to get to the bottom of the issue is instructive as a campaign that combined research with social action and a clear target.

David Crane described some of the research necessary to move the campaign forward. The first step was background research on New York Apple Tours. "You did a LexisNexis search and you find that his [the owner's] family company had the biggest fine ever from the EPA [Environmental Protection Agency]—and then you make connections with local politicians. Some of them are quite good—Tom Duane's office. And you start finding out about other violations."

Crane and company dug through the city archives for court cases in which the group might have been involved. "Basically standard private investigator techniques—look for things that are in the public information. But we found three things he'd [the owner] done which were really awful—and now he had these buses. But you got to have this information, you have to have your facts down because if you don't few reporters will take an activist seriously."

This research helped We Can't Breathe bring their case to the media. "First of all you can impress reporters by giving them facts and pointing them at real facts, even if they don't use the information," explained Crane. The reaction was "'Oh my god, you've done my footwork for me!' And this was stuff that we learned in ACT UP. You put together a nice glossy flier, and on the left you've got your press release and you've got a one-pager, like an FAQ. And then on the right, you pad it with all of the media and other stuff you've been able to find, other stories. And slap a nice sticker on the front."

As the campaign churned forward, the pieces helped explain the brazen behavior of the company. "We were after this guy [Hayim Grant, the President of New York Apple Tours] for a year or more; we did a lot of things and we hadn't gotten a whole lot of media action, but then the day that one of his buses struck a man and killed him when they were off their route and it was not legal for them to be there, and it was basically a hit and run 'cause the driver didn't even know it had happened, my phone started ringing off the hook because I'd always been the media contact person. So all these reporters had clearly held on to this information. And as soon as this happened they were calling me for what happened. 'Will you make a statement?' And I was saying like, 'It's terrible that it finally came to this that he's literally killed someone, but he's been killing people for years slowly with his damn polluting buses.'" Many of the media reports contained information Crane and company had collected doing sleuth work on the company (Chivers & Forero, 2000; Colangelo & Ingrassia, 2000). New York Apple Tours, which was in violation of many EPA and city rules, was forced to shut down and leave town.

❖ ❖ ❖ ———————— ❖ ❖ ❖

The Advocate as Researcher

As the accounts above suggest, change research tends to challenge social hierarchies. While critics have been known to suggest advocates engage in confirmation bias, those involved note we use ethical methods for research, including the use of peer review, surveys of those with differing perspectives, as well as collaboration among peers. Without these steps, research risks taking shape as a form of propaganda.

None of this is to suggest we do not have our predispositions. As Grineski (2006) points out, there are few neutral participants in the process. Historian Howard Zinn (2002), who participated in early actions of the civil rights movement before writing their history, titled his memoir *You Can't Be Neutral on a Moving Train*. For Zinn, objectivity is less important than asking the right questions. For Zinn, the best way to do this was to be there, on the ground, observing and influencing history. Many scholars have taken this point to heart. The result has been an engaged approach to "militant ethnography" (Juris, 2007). Here, research is conducted in the name of at least aiding in the work of campaigns aimed at social change, not just documenting for personal gain. Those who practice such a method suggest that engaged participation informs their understanding in ways that less direct participation could not have provided.

For Luis Fernandez (2009), militant ethnography is all about being there, making sense of his experience. In an essay on anarchism and participatory observation, he describes trying to conduct interviews during a WTO (World Trade Organization) meeting in Cancun, Mexico, in 2003. "We kept interviewing people, but kept a close eye on what felt like a tense situation," he writes, in a major underestimation (Fernandez, 2009, p. 93). "Soon a small group of young activists began throwing rocks over the fence, which landed on the helmeted police. We continued with our interviews, feeling a bit nervous and sensing a clear shift in the mood of demonstration" (p. 93). The police start throwing the stones back. "[W]e could see medical crews disappearing into the thick crowd only to reappear moments later escorting individuals covered with blood seeping from head wounds" (p. 93). As medics move back and forth, he talked with one man about his struggle to hold on in the midst of economic tumult. Breaking from the interview, the man commented on the circumstances of the protest. "'Somebody is going to die today. And it's going to be a good horrible death.' The truth of the statement almost knocked me over. He was right," Fernandez ruminated, observing himself in his interview (p. 94). For Fernandez, "these experiences only come from being there, by placing ourselves within and among the lives of those who suffer, by running risks and by placing ourselves among those who suffer" (p. 94).

Fernandez's (2008) writing serves as a case study in movement participatory observation. "Early on, I adopted a combination of approaches: one methodological, the other ethical" (p. 39). This work combines grounded theory with a multi-site ethnographic approach. "The ethical approach derives from the sociological tradition of *verstehen*" (p. 38). Herein the researcher approaches his research subject with "deep connection with those one studies," "empathy, compassion, and understanding" (p. 40). The method builds on notions of reflexivity. His thoughts about knowledge and participation help propel the ethnographic narrative away from notions of objectivity or scientific method toward the observation of self and other. "Instead of adopting a stance of objectivity, then, my methods deliberately blur the distinction between protester and researcher," he writes (p. 41). "I deliberately blurred the boundary between observer and observed, hoping to induce in myself the fears and stresses that the police inflict on protesters as they employ the mechanisms of control. This approach worked well, producing intense emotions" (p. 41). These feelings "fueled my analysis" (p. 41). Such an approach is equally appropriate when studying community projects. In this way, Fernandez and the other militant ethnographers function in much the same tradition of Henry Mayhe, Friedrich Engels, and even Upton Sinclair's novel *The Jungle,* which take on the working conditions of their respective times. The realistic descriptions of the miseries of poverty found in each volume pointed to the need for an explicit social reform agenda.

A few words about Sinclair's participatory observation research for *The Jungle* are instructive. Throughout 1905, Sinclair dressed in working clothes, carried buckets, and infiltrated packing plants in South Chicago. After months of research, he took his notes to Princeton, where he spent nine months writing a novel about what he had witnessed. His aim was to educate the masses about a system of exploitation and accumulation that consumed countless lives of workers who toiled in its factories, leaving them to suffer the ravages of blindness, disease, and ill health. *The Jungle* was so influential in its day that it served as a catalyst for a government investigation of the working conditions in the meatpacking plants in Chicago's "Back of the Yards" neighborhood. Before the work was published, progress on legislation to fully enforce inspection standards for meat had stalled in Congress. After the novel's publication, President Theodore Roosevelt invited Sinclair to the White House, and consumer protection standards moved through Congress, leading to the passage of the Pure Food and Drug Act and the Beef Act. The result was an improvement in labor conditions for food workers and inspection standards countrywide (Elliot, 1990; Liukkonen, 2008).

The working conditions Sinclair described inspired generations of reformers to identify the root causes of a problem and to seek to rectify them. Some sought administrative remedies for dangerous working conditions. Sinclair, on the other hand, sought to indict the system that seemed to perpetuate these problems (Elliot, 1990).

Enter a University of Chicago–trained sociologist named Saul Alinsky. Alinsky began his career as a community organizer in the 1930s in the same Chicago neighborhoods Sinclair had described in *The Jungle* (J. Bennett, 1981, p. 215). Conceptions of community and politics lay at the core of Alinsky's organizing approach; he believed that the cornerstone of effective organizing involved understanding and respect for "community traditions" (Alinsky, 1969). Throughout his years working in the Back of the Yards, Alinsky helped recruit and organize local leaders who understood and could clearly articulate common interests among the diverse groups of workers living in the neighborhood, made up of Serbs and Croatians, Czechs and Slovaks, Poles and Lithuanians. The result was the organization the Back of the Yards Neighborhood Council. The Council's raison d'être was direct action and fierce advocacy through sustained pressure campaigns. The Council pushed, cajoled, and demanded a place at the negotiating table. From there, the group negotiated for improvements in schools, housing, and working conditions, just as advocates had pushed for better working conditions after *The Jungle* was published (Horwitt, n.d.).

While Addams, Sinclair, and Alinsky are early exemplars of action research, recent years' examples from public health, AIDS activism, and global justice movement expand the story of change research (S. Epstein, 1996; Fernandez, 2008). The chapters that follow continue to consider these debates, highlighting examples of community research, ethnography, and participatory action research methods and the ways organizers approach communicating about issues, getting the word out to their communities.

7

Mobilization and Spreading the Message

❖

"**[T]**he media have become the social space where power is decided," social movement scholar Manuel Castells (2007) recently asserted. With the advent of user-friendly horizontal social networks, new forms of communication—community radio stations and the Internet—find expression (Juris, 2008). Text messaging and social networking sites have become spaces where social movements take shape, igniting uprisings from the Arab Spring to Occupy Wall Street. "[I]nsurgent politics and social movements are able to intervene more decisively in the new communication space," notes Castells (2007). And this is perhaps why the powers that be tend to restrict these social networks in periods of social unrest (Burns, 2011).

This chapter considers the ways movement stories find audiences, build communities, and spread messages. It reviews different forms of media activism, including theories of narrative, media, and language, as well as case studies of text messaging to organize a successful walkout for immigrant rights, Randolfe Wicker's Mattachine era work to advance more affirmative media coverage of gay life, video activism related to cycling, Occupy Wall Street, and ACT UP. Throughout, we see how media activism helps inject alternate perspectives into the public discourse.

The previous chapters highlighted the ways organizers identify an issue, study it, define it, make a claim, and discuss what to do about it. Having identified an issue, studied its roots, and outlined an alternative solution, it is up to organizers to get the message out there. Sometimes the claim involves a solution; in others it involves a critique. A bike ride results in a clash with police; a lonely plaza is taken over by dancing bodies making a claim about inequality. Stories about these gestures often begin with a pithy press release and a few snappy quotes. This is where communications—street theatrics, a text, phone call, a YouTube video, a Twitter feed, email, or Facebook post—help move an issue forward. There are multiple means with which to narrate and communicate movement aims. Here, organizers actively reframe problems into compelling stories. When done well, such communication invites others into involvement and engagement with a cause. Social networks help to connect research about claims into movement mobilization (Juris, 2008). Increasingly, research, video documentation, and press and communication strategies function as vital movement approaches, linking communications with strategies for spreading the word about community issues.

Much of the process begins with a narrative (Fine, 1995). Perhaps the purest form of communication is storytelling. Organizing is all about this process. Stories of both oppression and hope for something better move campaigns forward as people talk with each other, sharing news with friends. Along the way, both listeners and tellers can gain allies as community expands around the narrative (Plummer, 1995). Stories help give us meaning, help us cope, and provide direction for the future. These stories move from one person to another, from door to door, even from text to text.

Text Messaging, Media Activism, and Social Justice

Consider the story the California high school students who helped organize the 2006 student walkout in Los Angeles, which saw thousands of students leave class to protest proposed anti-immigrant legislation. "It all began on Sunday morning. . . . I was on MySpace. That website was a real big help in getting the word out," he explained (Chayko, 2008, p. 194). There was an online slideshow showing pictures of rallies and walkouts taking place all over the country. Those on MySpace started talking about a call for a national walkout the next day. "[I]mmediately, I had to call a best friend of mine, Miguel, and as soon as we called him, we spent the rest of the day just calling, texting people on their cell phones, emails, and by anywhere" (p. 194). While some hesitated, others were enthusiastic, asking for more details. "Tomorrow." Many were hesitant. "I was emphasizing to them, 'Well, as little time as we've got . . . just call anybody you know. I mean, call your whole phonebook, in your cell phone. Email everybody, all your contacts.' In the end everybody was for it" (p. 194). Texting and phone calls served as an organizing point that grew as others passed the word. "[I]t was one of those things, like a spider web that just kept growing, a network of people that just kept telling more and more people" (p. 194). Over a million people would take part in the rallies and walkouts of April 2006. These rallies grew from social networks, which helped support and expand labor, environmentalist, feminist, peace, and global social justice movements (Chayko 2008, p. 195). Their activism helped transform the story of immigration, moving a national dialog away from punishment toward solutions.

The rise of social media has eliminated many of the impediments to direct communication. It was not always this way. The notion that regular people could influence media was not a common idea until the social movements of the 1960s. The early gay, lesbian, bisexual, and transgender (GLBT) movement created its own publications to spread the message of the movement. New York Mattachine Society member Randolfe

Tools for a new kind of a revolution at Occupy Trinity.

Source: Photo by Venus Asa Rivera-Pitre

Randy Wicker, Craig Rodwell, and Renee Cafiero picket at the Whitehall Induction Center on September 19, 1964, to protest the military ban on homosexuals. This small rally was the first public protest for gay rights in U.S. history. "Homosexuals died for U.S. Too" declared Renee Cafiero's sign.

Source: Used with permission of Randy Wicker

Wicker recognized that social change would take place through a media-filtered lens. Through direct action and media advocacy, Wicker helped the movement open public space and debate to queer voices, challenging narratives of homosexuality as disease.

"[T]hey had these psychiatrists on WBAI [a listener-supported radio station in 1962]," he explained in an interview with me. "They were saying that they could change any homosexual in just eight hours at $50.00 an hour. That's what they were saying. I thought, these people don't know anything about homosexuals. I went to WBAI and confronted the program director and said that the program was an absolute outrage. They are out there fishing for clients and suckers. We can speak about homosexuality in a much more informed way than those jerks out there selling snake oil."

Wicker talked the producers into letting him help bring a group of homosexuals on the air to speak for themselves. The result was a panel aired in the summer of 1962, and subsequently covered in the *Herald Tribune*, the *New York Times*, and *Variety*. "As a result," says Wicker, "some conservatives went to the FCC and said, you've gotta revoke WBAI's license. They're putting perverts on the air. And the FCC ruled homosexuality is a legitimate subject for discussion on the airwaves." Soon, "the phone was ringing off the hook at the Mattachine Society." The media strategy brought many gays out of the closet and onto the airwaves, and eventually the streets and the movies (Schiavi, 2011).

With the Stonewall Riots of June 1969, new cohorts of queer activists joined the movement for Gay Liberation. Many borrowed from Wicker's recognition of the capacity of media to influence both positive and negative understanding of queer experience. Few contributed more to this project than Vito Russo, whose very life, art, and activism helped inform understandings of queer life. He defined activism as "the commitment to bring about change in the present, rather than theorize about change in the distant future" (as quoted in Schiavi, 2011, p. 78). Like Wicker, Russo recognized that the process took shape through filtered images, mediated discourse, as well as cultural production. "I always said that [liberation] would happen in social ways," explained Russo. "I didn't give a shit about changing the laws, although I knew it had to be done, but that you don't change people by changing laws. . . . [T]he way you reach people was through media" (p. 97). Russo studied cinema, writing the *Celluloid Closet*, a book that helped tell the story of queer imagery in film. Before he died, he worked on the ACT UP media committee, making masterful use of media to communicate movement goals.

Organizing and Narrative

As the stories of the L.A. school walkouts and Wicker's WBAI radio show suggest, organizing is often shaped through compelling narratives, which compete with widely held beliefs, while inviting people into the process of social change. Here stories and activism help us find meaning within our lives and struggles, as well as shape interpretations of social problems. A few words on the concept of narrative are useful in situating the bundles of stories that increasingly support both social movements and community practices (Polletta, 2006).

These narratives contain tips for the way one looks at the world, hence their efficacy for students of community projects. Philosopher Richard Rorty (1982) posits that some of the most important philosophy taking place today occurs within these transformative narratives and practices of self, these texts of people's lives and struggles.

"Throughout history, story has been used to teach, to entertain, to express, to advocate, and to organize," note Natash Friedus and Ceasar McDowell (n.d.) in their Narrative and Community Building class. "It is through the sharing of stories that communities build their identities, pass on traditions, and construct meaning." As Ken Plummer (1995) points out, stories bring people together, attracting audiences, while building a common language and perception.

This was certainly the case for the Common Ground Collective, an anarchist inspired relief organization formed shortly after Hurricane Katrina devastated the Gulf Coast in 2005. "On September 5, 2005, a day of trials by fire against hope, Malik, Shanon and I cofounded the Common Ground Collective," explained Common Ground cofounder Scott Crow (2011, p. 62). Crow and company were aware that those in the Gulf had not only suffered the devastation of the storm, but also watched aspects of their culture attacked and ridiculed. Crow and company understood they alone had the right to control their own histories. "We would help communities to tell their stories and we would tell ours, so as to move people to action," noted Crowe (p. 62). Common Ground Collective was a place where people could take control of their own stories instead of having someone else write them out of history. This would inform the collective and their efforts at disaster relief. "Part of shifting culture is changing the stories we tell others and ourselves," wrote Crowe (p. 130). "[W]e must develop our own narratives about our actions and what we imagine about the future," he argued, noting, "Communities and movements gain power in telling their own stories. If we tell our own stories we rebel against being defined by those who don't know us, such as the government, corporate media, or others with ideological axes to grind." In sum, "By consciously telling our stories we are about to reconnect with people in the real world, because it is in language they can see themselves within" (p. 130). Through Common Ground, a new model of care-informed narratives of disaster, anarchism, and radical public health took shape, informing relief efforts for the decade to come (Shepard, 2013).

This is a community-based model of care, where "people know by stories," echoing John McKnight's (1987) point. In these ways, stories help us both assess changing conditions of communities as well as move forward. They help us define and identify with our communities, by teaching ourselves and others who we are. In a diverse society, stories help us make sense of an increasingly complex social fabric with multiple perspectives on reality (Plummer, 1995).

Shifting understandings and interpretations of stories of power have everything to do with definitions of illness, health, and human feeling. For example, until a generation ago, the American Psychiatric Association (APA) advanced a storyline that homosexuality was an illness—hence the assertions of the psychiatrists on the WBAI broadcast. This is despite the fact that the field's founder, Sigmund Freud, suggested homosexuality was neither something to be condemned nor applauded; it was a regular part of human expression. Wicker's assertion of the right to his and his community's own narrative reframed the debate. Much of movement organizing is about storytelling as activists experiment with new stories and alternative ways of living in the world. Be it a press release, story, movie, or video, the creative expression of movement narratives serves as resistance to dominant narratives of the culture (Jimenez, 2010). "Narratives are stories of resilience, giving voice to subjugated knowledge displaced by dominative truth," writes Dennis Saleeby (1994, pp. 352–353). "Narrative writers can restore/re story themselves in their narratives." The same process takes shape when groups connect, form friendships, and networks (Nardi, 1999). "Narratives can nurture political resistance among repressed and subordinated groups by providing group members examples of historical precedents of individual and collective resistance, as alternative explanation of the group's condition," notes Richard Couto (1993). Paolo Freire (2000) echoes this point, arguing, "Narratives can be acts of social and political defiance, bring acts of meaning into larger world" (pp. 93–94).

CASE STUDY
Jay Blotcher and the Stop the Church Protest

Jay Blotcher recalls the activism he did as a member of ACT UP in the late 1980s and early 1990s. At the time, there was no treatment for people with HIV/AIDS. Death rates among high-risk groups were only increasing. "And when you're dealing with something like that either you break down and cry and crawl into a hole or you stand up to it defiantly and you blunt the sadness with humor, sarcasm, with black comedy, drag, with defiant, spit in your eye street theatre," notes Blotcher, recalling his work as media coordinator for the group during one of their most controversial campaigns, the Stop the Church Action. With this December 1989 action, the group protested the church's repressive approach to HIV education and reproductive rights at St. Patrick's Cathedral in New York City. "I was on the outside. I was handling media that day and it spiraled out of control. It went on for weeks and weeks afterward." During that time, Blotcher helped propel the activist narrative through the newspapers and television in the largest media market in the United States. He recalls it as an important moment in which media activism worked.

We effected a complete 180 degree turnaround. And it regards Jason DeParle. So Jason DeParle, of The *New York Times*, called me up and said "what's ACT UP stand for?" And I said I'm rushing off to a meeting, it's the last meeting before the action, join us. So he came there. Drank in the color of it all. Came to the demo the next day. And over the next week or two, he called me. I gave him a list of people he should talk to. It was very, very thorough. After the Stop the Church demo, the world hated us. "Oh, it's just awful what those nasty gay people did to you." I knew this was going to be difficult. For three weeks before the demo, I sent out information to the media explaining why we were doing what we were doing. There was no scenario for [protesting] inside [the church]. The inside demonstration was an inside last minute plan by an affinity group of ACT UP. It wasn't part of the overall plan. And that's what got everybody worked up, that they had gone inside and interrupted the mass. I had all this information [on attempts by the church to adversely influence HIV prevention policy]. And in a true testament to the idiocy of the media, none of this information was cited when they did reports after the demo.

All they were focusing on was the shock value of the people who had gone inside. So our message got lost. And we were reviled all over the place. I got media calls from as far as Belfast. I was on a radio with the Belfast BBC. Everybody was up in arms. And also gay organizations and AIDS organizations began to distance themselves from us during those two weeks.

That was on a Sunday. On the following Wednesday, we had an emergency press conference. My predecessor convinced me; he said, "you know Jay, this thing is still burning red hot." He said, "you have to have a follow up press conference." I said, "really?" And he said, "Definitely. We have to remind people why we did what we did. They're just blind with rage right now. And the issues are disappearing. There were reproductive rights. . . . The issues education (position on HIV prevention)."

Throughout December, the city media pilloried the group. Yet Blotcher continued to push the ACT UP counter narrative, explaining why they did what they did, why the world needs effective HIV education, based on evidence, not religious dogma.

On January 3rd, 1990, Jason DeParle's feature story, "Rude, Rash, Effective, ACT UP Shifts AIDS Policy" finally came out. It was at the height of the hate-in, the hatred for ACT UP by everybody. And it appeared on the front page of the Metro Section of the *New York Times*. And it said something like, "rash and drastic, ACT UP nevertheless effects change." And it was as close to a Valentine as the stick up its ass *New York Times* is going to give. It listed all the things that we had done to change the face of the epidemic, to empower people, to help people with AIDS. It said yeah, sometimes they go off a little bit, but what affirmation. And what followed that was, Phil Donahue called and said, "I want you guys on." And this is because of that. Several members of ACT UP went on and got to talk in a more reasonable level about why they do what they do. And the thing that we heard from people was that they had never seen ACT UP until then. If you're not from out of New York, you were unlikely to have seen what ACT UP did. This stuff was beamed all over the planet. And they saw angry fags. And people had only seen what they thought gay people were, limp wristed little nellies. And god knows, we are that. And that showed them that we were angry, that we had an energy. And we were a formidable adversary. . . . And the perception changed. People started to think I guess we have to take these people seriously.

Over and over ACT UP propelled its storylines through media outlets that communicated its goals. Members of the group pushed these messages in multiple forms, filming every protest they created with their own video crew, DIVA TV. Members of ACT UP would later send these videos to television stations or films, such as *How to Survive a Plague*, nominated for an Academy Award. In most cases, the group put their messages on propaganda, signs, even their bodies, created a spectacle that garnered the attention of independent and corporate media. In other cases, the group brought a message that they hoped other media outlets would communicate when they filmed ACT UP's action.

During the Republican National Convention (RNC) in 2004 in New York, a dozen activists from ACT UP stopped traffic in front of Madison Square Garden and stripped naked, the words "THE NAKED TRUTH: EMPEROR BUSH HAS NO CLOTHES" painted on their bodies. In terms of AIDS, "the emperor has no clothes" the group explained. "Stop AIDS Now." Sean Berry was one of the activists who participated in the street action. "We figured that in New York, especially at an event as important as the RNC that drew so much opposition from all corners of the city and from around the country, we had to do something different and outside anyone's experience. And that's difficult to do in New York, 'cause you see everything," noted Berry. "One thing you do not see as much these days is naked people in an intersection in front of Madison Square Garden."

"I have to say what worked best was that it was so easy to get media because it was about sex," noted Cyndra Feuer, who coordinated media for the action. "Ultimately it didn't have to be about sex, but we billed it as about sex. So it was so easy to get media. When I did the press releases I used the word 'naked.' That's what gets them to come out. We've discussed doing it more than once. But once you do it, I don't think you can pull that tool out for a while. It works because it's sensational."

Sean Berry elaborated. "We wanted to get the attention of our targets, which included President Bush, and the members of Congress that were there. But that we had to do something that would shock them, but at the same time was something which was comfortable for us. So at least as petrified as I was about the action, at the same time once it goes down, once you lock the chain or in that case, drop your pants, you enter tranquility. You start chanting and wait for the cops to come."

The following day's *New York Daily News* front page featured a photo of the naked protestors and their slogans from the backside, accompanied by the headline: "A New York Welcome to the GOP. Well, This is the Naked City" (D. Epstein, Lemire, & Becker, 2004). ACT UP was one of the most effective groups during the entire week of protests. Their long-time facilitator Ann Northrop explains: "I was at the naked protest, which was certainly one of the most original things that happened there. I was there as sort of a support for them to negotiate with the cops and that was quite an original event. Then the same group essentially got into Madison Square Garden. Their breaking in there was again the most original event. It only took a dozen of them in each case." While activists targeted policymakers, they hoped media would cover their message. It this case, it created an echo chamber with paper after paper covering the action. The hopes and limitations for such pranks to effect social change are many, noted Cyndra Feuer:

> It's going to break through all the media that you are bombarded with on a daily basis. It's going to somehow break through all of that shit. First of all, on a very logistical level, how do we get media to cover our event? No one gives a shit about girls who are going to lose their jobs or the Central American Free Trade Act [CAFTA]. So then, it's really about trying to come up with the cleverest way to get them with their cameras to cover our message. Every time it's like, What do we do this time?

What hasn't been done? What's going to be sexy? What's going to be image? So it's about what's going to cut across all the crap.

Over the years ACT UP was effective at moving media to cover their actions. They were certainly not the only activist group in town to do so. Throughout this period, members of ACT UP would collaborate with other groups to help link gestures of direct action with media.

Media Activism 101

"I immediately started going to the Monday night meetings. Within a few months, I was chairing the actions committee," recalled ACT UP veteran Andy Velez, describing his initial days as a media activist. "I became involved in the media committee. Mike Signorile and Jay Blotcher, they had been pals in college. And the three of us began going to the media committee meetings that Vito Russo was heading." A quarter century later, Velez is still active in countless movements, from ACT UP to Queer Rising and Occupy Wall Street. He describes how to handle media during a street action: "As far as sound bites are concerned, you have to learn how to say headlines. And you learn early on not to answer the question you're asked by a reporter. You answer the question they should have asked." In this way, those doing the organizing are injecting their own issue into the story. "You can even say to them, 'that's a really important question, but the one you should have really asked is.' And then you say what you were going to say as briefly as possible so that they can't really cut it out." After all, "they are either going to use you and you are going to get across your message or they won't be able to use it. Most of the time, they end up using it." Some keys to effective use of the media follow:

- Identify two or three talking points before an action.
- Learn them, rehearse them.
- The first should be your name, your role with the organization you are speaking for, and what the group does.
- The second point should be why you are doing what you are doing, what it means, what you want to see happen, the change you would like to see.
- Finally, the third point should elaborate on the second point. Keeping to three points is useful as reporters will use only a sentence or two in a story.

Television can be shorter; radio longer. But it is important to be precise.

- A well-prepared and concise message is vital. The better prepared an interview, the better the chance to achieve a given goal.
- Try to look at the reporter and minimize body movements.
- Have fun and make it short. This reduces the chance that one is misquoted. If one goes on too long, the wrong point may be highlighted by the reporter.
- And finally, bring eye catching art or images to actions to draw the media to cover a story (Cooper, 2002; Ruckus Society, 2011).

"We were really good at presenting things in an eye catching way," notes Velez. His point has long been it is useful to be confident in one's story, serious enough to use some humor and direct action to make a point. For example, in 2008, Velez brought these media techniques to fight a city policing policy that targeted gay men. "When the handcuffs clicked on my wrists on October 10, 2008, energy was released within me that connected me directly to the spirit of the Stonewall rebellion in late June of 1969," declared Robert Pinter, a victim of a false prostitution arrest. In the weeks afterward, members of ACT UP and the Queer Justice League joined in a coalition to fight the tactics of the New York City vice squad. Throughout 2008 the NYPD vice squad entrapped at least 30 men for prostitution after exiting Manhattan adult video stores with undercover officers who initially approached them for consensual sex. The city used these false arrests as the evidence in nuisance abatement suits against the stores to close them down. The arrests were part of a quality of life campaign, sanitizing signs of public sexual culture in New York (Crimp, 2002). In response, Robert Pinter founded the Campaign to Stop the False Arrests. The group held rallies from February through June of 2009 and his case drew the notice of media. The group highlighted a crackdown on cruisers, loitering, and signs of public sexual culture.

Andy Velez helped organize the rallies around the false arrests. "One thing one has to give up with such activism is a sense of good taste," Velez noted, describing an ethos that runs through queer activism. Of course, this requires letting go of shame, learning to speak up, and coping with embarrassment. Yet, he suggests it is worth it.

Velez described a brainstorming session during the meetings over the false arrests. In it they discussed whether to obtain a permit for a rally in Sheridan Square, which would push the action out several weeks. Velez had another idea. He said, "What are you waiting for? Too much time . . . You know what? Valentine's Day is coming up. I think we need to give the Mayor a Valentine. We should go to his house on 79th Street." So the following week, a relatively modest number of people attended the rally in the cold. "But it happened to be a day in which the media was hungry for something," Velez continued. There were as many journalists as activists. "We got huge coverage and a meeting the following week with the Mayor's office. It was mostly damage control." While the NYPD has been cracking down on visible signs of public sexual culture for years, suddenly they were apologizing. "We embarrassed the Mayor who wants to be god and be re-elected," Velez explained. "That's not stuff he wants to hear, even from crazies. That's why that meeting came about. And [NY Police Commissioner] Kelly has backed off." The charges against Pinter were dropped.

Velez and I talked about the ACT UP approach that he helped support. The push started with a simple request—pills into bodies. This was supported by research, direct action, mobilization, media, and some fun along the road. It borrows from the work of a generation of activists who put themselves on the agenda through direct action and eye-catching stunts. Arthur Bell, who ran the media for the Gay Activist Alliance helped hone the art of the zap, in which activists confront opponents. "He taught me that following the rules doesn't really guarantee you respect," explained Vito Russo. "[I]t is not tasteless to stand up and be who you are" (Schiavi, 2011, pp. 224–225). Andy

Velez concurs. "So what is conventionally good taste and manners, forget about it. . . . You have to be willing to tolerate embarrassment, discomforts of different kinds."

"Now ACT UP remains and I think this is a glorious thing, a non-violent organization," Velez continues. "We certainly were and are very confrontational. Yet we certainly never used physical violence against a person. But we did learn early on how effective and powerful it is to embarrass people. So you can do way more with the photograph of a corporate president or the *NY Times* owner and do a march, not just outside their office, but their home. Nobody, including Punch Sulzberger [publisher of the *NY Times*], liked being embarrassed at home in front of his neighbors."

Velez created a Warhol-like portrait of Sulzberger to highlight limitations in the *Times* coverage of the AIDS epidemic. "We got a picture of Sulzberger and I did a black and white copy of it and colored it in sort of Andy Warhol Day-Glo style. But I added a toilet plunger and the message was: 'Cut the Crap Punch.' At that time, the *Times'* coverage of the epidemic was so pitiful and lame. They were still hemming and hawing about using the term gay. And, of course, this epidemic swept a lot of that stuff away because the numbers were so huge. And then people at the *New York Times* itself began dying. And that made a difference. And the *Times* slowly began changing."

On Media and Language

One of the most important ingredients of a direct action campaign is the coordination of the actions within the group's message. As the accounts by Wicker, Blotcher, Berry, Feuer, and Velez highlight, language matters in campaigns. Once the issue is identified, activists go through the process of framing, communication, and messaging to determine how the issues are understood and translated into action. Much of the process begins with stories, particularly from the point of view of the community in need. Here, regular people start to reconstruct social reality from their own perspective, history, and point of view. "[R]eframing social issues is a fundamental element of any kind of social change activity," argues social welfare scholar Loretta Pyles (2009, pp. 114–115). This is why slogans, such as Housing Works, More Gardens, Drugs into Bodies are so effective. When activists make a clear argument, such as "preserve the gardens," which resonates with the community, they help win the message war over an issue. The point of media and communication is to use messaging that translates policy wins (R. Shaw, 2001).

Words are reality-creating machines. So, "the language that one utilized in organizing work may be the most critical component of community organizing practice," notes Pyles (2009, p. 114). "Language frames issues, and it communicates messages to constituents, targets, and the general public" (Pyles, p. 114). It also informs how social problems and policies are defined, understood, and implemented. When homelessness is defined by social workers in terms of a lack of services, the solution is more services; when it is defined in terms of loitering, the result is usually a correctional solution involving jail time. Countless social policies from welfare ("personal responsibility and work opportunity") to tax policy are framed with similar conflicts in terms of language. Conservative think tanks have spent over 3 billion dollars since 1970 to influence the ways people understand and frame social issues. Conservatives often win with their approach to framing issues around family and values, generating support even when the data and political support for issues such as global warming are against them, framing issues using feel-good terms such as "health, clean, and safe" that are favorable to their interests (Pyles, 2009, p. 115). Hence the support for the 2003 Clean Skies Act, which proposed to increase pollution. Activists have to challenge Orwellian uses of language that turn the meanings of policies on their head so they support the opposite of what they appear to support. The goal is to subvert predominant paradigms. Rather than "prostitution," advocates favor the term "sex work"; instead of "promiscuous," sexual civil liberties activists favor the term "sexual generosity." Hence the chant: "Unemployment and inflation/Are not the result of immigration. Stop it! Get off it/the real problem is profit!" to reframe immigration debate away from stigma toward more systemic issues. This is what is meant by "break the frame," explains Pyles. "Once the old frame was broken, participants constructed new frames to explain events . . . these 'reframing acts' are the first steps in calling attention to injustice and as a prelude to collective action," notes Pyles (2009, p. 114). "Framing acts should be strategic, with an eye toward a larger social change agenda. This can be facilitated by developing an understanding of social problems as interconnected rather than separate, isolated problems" (p. 114).

Video Activism

Throughout this chapter we have explored different ways of using media to communicate issues to multiple audiences. Activists use texts and tweets, as well as emails and phone trees, to connect people with social networks, where ideas expand as they find larger audiences. Through this organizing, ideas are communicated to multiple audiences, including newspaper readers, policymakers and the general public (McAdam, 1996). Sometimes activists communicate their messages through the media. At other times, they create their own media—via blogs and videos—that they distribute through social networks, YouTube, Diva TV, Independent Media Networks, community newspapers, and websites. Do-it-yourself activist media change understandings of social problems.

One of the most important tools of any activist today is the video camera. One of the earliest examples was the video of Rodney King beaten by members of the Los Angeles Police Department. When the video failed to help convict the officers of brutality, riots followed. Since then, however, video has become a vital tool for activists to counter official accounts of police action.

In short, the video camera has changed the world of activism. When a photographer filmed a conflict over curfew in a park in the Lower East Side of Manhattan, the experience changed his life. "Videotaping the '88 park riot turned me into an activist," confessed Clayton Patterson (2012). His video documented police abuses that the city had denied, later forcing the city to reclassify the event as a "police riot," compelling witnesses to come forward, and leading to congressional action over police abuse.

Let me cite a personal example: In 2003, a group of us planned to protest war profiteering at the Carlyle Group, a financial group that profited through its connections with governments and defense contractors. The scenario was simple enough. The protestors would converge, dressed like vampires, at the Carlyle Group offices on Madison Avenue between 58th and 59th Streets.

The demonstration was supposed to start at 8 on Monday morning. I was running late. Running down from the F train at 63rd, I'd lost the exact address of the protest. So I just followed the roars of the crowd and the riot police I noticed running through the streets. Within minutes of my arrival, we were arrested and taken away. When the city claimed we were blocking egress to the building, we produced video evidence that supported our claim that people had plenty of room to come and go. Our cases were eventually dropped by the city. With video evidence in hand, we sued the city and won a sizable settlement (Shepard, 2011b). Our cases were anything but unique. Throughout the period, video evidence helped challenge accounts of street arrests (Dwyer, 2005a).

Take the case of Chris Long, a New York cyclist who was arrested during a July 25, 2008, Critical Mass bike ride in New York City. The police charged Long with attempted assault and held Mr. Long for 26 hours in jail. Only after leaving jail, Long found a video of the ride showing he was violently knocked off his bike by a rookie policeman as he rode through Times Square. A tourist had filmed the incident and passed it on to Bill DiPaola, the founder of Time's Up!, a New York environmental group. DiPaola took the video and collaborated with Time's Up! and the Glass Bead Media Collective to distribute it. A veteran of the squatter and garden movements, DiPaola had seen the power of video documentation in the past. He had himself taken videos of gardens and squats being destroyed by city officials. Recognizing the influence of corporate media on public perception, DiPaola began to bring a video camera to almost every action in which he took part. While corporate media might not cover the actions in which he was involved, activist media might. This evidence was also useful to activists countering claims of the city. When the video of Chris Long's arrest was distributed through YouTube, it immediately went viral, with authorities seeing evidence that challenged official accounts suggesting that Long had assaulted the officer (Dwyer, 2008a). A recent Google Search for "Chris Long assaulted by police on Critical Mass" resulted in over one million hits. Search results tell the story of the ensuing legal battle over the video of differing accounts of that summer night. "Video of Cop Assaulting Cyclist at Critical Mass Ride," declared a report in the *Gothamist* on July 28, 2008. "NYC: police assault of Critical Mass cyclist probed," noted the World War 4. By September, charges against Long were dropped. Reports began to rewrite the narrative of the event, suggesting "Critical Mass Bicyclist Assaulted." A subsequent press release by Time's Up! was later picked up by a blog that declared, "Time's Up demands end to police harassment." The press release offered a more nuanced statement of what had happened (BikeBlogNYC):

Officer Caught on Video Knocking Critical Mass Cyclist off Bicycle Is Indicted. Time's Up! and civil rights activists demand an immediate end to NYPD's campaign of harassment toward cyclists

New York, NY (December 16, 2008)—NYPD Police Officer Patrick Pogan, who was caught on video aggressively knocking cyclist Christopher Long off his bicycle during the July 25, 2008, Critical Mass bicycle ride, has been indicted on five charges, including Falsifying Business Records and Offering a False Instrument for Filing in the First Degree, both Class E felonies, and Assault in the Third Degree, a Class A misdemeanor. The felony charges stem from the false arrest report and criminal court complaint that Police Officer Hogan [*sic*] allegedly filed about the incident. Officer Pogan's aggressive behavior and subsequent falsification of official documents are not *isolated events in NYPD's dealings with cyclists.* [emphasis added]

"This indictment is an important first step in the process of achieving accountability over some NYPD officers who continue to violate the civil rights of Critical Mass bicyclists. Perhaps, the indictment will send a strong message that it is no longer acceptable for police officers to take the law into their own hands vis-à-vis Critical Mass bike riders," states Civil Rights Attorney Norman Siegel. Since the 2004 Republican National Convention in New York City, civil rights activists and cycling advocates have long seen a pattern of excessive force and harassment against cyclists from even the highest ranks of the NYPD. "We hope that with this indictment, Mayor Bloomberg will now direct the higher-ups at the NYPD to discontinue their pattern of excessive force and dangerous tactics against cyclists and instead work with cyclists to make the ride safe and encourage non-polluting transportation," states Judy Ross, spokesperson for Time's Up!.

In the months that followed, official accounts of the story were dramatically impacted by the work of video and cycle activists. The officer involved in the case was eventually dismissed from his position with the NYPD and convicted of lying about his actions in the case (Eligon, 2010). Long successfully sued the NYPD, winning a settlement.

Occupy Wall Street and the Media

The advent of cheap technology has transformed the activist stage, bringing spectators and participants into the movement from around the world. When Occupy Wall Street (OWS) began an encampment in Lower Manhattan in the fall of 2011, live-stream video brought the drama of the streets to millions of spectators around the world. This footage brought live coverage of meetings, interviews, street demonstrations, and confrontations with police into the computers of thousands of viewers per second. Participants brought videos and cell phones, sending the images out to the world.

Vlad Teichberg is the creator of Global Revolution TV, which broadcast OWS-related content. He reflected on the approach. "It creates an instantaneous eye than cannot be censored. . . . It is one of the most honest forms of journalism because you can't even go back and edit yourself" (Moynihan, 2012). This helped spread the word about the protests around the globe, inviting new participants to join and politicians to take the actions seriously, as the movement grew stronger.

By the second week of the protests, police did not know what to make of the growing movement. "All day, all week: Occupy Wall Street!!!!" participants chanted, marching through New York's financial district, to Union Square September 24, 2011. At 12th and University, the march was met with arrests and police brutality. There, photographer Brennan Cavanaugh was arrested for taking pictures, along with another eighty participants, some enduring pepper spray and spending the night in jail.

Cavanaugh's offense: documenting a protest. We see here that while it does entail some personal risk, the ubiquity of cameras can help portray an event in a way that is not viewed simply through the "official" lens.

The Occupy Media Center was initially stationed right in Zuccotti Park. It functioned as an echo chamber for ideas, propelling a constant flow of live stream videos, photos, press statements, images, and stories.

Source: Photograph by Brennan Cavanaugh

Throughout this chapter we have reviewed different forms of media activism, including theories of narrative, media and language, as well as case studies of text messaging to organize a successful walkout for immigrant rights, Randolphe Wicker's Mattachine era work to advance more affirmative media coverage of gay life, video activism related to cycling, Occupy Wall Street, and ACT UP. The point is media activism helps project different points of view into the larger public discourse. Jürgen Habermas (1962/1991) suggested that the ideal of democracy is that everyone enters a public sphere where debate can take place. Yet Nancy Fraser (1989) and Douglas Crimp (2002) have long noted that differing outsider groups have limited access to this arena of public opinion, debate, and democratic participation. We have seen that effective use of the media—both

The last shot Cavanaugh took before his arrest at 12th St. and University, September 24, 2011. Media activism has its challenges, including the risk of arrest for those willing to cover the story as they see it. Such stories challenge official accounts, moving the storyline of street actions in favor of activist lines of thinking and action.

Source: Photo by Brennan Cavanaugh

in terms of knowing how to work mainstream media as well as using social media—can be a great leveler in this regard.

While media, messaging, and communication are essential parts of a campaign. Their vitality is limited without organizing or interaction with multiple forces, including direct action. Media and direct action work in mutually supportive ways. In the following chapter, we will see just how that works.

Direct Action and "Getting the Goods"

Gandhi wanted to end colonial rule in India. So his followers made salt, challenging the British prohibition again the practice. Civil rights activists wanted to battle a system of oppressive Jim Crow-era laws. So they risked arrest by sitting to order meals at segregated lunch counters. A group of young people recognized that the U.S. political system was overly influenced by money. So they started sleeping in a small park in the financial district of Manhattan, and the world recognized a gap between the 99% and the 1%. Much of organizing is born of just such gestures of freedom. These actions create counter-reactions, tension, and ruminations essential to any campaign. The driving force behind many community projects is a spirit of direct action. This practice is the subject of this chapter.

The point of nonviolent civil disobedience, or direct action, is that every person has resources and power to engage in actions, however large or small, to support freedom of the body and social imagination. Direct action is not only a mechanism used to compel others to alter their positions. Practitioners often see themselves as enacting the values that are important to them through these same gestures. Fellowship, convivial social relations, and nonhierarchical forms of community building are also realized through direct action. The practice is used by liberals, revolutionaries, religious groups, and those on the Left, Right, and center of the political spectrum. Yet, it is often social outsiders, those typically prohibited from or with limited access to legal participation in institutionalized politics, who tend to favor this approach. Direct action takes shape as blockades, encampments, occupations, vigils, street theater, refusal to salute officials, and even property alteration. This process is constantly reinvented (K. Moore & Shepard, 2012). More than anything, however, this approach is inspired by an impulse toward freedom.

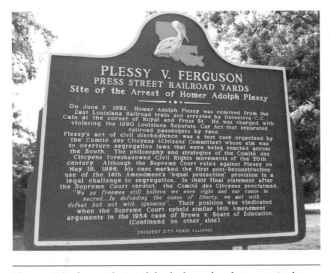

The practice of nonviolent civil disobedience has deep roots in the history of social movements.

Source: Photo by Erin Texeira

"Those who profess to favor freedom, yet deprecate agitation, are men who want crops without plowing up the ground," explains Frederich Douglas, in a quote on the AIDS Coalition to Unleash Power (ACT UP) Civil Disobedience Manual (n.d.). "They want rain without thunder and lightning. They want the ocean without the awful roar of its many waters. This struggle may be a moral one; or it may be a physical one . . . but it must be a struggle. Power concedes nothing without a demand. It never did and it never will." Going along to get along only serves the interests of the powerful. "[F]ollowing the rules doesn't really guarantee you respect," noted ACT UP's Vitto Russo (Schiavi, 2011, pp. 224–225).

"Sometimes people who appear powerless and stymied have used social movements to transform the problems they face—and history and society as well," notes Jeremy Brecher (2012, p. 7). "The U.S. sit-down strikes of the 1930's forced U.S. corporations to recognize and negotiate with the representatives of their employees. The solidarity movement and its general strikes led to the fall of Communism in Poland and helped bring down its demise throughout Eastern Europe and the USSR. The Arab Spring overthrew dictatorships in Tunisia and Egypt and reshaped the power configuration of the Middle East" (Brecher, 2012, p. 7).

"Non-violence is essentially non-cooperation. It expresses itself in the refusal to participate in the ordinary processes of society," notes 20th-century theologian Reinhold Niebuhr (1932, p. 240). According to the Midwest Academy, direct action takes place when "[t]he people who have the problem take action to solve it." Direct action-based community practice is "characterized by active resistance to existing or proposed laws or policies (Hanna & Robinson, 1994, p. 10). Sometimes, it takes place independent of a campaign or is part of a multi-method organizing campaign, complementing direct services or advocacy.

With many contemporary campaigns, there is little chance that organizers will ever have access to the negotiating table. Instead, they move ideas forward by way of creative direct action, accompanied by press releases outlining alternative proposals. When effective, these campaigns create stories that take on a life of their own. Sometimes such action involves a creative performance during public hearings, while in other cases it involves a creative disruption that cultivates the kinds of "creative tension" around an issue Martin Luther King (1963) suggests moves a campaign.

This chapter considers the ways in which organizers choose targets for actions. It offers a short history of media support for direct action, a review of the ethical choices faced by those involves, as well as applications of the practice to social services. Examples from the U.S. civil rights, abolition, and anti-war, as well as contemporary groups such as the Radical Homosexual Agenda, ACT UP, and Billionaires for Bush, follow. The International Workers of the World, founded in 1905 on the notion that all workers everywhere should be united, coined the slogan "Direct Action Gets the Goods." It still does today. Yet it is perhaps the most complicated of models of social action, for it straddles a divide between reformist and radical politics. Instead of lobbying for actions by others, it suggests the answers to our own problems can be found in our own actions (Graeber, 2009). It represents real power, often engendering potent or violent reaction from those in power. But when done with savvy and intelligence, it gets results in ways few other approaches can.

A Short History of Civil Disobedience

Civil disobedience is by no means a recent practice. People have long used whatever resources they had to resist mechanisms of oppression. The Greek women in Aristophanes' play *Lysistrata* (ca. 411 BCE) withheld intimate contact to force their husbands to end the Peloponnesian War. Other early forms of direct action include peasants' refusal to plow fields unless their demands were met; workers who went on strike; soldiers who collectively refuse to fight; and public mockery of officials during festivals. Anarchist movements were early proponents of the model, rejecting the legitimacy of the state and advocating the organization of individuals into self-governing groups (Brecher, 2012; K. Moore & Shepard, 2012; Scott, 1985, 1990).

The 19th-century Abolitionist movement is a classic early American example of civil disobedience. A decade before John Brown's raid at Harper's Ferry, Henry David Thoreau delivered a lecture titled "Resistance to Civil Government," later publishing it as the essay titled "Civil Disobedience." Like Brown, Thoreau favored the abolition of slavery. While this view had many proponents, relatively few favored the use of militant tactics. "All men recognize the right of revolution; that is, the right to refuse allegiance to, and to resist, the government," Thoreau urged early in the essay. "[W]hen a sixth of the population of a nation which has taken to be the refuge of slavery are slaves . . . I think that it is not too soon for honest men to rebel" (Thoreau, p. 12).

Instead of the ballot, Thoreau challenged supporters to vote with acts of freedom, noting, "Unjust laws exist: shall we be content to obey them, or shall we endeavor to amend them, and obey them until we have succeeded, or shall we transcend them at once?" (p. 17). This philosophy has served as a grounding point for countless movements.

One particular adherent to the principles of civil disobedience was Mahatma Gandhi (1869–1948). He led the Indian Independence Movement to challenge the British system of colonial rule. His approach to civil disobedience, dubbed Satyagraha, or "the way of truth," combined tenets of Hinduism with calls for refusal to participate in unjust laws. This method was designed to appeal to the moral goodness of opponents, with adherents willingly accepting the consequences of their noncooperation with unjust systems (K. Moore & Shepard, 2012). The whole world watched the police react to his campaign, with his followers willingly submitting to the assaults of the British without responding in kind. It made for thrilling political theater. "Non-violence, for him, has really become a term by which he expresses for the ideal of love, the spirit of moral good-will," noted philosopher Reinhold Niebuhr (1932). "This involves for him freedom from personal resentments and a moral purpose, free of selfish ambition" (p. 246).

The success of this nonviolent model of social change, which helped dismantle British colonial rule in India, inspired movements worldwide. In 1942, an American Quaker and pacifist named Bayard Rustin suggested this approach was needed to take on the Jim Crow system in the United States. This Gandhian model of nonviolent civil disobedience would become the driving force of the civil rights movement. Over the next two decades, Rustin helped move this agenda, teaching his disciple Martin Luther King Jr. the Gandhian approach to nonviolent civil disobedience. From the mid-1950s to the 1960s, civil rights organizers, including Rosa Parks, Rev. Martin Luther King Jr., Ella Baker, Myles Horton, James Bevel, and James Lawson used nonviolent methods including sit-ins, freedom rides, and mass arrest in their campaigns to fight segregation. By 1963, Rustin helped organize the March on Washington, setting in motion the end of the Jim Crow system in the U.S. South (D'Emilio, 2004; K. Moore & Shepard, 2012).

In subsequent years, countless movements crafted their nonviolent organizing approaches into distinct models of practice. Some followed the civil rights model of grassroots peoples' movements. Others emphasized building a just, peaceful, sustainable society. Some favored models of personal development, espousing nonviolent lifestyle choices (Graeber, 2009; Pyles, 2009). Many functioned as earnest gestures of opposition to injustice. For example, throughout the 1970s and 1980s, many in the anti-nuke movement followed their Christian faith to oppose the creation of nuclear weapons. Renowned campaigns targeted the Lawrence Livermore National Laboratory in Livermore, California, and PG&E's Diablo Canyon energy plant near San Luis Obispo, California. Here, activists used multiple tactics to block the construction of the plants, creating carnivals as well as experiments in direct democracy to oppose weapons and violence.

As noted, direct action is not limited by ideology. By the 1980s and 1990s, AIDS activists helped reinvent repertoires of nonviolent civil disobedience, mixing earnest forms of confrontation with satirical, often irreverent street theatrics. This link between celebratory and carnival-like action found expression in multiple forms within global justice movement, often taking transnational forms (K. Moore & Shepard, 2012; Shepard & Hayduk, 2002). Simultaneously, religious groups, such as Operation Rescue, made use of direct action to oppose abortion. In 1991, Operation Rescue started the Summer of Mercy, a wave of direct actions to block access to an abortion clinic in Wichita, Kansas. Eighteen years later, Dr. George Tiller was shot and killed by a man with contacts within Operation Rescue. The questions about direct action and ethical practices are many. But most agree that acts of violence, such as those by Operation Rescue, tend to betray the Gandian repertoire of nonviolent civil disobedience.

Other uses of direct action by conservatives include the successful use of disruption to block the recount of the ballots during the Florida election recount after the

2000 presidential election during what was dubbed the "Brooks Brothers Riot." More recent examples included the Tea Party approach to disrupting town hall meetings during the protests against health care reform early in the Obama administration. Throughout the years, the practice of civil disobedience has remained anything but static, as different groups experiment with tactical innovations of the practice (Moore & Shepard, 2012).

Some Practical and Ethical Guidelines for Direct Action

Starting in the late 1980s, ACT UP experimented with different methods of direct action. Any number of different movements informed this work. Quakers, veterans of the Women's, anti-war, anti-nuclear, and earlier LGBT movements mentored and trained ACT UP. Through this, the group established a series of "Guidelines for Direct Action" in its Civil Disobedience Handbook (n.d.): The group was clear it could not guarantee the safety of all participants at an action. Outside factors such as police and the legal system were out of its control. What it could control were its own plans to execute a direct action. Still the group sought to protect activists involved by organizing support and advocacy structures for those involved if problems arose. *Guidelines for Civil Disobedience* included a few of the simple points:

1. Those considering civil disobedience [CD] should take direct action CD training and join an affinity group.

2. At a demonstration, act with love for everyone, including bystanders and even police. Individual or group actions that endanger the well-being of others should not be undertaken.

3. Those considering acts of property alteration should do so openly and with legal advice, taking responsibility and care. Make sure not to put others in harm's way.

As the ACT UP guidelines for civil disobedience imply, this practice involves any number of tactical as well as moral decisions (Neibuhr, 1932). The code of conduct for social service providers calls for us to be aware of local laws and be ready to challenge those that support injustice: Human service professionals advocate for change in regulations and statutes when such legislation conflicts with ethical guidelines and/or client rights. "Where laws are harmful to individuals, groups or communities, human service professionals consider the conflict between the values of obeying the law and the values of serving people and may decide to initiate social action" (National Organization for Human Services [NOHS], 1996).

Everyone involved in advocacy is faced with a challenge: will they follow rules or policies they personally oppose or seek to change them? Many have chosen the former rather than the latter. Radical historian Howard Zinn (1970) suggests this is a problem in itself:

> Our problem is the numbers of people all over the world who have obeyed the dictates of the leaders of their government and have gone to war, and millions have been

killed because of this obedience. And our problem is that scene in *All Quiet on the Western Front* where the schoolboys march off dutifully in a line to war. Our problem is that people are obedient all over the world, in the face of poverty and starvation and stupidity, and war and cruelty. Our problem is that people are obedient while the jails are full of petty thieves, and all the while the grand thieves are running the country. (H. Zinn, 1970).

Human history is full of examples, however, of those who have not chosen to go along to get along. Let's consider the case of John Brown, mentioned earlier in this chapter. On the 16th of October in 1859, Brown and a group of abolitionists took over an armory in Harper's Ferry, West Virginia, where they hoped to use the weapons to force an end to slavery. Brown was tried and eventually found guilty of treason.

Brown told the court,

I have all along admitted the design on my part to free the slaves. I intended certainly to have made a clean thing of that matter, as I did last winter, when I went into Missouri and there took slaves without the snapping of a gun on either side, moved them through the country, and finally left them in Canada. I designed to have done the same thing again, on a larger scale. That was all I intended. I never did intend murder, or treason, or the destruction of property, or to excite or incite slaves to rebellion, or to make insurrection.

Yet, this is exactly what his actions triggered. "Had I interfered in behalf of the rich, the powerful, the intelligent, the so-called great, or in behalf of any of their friends . . . it would have been all right" (J. Zinn, n.d.).

While history tends to be kind to those who engage in civil disobedience, rarely are courts (Pyles, 2009). "This court acknowledges, as I suppose, the validity of the law of God," reasoned Brown. "I believe that to have interfered as I have done as I have always freely admitted I have done in behalf of His despised poor, was not wrong, but right. Now, if it is deemed necessary that I should forfeit my life for the furtherance of the ends of justice . . . I submit; so let it be done! I feel no consciousness of guilt" (J. Zinn, n.d.). Over the years many, such as Henry David Thoreau, would suggest that in a world of unjust laws, it is the moral person who ends up in jail. Many feel that this is a necessary price to pay for their willingness to take direct action.

Direct Action: Theory and Practice

The International Workers of the World's slogan "Direct Action Gets the Goods" highlights an important dynamic of this practice. Here, gestures of freedom, of building something better with one's actions are thought to prefigure new models of living. They take shape through blockades, the occupation of a welfare center, the creation of a community garden out of a vacant lot, squatting a building, or even giving away free food in a park. These gestures allow users to disrupt everyday mechanisms of power and injustice while repurposing spaces for alternative uses (K. Moore & Shepard, 2012; Pyles 2009). They also serve as exemplars of experimental forms of community building. If bike riders want to create a system of non-polluting transportation, the gesture—the group bike ride—reflects the external aim. For housing activists, direct action means creating squats or homesteads for people to live in; for community gardeners, this means planting more gardens. For Gandhi, this meant making salt. For Rosa Parks, it meant sitting at the front of the bus in violation of social convention.

"Activists who engage in direct action may be initially marginalized by society and only later appreciated," notes social welfare scholar Loretta Pyles (2009, p. 130). After her gesture, Rosa Parks found herself in jail. Today, her image is on a postage stamp. Acts of personal freedom often provoke the wrath of the state. But these acts also gain power as more and more people assert and act on creating the change they want, rather than just bemoaning the things they are against.

According to the Midwest Academy, a community activist training group, direct action organizing can include (1) direct services; (2) education for action involving teaching and research; (3) self-help programs in which people form mutual aid networks to help each other clean up neighborhoods, babysit, and more; (4) advocacy, including proposing laws; and finally, (5) direct action in which those who have a problem take action to solve it.

Direct action casework (Groves, 2003) builds on this scheme. It is a means of using direct action to push for the needs of those in one's caseload. This is aggressive case advocacy. Born with the National Welfare Rights Organization (NWRO), it helped those receiving services to access the benefits they were entitled to. After all, without legal advocacy as well as a movement behind it, rights-based frameworks only go so far. "Rights proclamations and legal entitlements by themselves haven't abolished poverty in the world," notes Frances Fox Piven. "And it won't be abolished until people themselves become a force" (Shepard, 2008b, p. 7). For NWRO, this meant organizing, helping the poor feel their own power, and breaking down stigma. Piven recalled a moment when a group of women on welfare went to advocate for services, in this case clothing, which they were legally guaranteed, but that few took advantage of because they were meant to feel stigmatized by the handout. "[O]ur plan was that the mothers would come with their children and sit in until they got school clothing grants," noted Piven (p. 12). Many did not want to participate, yet over time, these women started supporting each other, realizing they had every right to make claims on benefits. So the group held the "demonstration and got the school clothing grant" (p. 12).

Over the years, countless groups have pushed the link between direct action and direct services, connecting advocacy with direct action tactics, including street blockades and occupations of welfare centers when programs faced cuts (Mail on Sunday Reporter, 2012; Phelan, 2010). Others have linked the philosophy of nonviolence with new modes of clinical practice organized around nonviolent communication (Rosenberg, 2003).

CASE STUDY

Eustacia Smith—Social Ministry to Direct Action

For social worker Eustacia Smith, the journey to direct action began with her Christian faith. This is not an uncommon experience (Addams, 1910; B. Epstein, 1991; Niebuhr, 1932). After growing up in the church in the U.S. South, Smith was sent to New York as a missionary for the Southern Baptist Convention. "Worked for a church in the East Village, and at some point got kicked out of the church cause of my lifestyle. I pretty much transferred all of my passion and energy around religion to activism. But also the religion itself was always focused for me around activism and social types of ministry." For Smith, this practice was not about evangelizing; it was "about meeting people's needs." That is the part of the tradition she continues to embrace. Doing so, Smith followed a tradition from Dorothy Day to Jane Addams, who linked the politics with a social justice gospel. "I took all the messages from church that I feel like still are the things I believe today about being non-judgmental towards people, accepting people where they are. So things that for me seemed like matched up with activism and sometimes also with social work values. The other thing that got me into activism is just people that I ended up meeting. I worked in a homeless shelter." There Smith came in touch with activists—peace activists as well as AIDS activists. "I was doing more of the social working. I was in social work school and I was volunteering a lot." Over time, Smith gravitated more toward the direct action side of this practice. "My very first direct action was when the city was kicking the homeless people out of Tompkins Square Park. The church that I worked at was in the East Village and was right around there, and we worked a lot with the homeless people in the neighborhood. We did a sit-down meal every Wednesday out of the church storefront." At the time, Smith was involved with the East Seventh Street Baptist Church, commonly referred to as the Graffiti Church, in the East Village of Manhattan. "But it really reached out to the community [at large]. It was pretty much made up of the homeless people that went in the park, the low income people from Alphabet City or just the people in the neighborhood at that time." Through this church, Smith became involved in a campaign to keep the homeless from being evicted from the park. "There were a lot of community neighborhood meetings, community group meetings. And then the civic community board meetings, there were a lot of people that were members that weren't necessarily in favor of them kicking the homeless people out of the park." Smith participated in street marches with her church. "There was an organized action of people sitting in the park and not leaving on the days they were closing it." Smith was one of a group of activists who refused to leave when the police asked everyone to leave. "That was my first time getting arrested." Throughout this period, religious communities were joining local housing and community activists fighting the displacement and criminalization of the poor. On most occasions, the police refused to arrest anyone.

Smith became more and more involved with housing activism, which also connected her with movements related to AIDS/queer activism, social services, and harm reduction. "I was interested in working with homeless people. And partly, when I did the church work, a lot of the ministry there was focused on homeless people, because there were so many homeless people in the neighborhood."

Through these years, Smith spent a great deal of time thinking about what it would be like to be homeless. Her family took different forms as she grew up, as her mother had several marriages.

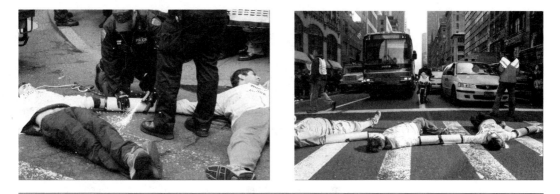

Smith and company were arrested as they blockaded the street corners of Fifth Avenue at 47th Street, stopping traffic flow for almost an hour. They used PVC pipes to hold themselves. The action inspired a wide range of reactions.

Source: Photos by Fred Askew

"And then she went to being a single parent," recalled Smith. "[A]nd we had nothing, and she was on welfare, and I was getting free lunch at school. And that definitely impacted me. Because I remember sitting in class and having to raise my hand in order to get the lunch, so everybody knew that our family was on welfare. And there was definitely a stigma around that. That struck me." Direct action would be a way to apply her own experience to getting results for others. As the AIDS crisis continued, many took a similar tack, organizing rallies, zaps, sit-ins, and street actions over the right to housing for people with HIV/AIDS. Many of these actions resulted in increases in the social policy net for people with AIDS (which the chapters on harm reduction in Part III will expand on).

Over time, Smith would establish a reputation as one of the foremost proponents of direct action in all of New York City. She described her approach. "It means it's an active form of resisting oppression. Non-violent sounds passive, but really it's making an active decision. And direct action can take many forms. Like civil disobedience is part of direct action, but it includes a whole range of other activities, like marches, whether they're permitted or not; like pickets—often union organizing does—basic flyering, fun zaps, fast zaps. You have all that kind of stuff. Street theater."

By the late 1990s, Smith became involved with a direct action group known as Fed Up Queers (FUQ; Mattilda, 2004). Some days the group used graffiti to bring pro queer messages into public space. The hit-and-run gestures were both playful and telling. The group helped repaint "the first AIDS memorial ever," explained Smith, referring to a stencil FUQ drew in the streets of the West Village of Manhattan. "[I]t was just a pink triangle that said, 'For Bobby, with love.'" It had been there for almost two decades when the city took it away in 1999. "The Jane Street block association decided they didn't want it on their block. They took it away. And so we repainted it. It gotten taken away again, and so then we repainted it all over the block." The group placed stickers with slogans such as "If You Don't Like Whores Then Get Out, We Were Here First!" critiquing gentrification. Through such gestures the group fought manifestations of collective stigma, as well as cultural erasure. At its peak, the group ignited waves of protests after the police killing of unarmed immigrant Amadou Diallo in 1999 (Shepard, 2009).

According to Smith's colleague in Gay Shame (n.d), these gestures "utilize hands-on intervention to directly challenge hierarchies. By using spectacle to expose hypocrisies, direct action terrorizes the status quo and revitalizes public space. In the process, it builds a delicious and defiant culture of resistance. Direct action encourages people to push the boundaries of acceptable behavior in order to create new possibilities for organizing, self-determination, and activism."

Over and over, the group challenged oppressive mechanisms of everyday living. "One of my favorite actions that we did was the red paint action," recalled Smith. "There was a dyke who was attacked outside of a bar in Park Slope. And there were some injuries; it was a pretty big attack. So we went to the intersection where the bar was, and we took gallons of red paint and we just poured red paint in the street. But then of course as cars drove by it spread. And then we wheat pasted posters so that people had some information about what it was about. No one did get caught doing it." But everyone whose car spread the red paint was made aware of the violence of homophobia. Ultimately, one of the purposes of a direct action is disrupting mechanisms of everyday living and power, creating the kind of "creative tension" necessary to unsettle the status quo (King, 1963). While some campaigns are designed to compel government to move, others, such as those described by Smith, are meant to bring attention to a long-dormant problem or cases of neglect (Pyles, 2009, p. 131).

❖ ❖ ❖ ———————— ❖ ❖ ❖

While the practice may seem occasionally anarchistic, there is a method to the approach. Effective practitioners consider a few basic criteria before moving forward. The first—the campaign's goals—will direct action move a campaign closer to its goals or set it back? Other considerations include organizational dynamics, constituents, allies, opponents, targets, and tactics. Who is the group going after and why? And does the group have the capacity to pull off the action? What tactic should the group employ from their bag of tricks? Tactics include boycotts, which utilize consumer power; strike or zaps (loud disturbances), which use disruptive power; or bird-dogging, in which groups target specific individuals. This "can be very effective," notes Loretta Pyles (pp. 130–131). Yet every action creates a reaction worth considering. Sometimes these reactions produce positive outcomes. At other times they trigger hostile reactions and legal complications worth anticipating.

Action, Reaction, and Narratives of Disobedience

More than any other form of practice, direct action raises many moral and ethical questions (Niebuhr, 1932). Before engaging in this practice, King (1963) suggested practitioners assess both the problem at hand as well as their willingness to take the risk of putting themselves in the morally and legally difficult situation of breaking the law and risking legal penalties. King advised those considering it to (1) fully assess the state of the problem they are challenging, (2) negotiate with decision makers before moving forward, (3) purify the self, and (4) take action.

Every action creates a reaction (Alinsky, 1969). To engage in direct action is to invite policymakers to change their mind. It also invites a punitive backlash. A civil disobedience from March 26, 2003, illustrates this point. The story of the case dates back to the days shortly before the beginning of the Iraq War. Ten days earlier, 24-year-old American peace activist Rachel Corrie was killed by a tank in Israel as she attempted to block it. In light of Corrie's death, and anticipating an imminent U.S. attack on Iraq, a group of U.S.

peace activists organized a civil disobedience action in the Diamond District of Manhattan. Under a signs stating "Witness to Israeli War Crimes" and a model of the armored Caterpillar bulldozer that rolled over Rachel Corrie, this group covered themselves in fake blood, chained themselves down across Fifth Avenue and chanted, "Occupation is a crime, from Iraq to Palestine." After police cleared the scene, 16 activists were arrested and charged with disorderly conduct. Stories from their action spread around the world.

Over the next two years, New York District Attorney Morgenthau's office asked for jail time for the eight activists with "previous contacts with the criminal justice system." Most of the "previous contacts" cited by the DA's office included cases that had been dismissed or sealed from prior years. The call for the use of dismissed charges was unprecedented. Twelve of the 16 activists received one-year discharges, with community service and court fees. The final four, Steve Quester, Kate Barnhart, Eustacia Smith, and Lysander Puccio, faced jail sentences for their actions.

Each of the four activists was allowed to offer testimony before Judge Stolz sentenced them on August 1, 2005. If ever there were an articulation of the acts of moral witnessing, the three testimonies offer as clear a narrative of the call for civil disobedience. They also highlighted the very real risks and complications of direct action–based practice.

"I am standing before you today with serious questions about our priorities as a society," began Kate Barnhart in her sentencing statement to Judge Robert M. Stolz. "I am the director of a shelter for homeless youth. We provide a safe place for kids who have fled from abusive families, been kicked out by parents who couldn't tolerate their being lesbian or gay or transgender, or kids who've just plain lost their families. . . . The young people who come to us are injured, sometimes physically, but always emotionally. . . . Our shelter consists of cots lined up in a church basement. Our annual budget is tiny. The hours are long, the conditions hard, and the work is—quite frankly—heart-breaking."

But, Barnhart explained, the staff does it: "I do it—because I believe that some things are more important than money or personal comfort or material gains and chief among those is the sanctity of human life. I was taught a long time ago, as part of my Jewish education that the predominant value of the Torah, the one situation which surpasses all the other commandments, is the preservation of human life."

After the judge read her testimonies in the ACT UP Oral History project, Barnhart suggested, "it should be clear that my commitment to this principle has taken a wide variety of forms during my life." This included working to raise awareness of atrocities being committed in El Salvador, "efforts to protect my peers from contracting HIV," and her "current work, keeping homeless teens safe from the dangers of the streets." Each action by ACT UP was informed by the same disposition. "The ACT UP action at the stock exchange was a desperate effort to lower the prices of AIDS drugs, at a time when hundreds of thousands of people around the world were—and still are—dying grisly, unnecessary deaths because they can't afford medication. The other . . . was in response to the horrendous killing of Amadou Diallo, an incident which provoked international outrage and protests at 1 Police Plaza." Barnhart echoed John Brown, concluding, "Your Honor, if standing up for the fundamental human rights—the right to live and to live in freedom—is a crime, then I am a criminal, because I cannot be anything else."

Eustacia Smith described a similar series of decisions in her sentencing statement. "Human behavior and action does not happen in a vacuum. There is a context in which I acted on March 26, 2003. Rachel Corrie, a young American humanitarian worker, had just been killed by bulldozers paid for by our tax support, for trying to defend a Palestinian home." She acknowledged the portrait painted of her as someone who acts carelessly.

> But I think you would be hard pressed to find a group of people who care more for the rights and safety of other human beings and who believe more in the sanctity of life. In fact the majority of our lives have been spent fighting for the human rights of all others. In your speech to my colleagues before you sentenced them, you characterized our action as irresponsible and talked of other forms of expressing our opinion that would have been "legally acceptable." I think the hundreds of people arrested during the Republican National Convention for simply walking down a side walk is a testament to how this system is making the kind of "free speech" you were referring to obsolete.

Smith noted that since she was arrested in 2003, some 1,786 U.S. soldiers had died in Iraq. Another 23,000 to 26,000 Iraqi civilians, including children, had died.

> And Rachel's family and friends have had to deal with enormous grief. There is a time for organizing a rally. And a time for advocating to congressional legislatures. There is a time for working in social service capacities and in social movements. And there is a time for civil disobedience. . . . Since the time of our action between 6 and 7 million people have died from AIDS because they lacked the resources to buy medication. Medication that could have easily been bought with the billions we have spent on this war. Since the time of our action, the estimated 3.5 million homeless people in the US remained homeless because we spent our resources on war rather than taking care of our own citizens. Since the time of our action, Marla Ruzicka, a friend and colleague of an organization I work with, who was a US citizen working with victims of the bombings in Iraq was killed in a bomb herself in Iraq. There are times in the course of history when the letter of the law conflicts with what is morally right. In these times, we must choose what is morally right. If the heroes in generations before me had not made the choice to overlook the letter of the law and do what was right, then there would have never been a civil rights movement. In the civil rights movement, streets were blocked due to civil disobedience on a regular basis. If my predecessors had not participated in civil disobedience then people with AIDS in this country would not have access to affordable lifesaving medication. Without the willingness of people to commit acts of civil disobedience, we would still be paying taxes to England. [W]ould you really want the world to still be in those places?

Smith concluded by speaking as a social worker and a Christian.

My actions have been driven by the vow that I took as a social worker and the values I learned growing up in the Christian faith. I believe that as human beings we have an obligation to use whatever resources we have to work for the health and safety and the human rights of others around us. I cannot turn a blind eye to injustice, particularly an injustice that I know intimately. . . . But when you know them intimately you must take action. The most immoral, I believe, even the most criminal action one could take is to know oppression and suffering of another intimately and personally and to not take action.

After the testimonies, Judge Stolz scolded the group for their unapologetic approach, but reduced their charges to a week of community service. Quester would note, "I'm immensely proud of my years in ACT UP, and am filled with admiration for people, like my co-defendants Staci and Kate, who remain active in the organization."

Shortly after the sentencing, Smith described her reasons for doing what she did, given the risks. "It was a combination of things; it happened right at the same time that the U.S. started the war in Iraq. And so there was a call for direct action around that. But also what had happened is that Rachel Corrie was killed in Palestine while trying to defend a home." Smith noted Corrie had been engaging in nonviolent direct action. "And she was run over by a bulldozer and killed. And it was clearly not accidental."

Looking back on the case, Smith worried legal battles would have a chilling effect on activism. "It was the first time actually in all my years of doing activism, and I didn't do anything different than I've always done, that I actually had to go to a trial. The case usually gets dropped, it gets lowered, you get an ACD [adjournment in contemplation of dismissal], and maybe some little bit of community service."

Speaking with Smith, I asked if the National Association of Social Workers had been of any help or support. "I guess I would say no," noted Smith. "They're just totally absent I think around issues like that oftentimes." Of course, that pattern was part of a larger historical trend. "The NASW and social workers in general focus so much on wanting to be considered professional clinicians . . . and on clinical work that a lot of the history of community organizing and social justice work has gotten left behind. That's sad. But the social work field is very behind on a lot of social movements lately."

Direct Action and Storytelling

Much of direct action is about a different form of community-building practice than that taught in school. Sometimes the practice even involves spending some time in jail. But its similarities to other community building activities are many. This is why it is important to go through it with some friends and comrades. Many activists recall building a sense of solidarity with others through the stories told going through the system. "We were taken to the court yard on Pearl Street, inside One Police Plaza," noted Brennan Cavanaugh, a volunteer with Time's Up! after being arrested during the Occupy Wall Street movement in October of 2011. "Then they took our bags outside, put us inside. I was put in a gang cell with about fifty guys. It's a special cell I've never seen before. There was the squatter symbol carved into the benches. There was the Missing Foundation symbol, and I also saw a sticker. It's a beautiful sticker from 1999, it says: 'New York City Rocks/ Critical Mass/ Reclaim the Streets' with a bunch of people holding a banner that says, 'Clean Air! Time's Up!' The other picture was of the guy on a tripod on Broadway. So I'm in this holding cell and I find this sticker and I'm home." Cavanaugh was immediately aware he was witnessing a short history of protests in the graffiti in arresting areas. "And they don't take them down."

Storytelling and direct action are vitally connected. "From the earliest days of the movement, personal story-telling had helped to build solidarity—and to put faces on OWS and better explain it to the outside world," note the Writers for the 99% (2011, p. 140) in their history of the Occupy Movement. "For many, a desire to exorcize associated frustrations—toward positive ends, if possible—was deeply motivating" (p. 140). Storytelling is both part of the internal conversation and community building of many a movement, as well as the way movements communicate their goals.

As the cases above suggest, representation and media narrative help observers shape their understandings of a given political action. When done well, each action triggers reactions and counter-narratives. After the protest Steve Quester, Smith, and Barnhart took part in, photos in the media showed people spilling coffee on those lying down in the streets. Bob Kohler, another member of Fed Up Queers, noted that some felt the action was anti-Semitic. "The crowd was really hostile towards us," noted Smith. "We had a mock bulldozer that was made of plywood and cardboard and it got demolished by some of the people in the crowd—especially one man that just completely lost control and started beating it and pulling us." It is vital for a direct-action campaign to consider the ways stories are conveyed, the ways symbols communicate a message, even in the face of a potential backlash.

More than a press release or a policy report, direct action helps convey what is wrong or right. Yet, it must be part of a coordinated campaign, with a clear overarching story and message. Bayard Rustin defied the apartheid systems around bus seating, attempting to sit at the front of a bus years before Parks, and was beaten without the world knowing about his action. Yet, when Parks did so, her gesture of freedom was connected with a campaign, which propelled the action and its message reverberated through time, pushing the movement forward (D'Emilio, 2004).

Martin Luther King Jr. was aware of the image and the frame used to advance the narratives of the civil rights movement. He knew that the image of children being exposed to high-pressure fire hoses would bring public sympathy to the cause. Observers of movements have come to describe this as strategic dramaturgy (McAdam, 1996).

Andrew Boyd, the founder of the satirical group Billionaires for Bush, was acutely aware that social action can take on the feeling of a street theater piece. Yet, not everyone thinks that way. "[T]he guys who went through the Highlander seven-month course and then sat down at the Greensboro lunch counter, they understood theater." Boyd explains: "You didn't have to read Artaud. They understood it more from that tradition, of Gandhian theater. Gandhi understood theater." Yet political theater—the theater of democracy and direct action—takes on an entirely different kind of complexion. "It's more in terms of human drama and human power and chemistry," notes Boyd. "But nonetheless, it has this incredible impact."

ACT UP emphasized the point that activists speak not to, but through the media. The group emphasized the need for social movements to create their own media for their actions. The point was to advance the story of the actions being presented, using media for results, not just coverage (R. Shaw, 2001). Here direct action connects media with clear movement goals, which in turn influences social discourse and policy. With each gesture, effective activists are aware of who they are communicating their message to: potential recruits, those working within the movement, allies, potential coalition partners, media outlets, public opinion, and public policymakers controlling state action (McAdam, 1996). Not all actions are designed for media just as not all are designed for policymakers. But it is useful to know who is the target of an action and why.

By the 1960s, the New York Mattachine Society was increasingly influenced by the civil rights movement, borrowing tactics as well as political understandings. Randy Wicker was part of an action in April of 1966, when members held a sit-in to fight their exclusion from bars not under mob protection. They entered bars and announced, "We are homosexuals. We are orderly, we intend to remain orderly, and we are asking for service." The first few sites went without incident. At the fourth site, they were refused service. The *New York Times* story noted, "3 Deviates Invite Exclusion by Bars." The confrontation eventually led to a favorable ruling supporting homosexuals.

We have seen how a well-coordinated direct action can influence the way we understand a story. When New York Mayor Michael Bloomberg announced his plans to run for a third term as mayor in 2008, many were dismayed. But frustration in the streets was palpable. So, a group of activists, including myself, made a plan. We knew that the chambers of the New York City Council were full of photographers and media. We decided to disrupt the proceedings, bringing our message into the usually staid hearings. Concerns about our billionaire mayor undoing a popular term limit law and purchasing a third term in office, even when voters had clearly stated they opposed third terms for New York mayors, would be raised. After spending a late night painting banners, one of them declaring "Bloomberg to Democracy: Drop Dead," we entered the council hearings positioning ourselves between the cameras and the hearings themselves. Journalists would have plenty of room to photograph us before we were evicted. We leaked our story to a sympathetic blogger who came to the hearing with us. We carried the banner in our bags. Once the hearings had begun, we stood up with our banner declaring billionaires had ruined the economy, holding the banners as long as we possibly could, as the city press corps stood taking pictures. It took no longer than fifteen minutes before we were escorted out of the chambers. But that was enough time. By lunchtime, our friend's blog was up. "It's not about term limits; it's about fake democracy." Others disagreed: "The Radical Homosexual Agenda seen in Council this morning," declared the blog posted on jameswagner .com. Our story of the conflict between democracy and plutocracy became the storyline of the day. The dailies largely echoed the story from our friend James Wagner, whose blog offered the first story of the day. "Protesters briefly disrupt term-limits hearing," declared the *Daily News*. "Opponents of Mayor Michael Bloomberg's attempt to change term-limits law so that he can run again jumped up and disrupted a City Council hearing, yelling 'billionaires have ruined this economy.'" Later, *New York Newsday* declared, "'Bloomberg to democracy: Drop Dead': Protestors—and supporters—speak out at term limits hearing."

The point of the action was to highlight the message that democracy means more than buying TV ads to persuade more voters. "Democracy is not just a counting up of votes; it is a counting up of actions," notes Howard Zinn (1970). "Without those on the bottom acting out their desires for justice, as the government acts out its needs, and power and privilege act out theirs, the scales of democracy will be off. That is why civil disobedience is not just to be tolerated. If we are to have a truly democratic society, it is a necessity. . . . Civil disobedience founded this country. This is what the American Revolution was about." Yet, it's always useful to have a few lawyers, or those connected to lawyers, ready to think through how to position the argument of a movement in legal terms, to get people out of jail, and to reframe issues in short- and long-term ways. This is the subject for the next chapter.

9

Legal Strategies ❖

Direct action certainly secures wins—such as preventing a budget cut. But to effect deep institutional changes, a larger campaign, focusing on both long-term and short-term goals, is needed. Crucial in the long-term thinking of successful campaigns is a legal strategy. Civil rights activists, for example, were supported by the work of legal heavyweights such as Thurgood Marshall. His work helped bridge the gap between direct action and institutional change. Such inside-outside work helps campaigns to broker long-term wins. This chapter considers the ways organizers use legal strategies to move their campaigns forward.

The case studies throughout this volume highlight the work of organizations formed not only to change laws but to change the system. Dean Spade (2011) formed the Sylvia Rivera Law Project after he was arrested using the men's bathroom at Grand Central Station after a protest (Shepard, 2012a). As a transgender man, Spade felt like it was impossible to get a good lawyer. So he started a legal clinic for trans populations, often marginalized from social services. His is a story about social movements, direct action, and the ways social movements change the way we understand our relationship to social reality. There are many such stories of activists who did not get mad, they fought to make sure the same thing did not happen to others in similar situations.

According to the Miami Workers Center, a strategy action center working for the underserved in Dade County, Florida, social justice work involves four key components, described as the "Four Pillars of Social Justice Infrastructure." These are the Pillar of Policy, the Pillar of Consciousness, the Pillar of Service, and the Pillar of Power. These four aspects are found throughout the model described in this book. While the Pillar of Service involves vital services that keep people alive and thriving, the Pillar of Power involves organizing to support long-term success (Mananzala & Spade, 2008). Legal advocacy is a central part of this approach.

Legal advocacy helps move a campaign forward by connecting research with policy. "In order to become the hero/pain in the ass of an environmental saga, it is only necessary to be obsessive, compulsive, and workaholic, to have the instincts of a trained investigator, the dispossession of a trained bloodhound, and the skill of a research librarian," notes Loretta Pyles (2009, p. 129). "Combining plodding research and investigation with gonzo activism . . . [you must be] part Ralph Nader and part Abbie Hoffman" (p. 129).

Know Your Rights

Undergirding successful legal strategies for social movements is knowledge of one's rights, in addition to clear goals and parameters for succeeding. Sometimes this means knowing how far one can go in terms of civil disobedience that maximizes disruption without incurring criminal charges. In other cases, the point is to transform the system itself. In many cases, it means knowing what one has a right to and making sure one can get it. Piven and Cloward (1977) describe this as an enforcement strategy. The point is to know the ins and outs of policies and make sure those laws are being enforced. "Pursue the services that are on the books and also change the books," explains Frances Piven (Shepard, 2008b, p. 7). Groups such as Housing Works have pushed this legal, administrative strategy for years, litigating when the city failed to comply with its laws in order to force the city to do the right thing (Shepard, 2008a).

Such a principle is at the heart of direct action casework. Tim Groves (2003) notes that the method has three core components: (1) linking legal advocacy with social action, (2) charting an alternate practice to those offered by legal clinics or agencies, and (3) furthering the interests of those on one's caseload, with whom one is working. Their case is the reason one is there. The process begins when one knows one's rights as well as what one is guaranteed by laws. "By taking on the cases of people who are not receiving all the benefits they are entitled to under the law you create a legal backing to your demands," explains Groves. "By combining law with disruptive action you bring teeth to those demands." While those in power, the police, the lawmakers tend to pick and choose which laws to fully adhere and which can be selectively enforced, their choices are seldom scrutinized. Channels for redress tend to take years, if they happen at all. "Direct action casework is designed to cut through this to get people what they deserve," Groves follows. "Keeping business as usual is very important to the functioning of many institutions," notes Groves. "Our success comes from demanding that people receive what they legitimately deserve under the law and backing it up with disruptive action."

At times one just has to get a lawyer involved to support long-term successes. While community gardeners in New York locked themselves down to prevent the bulldozing of the Esperanza Community Garden on East Seventh Street in 2000, activists made contact with the attorney general, who put a temporary restraining order on the bulldozing of community gardens. This led to further protections (Shepard, 2012b).

When members of Occupy Wall Street were prevented access to Zuccotti Park by NYPD-erected barricades, they coordinated with the National Lawyers Guild to draft a letter to the city highlighting their legal right to be in the space unhindered by such barricades. Down the barricades came. The power of the judicial system superseded the law of might too often employed by police.

In other cases, simply knowing one's rights and conveying that knowledge helps create a more effective collaboration. Susan Wright, of the National Coalition for Sexual Freedom, runs S&M parties in large hotels. "When you explain it to the officers and the attorney general that we can stay within the legal parameters, we're finding that we just don't have any trouble at all," she explains. "Even with hotels, hotels love us. We come in; we pack the hotels like the Shriners do. We're really responsible people."

When activists with the New York City AIDS Housing Network found that the city was sending homeless people with HIV/AIDS out into the streets in violation of city law, rather than providing them with shelter, they contacted a lawyer with Housing Works, who interviewed the clients, discovered a pattern, and litigated.

On June 20, 2001, Judge Emily Jane Goodman issued a ruling in the case filed by Housing Works staff attorney Armen Merjian, charging contempt of court in *Hanna v. Turner*. Mr. Merjian filed the case after hundreds of clients of the City's Division of AIDS Services and Income Support were denied the emergency housing placements they are guaranteed under Local Law 49. The 17 clients involved with the case were all vindicated and granted relief.

"To know that these very sick individuals will be given some form of compensation for the many nights that they were forced to sleep in the streets is great news, but the trouble at the welfare centers still continues," said Bob Kohler, the most dedicated DASIS Human Rights Monitor. "Hearing this is definitely wonderful, but this is also just two days after the City left a homeless woman living with AIDS in a wheelchair without accessible housing so I can't get too excited about it."

"The DASIS Human Rights Watch will continue to ensure that the City complies with the Judge's decision in *Hanna v. Turner* and ceases to send sick people to false addresses and hotels where they are not registered," said Jennifer Flynn, then director of the NYC AIDS Housing Network and DASIS Human Rights Monitor.

CASE STUDY

Greg Berman and the Red Hook Community Justice Center

On World AIDS Day 2010, Charles King and a group of activists from Housing Works were arrested on the streets of Grand Army Plaza in Brooklyn, protesting cuts in AIDS services. Yet, instead of going to Criminal Court in downtown Brooklyn, where they were sure to face tough charges, they were taken to Red Hook Community Court in South Brooklyn. There the activists were released immediately.

The Red Hook Community Court is famous for just treatment of those moving through the system. The court is part of the Red Hook Community Justice Center, a multidisciplinary community court, that provides social services and prevention designed to reduce the revolving door of prison, parole, and reentry that plagues much of the criminal justice system today. The genesis of the court was the murder of Principal Patrick Daly in 1992. While principal of PS 15, he was killed in the cross-fire of a drug shooting while going to check up on a student who failed to attend school that morning. At the center of a waterfront neighborhood that had been the center of commerce for some three hundred years, by the 1980s the neighborhood was in disrepair. Most of the dock jobs had disappeared from the port community, and while many people simply moved away, others turned to the black market economy to survive. By the 1980s, the crack epidemic had overwhelmed the space. The neighborhood became the site of the NYCHA Red Hook Houses, the largest housing project in Brooklyn. A July 1988 article on crack in *Life Magazine* described the neighborhood as one of the "worst" neighborhoods to live in in America. The Red Hook Community Justice Center was an effort to get to get to the root of the problems in the neighborhood.

Greg Berman, the director of the Center for Court Innovation, described how the community came together to form the court. After Principal Daly was killed, the district attorney, Charles Hynes, hoped to get to the bottom of the issue. What was below the surface of the crime? How could the community prevent similar incidents? D.A. Hynes prosecuted the killers, but hoped to do more than just put another person behind bars. He wanted to deal with the underlying issues the killing represented. In the spirit of Research as Action (see Chapter 6), Hynes undertook a survey of the neighborhood that would function as a community-based needs assessment. The court started a community-based research process, sending messengers out to the community asking members to come to a meeting to talk about the strengths of the neighborhood, not just its limitations. Court representatives attended community council meetings, heard concerns about the need for housing, and listened. "Good organizations listen," notes Berman.

Throughout these conversations, researchers looked not only for problems, but for community assets. The strengths of the community were many. The physical environment was less dense than other parts of New York City. It had parks, fields, and an open waterfront. The neighborhood was and is full of multigenerational families. While the community suffered from the lack of jobs once the shipping industry had left, what remained was an indigenous leadership who were ready to lead the community into a new way of looking at itself. Berman and company reached out to this local leadership, organized a focus group with priests, educators, elected heads of the community board, and representatives from the Red Hook Civic Association, and said to them, "What would you like to see here?" Berman and company tried to be direct with the community about what he and his group could and could not do; they could not run a jobs program. What they could do was listen to people's concerns. Following the principles of participatory action research, they learned of the deep concern about the lack of jobs, the infestation of drugs, and the overall sense of despair in their neighborhood. The black market was finding its way into a community with few other opportunities or social spaces. What the researchers heard was that the courts were not helping residents deal with things; the midtown court was referred to as "misdemeanor court." The core feedback was that the courts need to focus on prevention, not wait for problems before they engaged. The city and criminal justice system was reactive. Red Hook could be different.

The idea of a community center took root, and in 1997, a youth court with a community mediation center was established. The goal was to get to the root of community problems around drugs, lack of services, and jobs. Referrals for services would be available at the youth court. In addition, the community would focus on creating community gardens and a community farm. These gardens, in addition to becoming aesthetic points of pride for the neighborhood, would also serve as places to send those going through the courts for community services—a much more positive environment than typically found. Outreach workers would go out into these spaces. The point was to engage people in the community instead of seeing them go through the revolving door of prison, parole, and recidivism. This was an approach with a long history in community practice (J. Bennett, 1981).

The Red Hook Community Justice Center was born out of these focus groups and conversations. The plan was innovative and ambitious. The Red Hook Community Court would work in conjunction with a think tank, the Center for Court Innovation. Instead of merely prosecuting people, the court would provide free services. It would deal with low-level offenses while attempting to reduce big ones. Its focus would shift from prosecution and incarceration to dealing with the underlying causes of the neighborhood decay. Since about 70% of the arrests involved the drug trade, the main goal became prevention: helping to reach out to the community and intervene before people found themselves in front of a judge. The court would address institutional barriers, choosing issues by consensus, gathering information, creating programming, and evaluating its own efforts. The court would offer social services, including case management and housing assistance.

Today, the Red Hook Community Justice Center serves 200,000 people in three precincts; one judge sees them all. The court tries to stay in tune with the surrounding community, regularly surveying the community, gathering information about issues from HIV/AIDS to trash dumping. Four principles drive the process: One, don't go into the community assuming you know what is needed. Don't be presumptuous. Two, use data to evaluate services on a quarterly basis. Three, ask people why they are involved in the criminal justice system. Four, address the problems presented.

After I finished talking with Greg Berman and the rest of the services staff, I was able to sit in court and watch the judge, Alex Calebrese, hear cases. One young teenager, an African American high school student, was facing marijuana possession charges. Calebrese listened to the case, dropped the charges, and reframed the hearing into a conversation about what the young man was going to do with his life, his education, and college plans. What could have been the beginning of a downward spiral for that young man instead became a forum in which he could be heard and made to feel that he was a worthwhile part of the community.

Later I thanked everyone and grabbed a cab home. My cabbie noted where I had been—and had something to share. "He's given me a bunch of chances. He's a good guy," the cabbie explained, referring to Calebrese. "And they have a lot of things going there, services, et cetera. At that other court on Schermerhorn Street, all they do is send people away." Laughing, I asked the driver, "Did they pay you to say that?"

While the Red Hook Community Court is a step in the right direction, the criminal justice system as a whole continues feed the big business that is the prison industry. Prevention is not the main thrust, it seems: punishment is. The example of the community court is a model worth emulating. Courts like it offer positive alternatives to the legal system, replacing jail sentences with referrals to services that prevent problems from happening in the first place.

❖ ❖ ❖ ────────── ❖ ❖ ❖

An Afterword

Legal strategies are a vital part of the landscape for organizers. Without such strategies, organizing campaigns are often limited. Police tend to work with the rule of force. So advocates need to hold them in check with the rule of law. While many aspire to change the system, short-term legal wins become part of establishing a stronger movement. Yet, the struggle for meaningful, institutional change can be a long one. Having a little fun along the way can lighten the burden, and help keep people energized over the long haul. In the next chapter, we'll talk about the ways organizers are fighting for the fundamental rights to life, liberty, and the pursuit of happiness with every action they organize.

10

From Joy to Justice

Mixing Fun and Community Building

Activists bring any number of motivations to their work. Often, they bring personal guilt, self-righteousness, or an impulse toward martyrdom—all negative motivations. "The fatal flaw of every group since the movement began," a frustrated Vito Russo mused early in the AIDS crisis in New York, "[is to] starve to death for the cause" (Schiavi, 2011, p. 240). To counter this, Russo turned to the movies, cultural activism, and outrageous forms of direct action. And, he was not alone in doing so. Throughout the history of social movements, countless players have turned to the intersection of art, music, culture, and even play to sustain themselves, as well as to imagine new ways of living. This creative, theatrical brand of street activism owes as much to 1960s era Situationism as to the distinct brand of activism Russo and company brought to the early years of the gay liberation in the 1970s. The direct action of the era took a far more outlandish, even carnival-like dimension, vacillating between the somber and silly, the serious and surreal (K. Moore & Shepard, 2012). Throughout the era, activists recognized that pleasure and fun were necessary parts of any movement. This play served both affective and instructive purposes, with street antics communicating messages and well as sustaining organizing efforts. Mixing fun, pranks, and cultural activism, those involved brought a sense of spontaneity and energy into campaigns for social change (Shepard, 2009). These components help communities of resistance and care in countless ways.

Activists get involved for any number of reasons, but for many, building a community is the most important outcome of their work. In other cases, it is a by-product.

Quite often, a true sense of community is the unmet need. While Rothman (1995) states that locality development, policy, planning, and social action are primary components of community development schemas, this framework neglects the sustaining function of community building. This is the piece that keeps people moving.

This chapter addresses the ways organizers build the *communitas* necessary to keep groups together and campaigns moving forward. Throughout the most serious of campaigns, organizers seem to find time to joke, perform, celebrate, enjoy culture, nurture themselves, and use joy in the fight for justice (B. Ehrenreich, 2007). This chapter highlights ways that groups have integrated elements of play into their organizing. It suggests that play has a rightful place here. For some, fun is an expression of authentic emotion, helping to infuse social protest with a sense of creativity that makes the "game" of social change intriguing and enticing. Through sustained involvement in the process, many report increased feelings of happiness, a sense of agency, and meaning in their experiences (Klar & Kasser, 2009).

In recent years, scholars, practitioners, and activists alike have come to recognize play as a vital component of the process of social work, learning and social change (Nachmanovitch, 1990; Reilly, 1974; Shepard, 2009, 2011b). The reasons for this are many. I recall being in training on the rules for child protective services in New York when a supervisor of children's services concluded a particularly grisly discussion of the abuses endured by children with a confession. She mentioned that she occasionally played with the dolls she kept in office for the children she saw. One of the attendees asked why. "Well, if you don't figure a way to play and get some of the stress out with the stories that come in your door, you are doing to be on Gilligan's Island," she retorted. "They are going to lock you up." Sometimes, then, play is a simple way of helping us stay sane. We all grow by finding a space for ourselves to grapple with the tragicomic continuum of modern living (Shepard, 2011b). We need to make sense of and explore the limits of our understandings.

"Sometimes social change work can appear quite linear—getting funding, identifying issues, developing a tactical plan, engaging in actions, evaluating actions, and then onto the next issue," warns Loretta Pyles (2009, p. 24). "This approach can unfortunately block out creative and innovative issues that can influence organizing. Thus, making space for art and creativity in social change work is very important."

When the Food and Drug Administration (FDA) failed to work with any urgency to approve new AIDS drugs, members of ACT UP started doing research on the problem with the drug approval system in the United States, conducting panels, discussion sessions, meetings, teach-ins, performances in clubs, and finally a takeover of the FDA in a mass direct action in October of 1988. Members of Jim Eigo's affinity group, Wave Three (named after a wave of activists willing to be arrested at City Hall earlier that year) wore lab coats to the action and occupied a building. "One new Wave 3 member was the performance and visual artist Brian Damage," recalled Eigo (personal communication, 2012).

> He designed the banner Wave 3 marched under that day, and the lab coats we would wear, emblazoned with the international symbol for biohazard. Brian was at that time using the symbol in his own visual work. A person with AIDS, Brian was acutely aware

that to much of the general public, he was viewed as biohazard. Brian's appropriation of the symbol recalls the earlier use of the concentration camp pink triangle by the Silence = Death Project. Members of Wave Three marched in lab coats with the bio-hazard symbol on their lab coats, highlighting the plight of people with HIV treated like bio-hazards.

Later that year a copy of the downtown magazine *WW3 Illustrated* included comic drawings by Brian Damage in its Biohazard issue. For Eigo that was "the most telling artifact of the day." That year Brian "would begin a long, excruciating hospitalization. The Biohazard Issue of *WW3* was on the stands when Brian, later that year, after another long hospitalization and several unchecked infections, died" (Eigo, 2012).

From the AIDS epidemic to struggles against global warming, art has long been part of social change work. "This creativity and joy has been a hallmark of organizing in post-Katrina New Orleans," noted Pyles (2009, p. 24). It is part of organizing around the world. The play of creating art often helps to bring a rambunctious spirit to the difficult realities of organizing—even in the darkest of circumstances, such as Brian Damage's. In this way, play infuses a spirit of freedom and resistance into everyday life and organizing.

"The best organizers, like the best parents, understand the value of play," notes social worker Melinda Lewis (2011). "We've all been involved in social movements that could use a serious injection of fun—when even a big rally is kind of a drag, it's a serious sign that something is wrong. Think about it; most of the time we need to ask people to stick with us for months, even years, and few people want to spend that much time with people who are not any fun. We need to nourish people's souls as we're fighting with them for justice, and that means learning to laugh, commune, and dance together."

At first this line of thought was difficult for Lewis. "My family of origin is, quite honestly, not too big on play. When you ask us what we're doing for the weekend, we'll respond with a to-do list. We're pretty much always working on something: paid employment, volunteering, housework, general self-improvement. We love each other, and we even have a good time together, but it's mostly in parallel labor."

Gradually Lewis incorporated play-based strategies into her work and organizing:

Thank goodness that I started my organizing work in a community that includes celebration and camaraderie as a core part of its culture. . . . [I]n my work with Latino immigrants, they showed me that taking time to eat meals together, to attend each other's family celebrations, to tell jokes, to make music and dance, to enjoy beautiful artwork . . . these pursuits are not distractions from community-building but integral components. . . . [T]hese were areas where [it] was best to cede all authority to the grassroots leaders for whom such play was more natural, and they organized some of the best parties and gatherings I've ever attended . . . finding ways to weave laughter and love into everything we did together—from planning sessions to poster-making nights to phone banks to trips to give testimony. And the relationships that we built were stronger as a result of attending to each others' needs as whole people rather than just our "serious" sides.

In this way, fun is integrated into community building. For many, it is a way of embracing a freer flowing approach to living, organizing, and confronting apparently insurmountable targets.

Defiant Laughter and the Power of Play

From the Suffragettes to the Black Panthers, Gay Liberation to Global Justice, and even the Brooks Brothers Riot disrupting the Bush vs. Gore recounts, countless movements have made use of forms of direct action, oft-times playful and even silly, in order to put new ideas on the social agenda. Toward the end of her work, *Dancing in the Streets: A History of Collective Joy,* Barbara Ehrenreich (2007, p. 259) offers a telling observation. "[W]hatever its shortcomings as a means to social change, protest movements keep reinventing carnival.... Almost every demonstration I have been to—has featured some element of the carnivalesque: costumes, music, impromptu dancing, the sharing of food and drink." For Ehrenreich, such forms of "collective joy" are an essential component of social movement practice. "People must find, in their movement, the immediate joy of solidarity, if only because, in the face of overwhelming state or corporate power, solidarity is their sole source of strength" (B. Ehrenreich 2007, p. 259). Many organizers recognize such activities offer a useful compliment to an ongoing organizing campaign. Without them, organizing efforts tend to lose steam, or worse become boring. Their addition increases means and motivation for long term participation. Still critics remain. Some say such tactics may alienate supporters. "The media often deride the carnival spirit of protests, as if it were a self-indulgent distraction from the serious political point," Barbara Ehrenreich (2007, p. 259) explains. "But seasoned organizers know that gratification cannot be deferred until after the "revolution." Despite the contention that ludic activities are counterproductive, movements continue to put the right to party, the right to pleasure, on the table as a part of a larger process of social change.

Letters from civil rights workers who participated in the Freedom Summer of 1964 suggest that dancing, beer drinking, singing, hooking up, and an unbridled sense of social connection were ongoing components of the civil rights years. The struggle to break down racial, social, cultural, and sexual barriers included a great deal of play and social experimentation. Those in the movement described these feelings and practices as the "freedom high."

"When you are locked arm in arm with your friends and you are running into a line of police and you tell them to screw off, why wouldn't that be play?" notes Frances Fox Piven (Shepard, 2011b, p. 18). The point is, fighting authority can be a joyous endeavor.

Monica Hunken, a cyclist with Time's Up!, reflected on the ludic qualities of activism. She recalled a fellow bike supporter cautioning her: "They have to know that we're serious about this issue." "Well, of course we're serious about the issue. You can be serious about something and be joyful. The action that we were doing was very joyful; we were celebrating life on earth together. We have to laugh and we have to sing, and we have to have all that humanity. We are the most human when we are in our embarrassed state, in our laughing state" (as quoted in Shepard, 2011a).

This is a point on which social theorists from Douglas Crimp (2002) to Slavoj Zizek agree. In a 2005 interview, Zizek specifically argued there is a rationale for such thinking. "The only way to signal you are serious, at the level of form, is to make fun of yourself," he explained. "This pseudo-Heideggerian jargon, we live in fateful times, the destiny of humanity is threatened blah, blah, blah—I think you cannot talk like that," Zizek elaborated (Clover, 2005). A sense of one's own absurdity is no impediment to engaging in serious tasks—in fact, quite the opposite seems to be more accurate.

In his 2007 work, *Infinitely Demanding*, philosopher Simon Critchley takes on the subject. Writing about contemporary ludic performance, Critchley (2007, p. 128) described some of the distinct logic in such activism:

> These comical tactics hide a serious political intent: they exemplify the effective forging of chains of equivalence or collective will formation across diverse and otherwise conflicting protest groups. Deploying a politics of subversion, contemporary anarchist practice exercises a satirical pressure on the state in order to show that other forms of life are possible. Picking up on my thoughts about humor, it is the exposed, self-ridiculing and self-undermining character of these forms of protest that I find most compelling as opposed to the pious humorlessness of most forms of vanguardist active nihilism and some forms of contemporary protest. . . . Politically, humor is a powerless power that uses its position of weakness to expose those in power through forms of self-aware ridicule.

"We all know that life is hard. We all know that there is war and blood and suffering," Monica Hunken continued at Left Forum. "That is so deep upon us and so weighted on our backs." This inspires the guilt-ridden, hair-shirted Left to reject the politics of fun, while embracing a politics of respectability. Yet, there is more to life than looking dignified. Countless movements, the Mattachine Society before Stonewall and the other pre-civil rights groups, called for their followers to look dignified. Yet, they rarely accomplished much until the Stonewall Riots or sit-ins challenged the moral bankruptcy of the system as it stood. When we play by the system's rules, few pay attention. The rules too often seemed stacked against us. If one embraces a politics of shame and dourness, hoping not to offend, rather than pushing back, we tend to lose. Countless movements have challenged this logic, from the IWW to the Gay Liberation Front, and many others.

For Hunken, the best way to cut through these barriers is with humor, storytelling, and highly participatory street performance. "We have to tap into that kind of playfulness in a way and not be afraid of it because we're the ones who know what is sad and really right. We have to be able to play with that glee and that storytelling" (quoted in Shepard, 2011a).

When ACT UP first began, many misunderstood its defiant gestures aimed at those in power, such as throwing blood or dressing like clowns at congressional hearings. But over time people began to reconsider why the group made use of such outlandish tactics. And public opinion shifted (Shepard, 2009). "You gotta listen to the crazies," Stonewall veteran Bob Kohler used to implore. From Feste in *Twelfth Night* to the fool in *King Lear,* there is a long tradition of the wise fool who usually gets it right. Usually it's a good idea to pay attention to the fool.

Play, Pleasure, and Cultural Resistance

At its core, play is about pleasure and resistance. After all, regular people locate their own power through the "secret realization of unmediated play," explains Hakim Bey (2003). It is a way for regular people to stay engaged and channel emotions about often larger-than-life challenges. "Do activists lead happier and more fulfilled lives than the average person?" ask Malte Klar and Tim Kasser (2009) in their article "Some Benefits of Being an Activist: Measuring Activism and Its Role in Psychological Well-Being." After conducting two online surveys of college students compared with activists, they were able to conclude social activism is positively linked "with measures of hedonic, eudemonic, and social well-being." Both studies indicated that "activists were more likely to be 'flourishing' . . . than were nonactivists." A third study found "the subjects who did the brief activist behavior reported significantly higher levels of subjective vitality than did the subjects who engaged in the nonactivist behavior."

"If it's true a rich man leads a sad life . . . That's what they say, from day to day . . . Then what do the poor do with their lives?" asks the British punk group the Clash, in their song "I'm Not Down." "On Judgement Day, with nothin' to say? I've been beat up, I've been thrown Out . . . But I'm not down, No I'm not down." Mick Jones, who wrote "I'm Not Down" with Joe Strummer, says that a band knows it has succeeded when people shake, move, and dance, move their bodies while they are making a political point. Then you know you are getting somewhere. Culture is often a common denominator that connects hearts and minds, ideas and social change. When the Clash performed they joined a tradition of cultural resistance, linking social movements and community organizing stretching from LeadBelly to Michael Franti, Woody Guthrie to Pete Seeger, Odetta, Billie Holliday, Tom Morello, to Tito Puente. Their songs inspired movements from labor to civil rights, punk, Global Justice, and Occupy. "Songs did a lot for unions, but the civil rights movement would not have succeeded if it hadn't

The Occupy Wall Street Guitarmy. Here, everyone shares the stage; everyone participates.

Source: Photo by Stacy Lanyon

been for all those songs," noted folk singer Pete Seeger, who participated in both movements. "They were sung in jails and on picket lines and parades. People hummed them when they were most beaten" (Kupfer, 2011). When people heard Odetta sing "Oh Freedom," they were willing to put their bodies on the line. These songs connected hearts and minds.

I remember listening to NWA's "Straight Outta Compton," and "The Revolution Will Not Be Televised" by Gil Scott-Heron as I was driving around Southern California weeks before the Los Angeles riots in 1992. And then the riots happened. With smoke still rising in the downtown sky, the songs sounded like a soundtrack for the broken windows and desolate streets of the city. They helped communicate the message that something was wrong and everyone needed to get involved. This message found its way deep into my body. Music can do that; engaging first our bodies and then our minds.

"It [cultural resistance] grabs a hold of you in a place, you never knew existed, shakes you to your core and shatters everything and shatters everything you hold as true. It is transcendent. Illuminating. Empowering. Emancipating," notes Antoninio D'Ambrosio (2004, p. xxiii), writing about the Clash. "What we all need to help us cope with a world that is anything but comfortable, is the kind of music that intoxicates you with crushing hooks that open up the mind with lyrics that make you think" (p. xxiii).

CASE STUDY

Mark Andersen and the Transformative Power of Punk

When the Clash played, they opened a whole new world for countless listeners around the world. Take Mark Andersen, an organizer, service provider, writer, and musician living in Washington, D.C. He first heard the Clash and other punk bands in the 1970s. Andersen said:

> I grew up in a rural working class context. I was just buried under the weight of all of this lack of opportunity. So, how do you even glimpse at another way to place yourself within this struggle. Well, for me the answer was music. That's what reached me. And particularly punk music. That's one of the great things that the arts can do. It can cut through the layers of fatalism. . . . It strikes so close to our core that it awakens some things that we might not be aware of—our own personal power to do something, and the chance to live a life that makes sense to us.

Through his immersion in punk music, Andersen was able to break an isolation that is so common in our modern life (Ollman, 1977). Music meant not being alone. Through it, horizons started to open for Andersen. "Just knowing that there were these crazy-looking free spirits, essentially, in New York City or London, it meant an immense amount to me. It was literally, for me, it was like a life preserver thrown. . . . I guess working first on a level of coming to affirm myself and to feel like what I feel inside is worthy and worth sharing, and then the level of I'm starting to share it. First with my friends, but then also starting into public speaking." Punk linked thinking and acting for Andersen.

I gave a talk on the ideology of punk rock music in the spring of 1980 at Montana State University, where I was going to school at that time—and there happened to be a janitorial strike that was happening on campus. I got a leaflet and I read it, and I was like this is righteous, these people are doing something that is meaningful and important and is a just cause. So I joined the picket line. And then I joined a student group that was working around that issue. One thing led to another. . . . Reagan was elected later that year. All of a sudden there were all of these issues . . . around abortion, Central America, nuclear arms . . . that I began to be involved with.

Andersen's story is one of many from those who started looking at the world from different angles after being moved by cultural resistance. More than dancing, the music helped nudge listeners into new ways of being. Paul Simonon, the Clash's bass player, was aware of the racist subtext of a subculture of skinheads, some of their fans. Yet, music altered this way of thinking. "[W]hen we play reggae, it's sort of like turning them on to black music—which helps lead them away from that racist feeling," noted Simonon. "Which is like changing them. . . . It's made loads of kids that would normally go around wrecking up streets and fucking up cars, form groups. They're doing something creative, which I think is really important—and they're enjoying it" (Duncombe & Tremblay, 2011, p. 170). Here, punk opened the way for a more affirmative approach to living.

"You could be part of something positive. Change can happen if you are willing to change yourself," notes D'Ambrosio (2004, p. xxiii). He saw punk as a movement that offered a choice. Instead of negation, it offered a "positive action" (p. xxiii). "Forget about waiting on the side of the road for someone to come along and pick you up. It was about DIY. Do it yourself not for yourself but for each other. Bonded together in what matters, forsaking intolerance, embracing justice" (p. xxiv).

The idea was that everyone could help build something and take part. "I was taken to a lot of protests as a child, or building the origami cranes with Pete Seeger. All that stuff, kind of sucks you in," confessed New York activist Kate Barnhart, who went on to join ACT UP and provide services for homeless street youth. She reveled in just being creative and responsive. "This was during the anti-nuclear war movement during the 70s. Pete Seeger would gather up groups of small children and we would all sit there making the origami cranes."

In this way, play, dancing, and the arts are also seen as resources used both to engage as well as create some levity in an otherwise difficult world. Social worker and political scientist Ron Hayduk worked as a recreation coordinator in a community mental health facility:

People that are manic depressive, schizophrenics, some significant mental health issues, how do you get somebody to kind of deal with their problems, their challenge in life, in a way that is right here now—OK, what do we need tonight, what do you need tomorrow—and not about their problem, about something's that's an alternative? It's incredibly therapeutic. Distract somebody from listening to voices. And yes, dancing or music or we're going to go to a museum or we're going to draw or just going to tell stories—it's therapeutic and it's fun. And all of a sudden we're telling jokes about somebody's mental illness and it's like they're in a different place.

Here, play brings a little lightness to a difficult situation.

❖ ❖ ❖ ───────── ❖ ❖ ❖

Many of the community approaches discussed throughout this text incorporate strands of cultural activism as part of community practice. In contrast to institutional settings, the emphasis of community practice is on capacity, collective effort, informality, and the acknowledgment of both tragedy and the need for celebration (McKnight, 1987). More than anything, they share an emphasis on participation. Folk singer Pete Seeger used to say this was what his life was all about (Kupfer, 2011). "There is something about participating; it is almost my religion. If the world is still here in 100 years, people will know the importance of participating, not just being spectators," explained Pete Seeger (Kupfer, 2011). "Millions of small groups around the world, that don't necessarily all agree with one another, are made up of people who are not just sitting back waiting for someone to do things for them. No one can prove anything, but of course if I didn't believe it had some kind of power, I wouldn't be trying to do it." Here, everyone is invited to take part. And those on the periphery are ushered into community.

Through cultural activism, Ron Hayduk found himself intrigued. "It's so much fun, and you can capture people's imaginations, and that's a powerful thing. If you can capture people's imaginations and say, hey, it could be this way, come join the party, it's fun! It's seductive, it's inviting. I mean people want to have a fun time, people want to be part of the party." And along the way, these dancing bodies get involved in community.

Hayduk recalled being inspired as he watched this movement blurred lines between public and private space. "I'll never forget being a part of a gathering of fabulously dressed, hilarious party animals that painted, or sort of did up a couple of subways in orange." The event was an all-night subway ride called the Orange Party. "People that got on that subway were like, Whoa, did I get on the wrong subway here? But immediately they were put at ease and felt that this is a fun atmosphere. There were people that just immediately engaged with us, joined in essentially. And that happens with Time's Up and biking. People will just join in. People sort of want to see what's happening. And that's engaging human beings who otherwise would not be engaged." The politics of play is not unlike inviting people in to a party.

Once engaged, those taking part gain, they expand their own collective social capital. "Social capital is developed through a network of trusting connections that members of the communities have with each other, as well as those outside the community," writes Mark Homan (2008, p. 36). "These connections not only create access to other resources, but they make it much easier to bring people together to mobilize their power. It can promote both social

A Time's Up! Occupy fountains bike ride. Don't ask for permission to disobey, notes the photographer Mickey Z.

Source: Photo by Mickey Z

action and community development" (p. 36). Social capital is a "store of wealth and assets . . . that store of behaviors and norms in any large group that lets its members support each other," notes Clay Shirky (2008, p. 222).

Early in his career, New York organizer Tim Doody struggled to find a voice, as many of the groups he worked with were organized within a strict hierarchy. "It was definitely top down," he explained. "There is a right answer." Eventually, Doody found his way into a far more creative niche with organizing.

> Environmentalists, all political struggles, have had a good history of creative resistance . . . the thing that started appealing to me more than anything else was, I had heard about this group called The Ruckus Society. This group trains people in creative tactics designed to garner media attention for political causes; and I went to this camp and it was just this mindboggling thing, people getting trained on climbing tactics, and how to rappel off of buildings while holding big banners, doing blockades in the streets and all kinds of street theatre. I remember the first street theatre I ever saw, there were drums, and it was intricate with narrative. And I realized, you don't have to just hold signs and walk in a circle on a sidewalk. There are a lot more options.

Doody has long been intrigued by music and pieces of culture in organizing. "It makes people stay longer. It completely changes a lot of things. During the World Economic Forum, we started the samba band protest in New York in 2002. And there was this entourage of drummers going down the street, all playing really good samba music, chanting: "NO WEF." With 50 drummers, people are more apt to go out in the streets. They are more apt to hear you. And it completely changes the dynamic. In this way, creative activism helps Doody fashion an affirmative image of the world he wants to see: "We're not just going out into the streets and saying no to something. We might be doing that, but we're also in the same process showing what we say yes to. This [is a] democratically driven protest filled with a lot of elements, including smiles, people watching each other's backs. It's filled with tons of creativity. It's a completely different feeling in the streets. And these protests are just one part of living dynamically in the city. It's one of the best things you can possibly use public space for."

Cultural Animation

Part of the work of organizers is to look for sources of cultural expression, find meaning in them, and use them to organize (Duncombe, 2007). The idea of culture can be thought of as both a set of meanings, ideas, and ways of acting as well as a product or performance, which contains and communicates a message (Duncombe, 2002a). "When you take the time to familiarize yourself with selected cultural characteristics, such as the history, values, belief systems, and behaviors of members of another ethnic group, you are acquiring cultural knowledge" explains Mark Homan (2008). "Like any other form of wealth, it must be recognized, valued, and used if it is going to mean anything," Homan (2008, p. 36) continues. Each community depends on different kinds of capital—social, environmental, human, political, and even cultural. "Cultural capital is the wealth that exists in communities from artistic expressions, understood norms and shared traditions, rituals and beliefs, which provide reference points, identity, and meaning to its members" (Homan, 2008, pp. 35–36).

Social work practitioners have long made use of forms of cultural animation. Put simply, cultural animation is "community arts work which literally animates, or 'gives life to,' the underlying dynamic of a community. The animateur is a community artist who helps people create and celebrate their own culture" by drawing on community aspirations (P. Reynolds, 1984). Others describe such practices in cultural activism as "culture jamming" (Lasn, 1999; Wettergren, 2009).

Much of the time organizer and grassroots groups are trying to shift the terms of debate and discourse. As John Sellers (2004), the founder of the Ruckus Society, explains, they are "branding themselves and trying to jam the brands of their adversaries and get them to the table and have enough momentum and leverage to change their behavior." Such tactics "can be really effective because they are very attractive to the media," he says. This is where the play comes in. "When you're smart, when you're funny, a lot of the time you are, 'using the master's tools to tear down the master's house.' And creating an intelligent, fun kind of public confrontation," Sellers explains. Through these techniques, counter-public groups are able to advance "a pretty radical message through the filter that is the corporate media."

"Culture is a really great tactic," notes James Tracey, who works as an organizer with the homeless in San Francisco and writes poetry. He has spent years integrating his creativity with organizing. When working with youth, poetry has helped build on an ongoing dialog. For Tracey, poetry is a way to raise different kinds of voices. It's a way to break down conflicts between analysis and imagination. It stimulates thinking, encouraging different kinds of questions and stories. And anyone who has access to a pen and a napkin can do it. No revolution would be complete without some poetry.

For Tracey, cultural work and organizing are part of the same game. "It's not one or the other—all joy versus the necessary organizing stuff." Creative politics gets people out:

> Culture and organizing go hand in hand. One of the big lessons the left had to learn is that human beings have multiple interests. Culture can address people as whole human beings. They can decide whether or not to participate in a movement for many reasons. Effective political art does this, while ineffective art simply rehashes slogans and is quite patronizing. [Here] art expands avenues for participation. Many people who want to make a difference don't want to do so on the frontlines. Instead sign painting, spoken word, and music engages people on the levels that make them feel most alive, and helps build a sense of purpose. Movements that use culture are sturdier. Their participants are prepared for the inevitable disappointments and set-backs because they come to see their work as something bigger—something worth doing for years of your life.

Culture serves as a focal point around which to build collegiality and connection while engaging with issues. Further, cultural resistance often speaks in less shrill tones than the often dour approaches, making engagement more accessible and fun (Duncombe, 2002a). John Sellers offers an example:

> One of my favorite things was working on the Anacostia River in Washington, which is usually considered to be the first or second most polluted river in the country. The predominantly African American neighborhoods around it are some of the poorest in the United States. Clear cut environmental racism, right? The river is super-polluted by toxic PCBs. The fish constitute a cancer death risk when eaten. But lots of folks around the river are so poor that they are still harvesting the fish for food. So one of the things we did was to hold a classic fish derby. They are done all over the country. People love to fish.

Having recognized this cultural resource—this love of fishing—Sellers and his colleagues sought to animate it, turning it into a resource for thinking about the environment. "Our derby was actually a 'Tumor Derby'. Rather than awarding prizes for the biggest catches, our prizes went to the fish with the most tumors and birth defects. It was a creative way to show the general public how crazy things had gotten in this river. I think one of the first things you learn in organizing 101 is to meet people where they are. I love creative actions that are anchored into mainstream cultural touchstones and then flipped on their heads and taken somewhere radical."

"[I]t is important to take joy from politics," writes social welfare scholar Steve Burghardt (1982, p. 2). "After all, if we are trying to change the world . . . our vision had better encompass a personal capacity that brings part of that vision to life before it miraculously appears somewhere in the distant future" (p. 2).

Organizing tactics "should be things that build the movement, that expand the base and involve people who are either bearing witness or who are a target," notes Sean Berry of VOCAL New York: "People are used to seeing picket lines and signs. And all that is important and we engage in those tactics. But, we believe protest should excite people. Transgressive actions should activate people. We often blame people, especially people who are directly affected, for not getting involved in issues that affect their lives. But if what we are doing is failing to engage them then that's on us. You cannot blame people for not joining the movement if the movement is not exciting."

People connect with social change in multiple ways. "I was going to study art, but it didn't seem really relevant to the world so I put that off," San Francisco organizer David Solnit explained as he discussed his roots in community organizing. Instead of going into the arts, the creative urge found its way into his activism. Over time, he was able to integrate the ideas of pacifism with the creative DIY culture of punk, queer activism, and anarchism, while participating in the anti-nukes movement. Cultural activism was a stepping stone to a much larger world for Solnit.

L. J. Wood, who worked with New York's Direct Action Network and later on the Toronto mobilizations against the G8, suggests that this mix of play, culture, and politics is most helpful when it serves as a complement to larger campaigns. "Basically, it's complementary. One of the things I've found in Toronto is there is a fair amount of hostility to some forms of creative protest. It's seen as not taking seriously the issues that the people are going through." The strength of the model is not seen as a substitute for a coherent organizing strategy. "I don't think it should be so oppositional, I think it's more creative when people can take advantage of the widest range of tactics," notes Wood.

Play as a Low-Threshold Entry Into Politics

Steven Duncombe (2002a, pp. 5–6) suggests that just these sorts of bits and pieces of culture provide a focal point around which to build collegiality and connection; it functions as an easy entry point, "the stepping stone into political activity." As actors support each other and gain new tools, other engagements in more formal political work become feasible. Creative activism helps actors connect with their work in a visceral, emotive ways. "[P]eople need to be inspired; they need to be motivated; they need to feel powerful; they need to have fun; [actions] need to be something that people want to join and be a part of," John Sellers explains. "I think that when you create attractive actions, when you create smart funny actions, I think humor is an incredible motivator and an incredible teacher." Part of the effectiveness of this approach involves a capacity to show the actors do not take themselves too seriously. "If you can show you can laugh at yourself a little bit and laugh at your adversary, you can bring it down to a very human form," Sellers elaborates. "It breaks down walls."

If done well, then, creative activism engages new participants. Organizer Matthew Roth described how he felt moved to participate and found a new power in himself:

> What I find so much more interesting about street theater and Billionaires for Bush type of things is the way it pushes me beyond my normal limitations. I'm not an actor, but I certainly am a performer, which is something I didn't know before I got involved in this. So it's taking this raw protean nucleus of energy and giving it some direction

Playing in a squatted community garden. Play is a low-threshold way to engage in multiple forms of activism.

Source: Photos by author

and then seeing what happens with that. I was always nervous with public speaking in school, but I don't remember being nervous with this.

I had been involved in other protests in college and stuff. But I had never been able to conceptualize why I loathed and felt uncomfortable in normal protest situations with the placards and the march and the chanting. And it wasn't until I discovered the politics of play, the politics of street theater, or how it discovered me, or how we came together at the same time, that I realized how I could use my energy in a way that I completely condoned everything that was happening. When I was standing behind a placard that says "don't do this" or "power to this" and people started chanting things that I may know or not, I never bought into it. It was a canned slogan. It's all these things that weren't authentic. They weren't spontaneous. And even though street theater has direction, it's still about spontaneity; it's still about authenticity in that moment and experience. It is about everyone taking part.

"The winning campaign, it works in two different directions at the same time," explains New York party promoter William Etundi, a veteran of creative activism. "Number one there is winning the campaign or the tangible goals, like shutting down this prison, saving this garden, stopping this law. Winnable, attainable goals are one element of movement building. The other element is creating a sustainable alive and active movement. This doesn't necessarily involve winning campaigns. It does involve being involved in a process that is working for people, for feeling heard, being respected, being interested and engaging . . . creating something interesting, engaging, and sustainable."

Here, street actions transform public space into a living, breathing work of art. Starhawk describes such a process in San Francisco:

We did a whole action here in San Francisco the year before called Reclaim the Commons. It was around a biotech conference. It was kind of in our home ground. We had prop-making parties there for months beforehand, where we propagated thousands of plants. At one point we took them into the street and created a blockade with them, creating a garden in the streets. We did a "really free market" where everything was free. We gave away organic plants, seeds, lavender, and chocolate in the middle of downtown San Francisco. And then at the end we took all the plants out and planted a garden in the Bay View/Hunter's Point.

The applications of such projects tend to depend on social and cultural contexts. "It's intriguing people. It's moving people," notes William Etundi. "Prison Moratorium Project uses hip hop in almost everything they do. They get young people from the neighborhood excited, working on things and knowing about the prison-industrial complex and this whole system and how it's working against them. It's super powerful."

One of the most potent contemporary models of cultural activism is the flash mob. During a flash mob in a hotel lobby, park, or public space, a regular day is transformed into a scene from a musical, as people break out in song, often with a political message. On July 30, 2010, a group of several hundred health care activists—most in the age demographic affected by potential Medicare cuts—appeared out of nowhere in Bryant

Park in New York City during lunchtime to perform a choreographed dance based on the Supremes' hit "Stop! In the Name of Love." "Stop! In the Name of Health, Don't Cut My Medicare," the "dancing grannies" sang as the Obama Deficit Commission debated cuts to Medicare, Medicaid, and Social Security. The day of the action was Medicare's 45th birthday.

Though having a good time, the grannies and their supporters said this was a life-and-death issue. One of the dancing grannies, Joan Pleune, 71, said, "Rehearsing for this choreographed dance is harder than getting arrested during the Freedom Rides of 1961." This veteran of the civil rights movement added, "But my health is threatened and I need the Deficit Commission to pay attention—expand, not cut, Medicare!"

Press releases went out citywide, with stories appearing around the country. The *Village Voice* called the action "the best protest ever." The flash mob communicated in ways that were engaging and thought-provoking. "It puts an idea in people's minds," explained Amanda Hickman. Rather than just being negative around an issue, such actions highlight issues in a more positive light. "It's accessible and engaging, and sustainable," explains Hickman. If a political message is dreary or condescending, people really do not want to pay attention.

"Organizers are basically communicators, and we need to know how to connect to mass culture instead or merely critiquing it," James Tracy concludes. "People turn to mass commercial culture for release, enjoyment, and pleasure. So dissident political culture must also provide release, enjoyment, and pleasure and somehow also add critical consciousness, solidarity and agitation."

The link between cultural activism and the politics of play helps engage and intrigue. It breaks down the barriers between spectator and performer, leader and follower, audience and the group members (Bakhtin, 1981). Culture is a strength and a stress reliever for people in many communities. It helps people from multiple walks of life take part in the process of building communities. Through such cultural exchanges, everyone is invited to join the chorus of democratic living (Kupfer, 2011). After all, this is what social activism and community projects are all about.

Part II
In Conclusion

In Part II we have looked more closely at the seven stages of community-based social activism. Through many narratives and case studies we have seen how each stage informs the others to form a solid working schema for successful social action. From simply identifying a clear goal to engendering the kind of spirit needed to sustain a long campaign, the seven stages, while not a lock-step rulebook, encapsulate the habits of mind and heart that create social change. We will delve further into their application in Part III.

Part III

Praxis

From Direct Action to Direct Services

Parts I and II introduced and sketched a model of action framing *Community Projects as Social Activism*. Part III considers the application of the model as organizers move from community organization to development, from the grass roots to organizational development, direct action to direct services and back again.

The challenges of organizational development are many. Gareth Morgan (2006) notes that organizations, spaces where human services are typically provided, often feel like psychic prisons. Many of the impulses that first spurred organizational innovation are lost with institutionalization. Max Weber notes that work in such organizations often feels like an "iron cage of despair." Others warn of the pitfalls of the nonprofit industrial complex (Incite, 2007; Mananzala & Spade, 2008). We have become a society

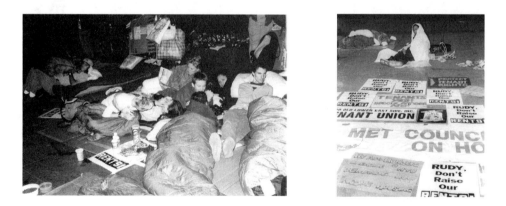

Facing rent increases, activists held a sleep out in front of City Hall on October 1, 2000, establishing the legal right to sleep on the sidewalk in New York City.

Source: Photos by Caroline Shepard

of institutions, cautions John McKnight (1987), bemoaning the loss of community spaces to such formalized programs. Part III of this volume considers the ways community practitioners have found to create services in an era when community-based services are increasingly under threat, bridging a gap between direct action and direct services and back again.

This section considers the overlapping nature of social action and services. Borrowing from both contemporary and historic case examples, it traces a history of radical social services from the Young Lords to Harm Reduction, ACT UP to Zapatismo and Occupy movements, bridging a gap between anarchism and its ongoing influences in larger organizing trends, including the age-old need for direct care.

As Dean Spade, founder of the Sylvia Rivera Law Project (SRLP), explains:

> In certain circles, doing direct service is considered reformist. If you want to be radical, God forbid you work within the system. Which is funny, considering the Black Panthers served breakfast. The Young Lords took over lead-paint testing trucks. There's a huge history of severely oppressed communities realizing that it's hard to raise your political voice if you don't have anywhere to sleep or anything to eat. SRLP is committed to providing people with some basic services.

Providing services is part of keeping a community well nourished, housed, alive, thriving, and pushing forward. It is the first step to building power. Throughout Part III, we highlight the stories of organizers who argue that there is room for direct action and direct services, community organization and service provision. Each brief chapter contains an example or two that build on the lessons and applications of the work's seven-stage model by illustrating the diverse ways a group of people can go from identifying an issue, to fighting for it, to doing something about it, and offering an alternative solution. These community driven solutions are the heart of community projects.

11

Social Movement to Social Services ❖

From the Black Panthers to the Young Lords

Some of the most radical and innovative social movement organizations have involved combinations of community development, social action, and service provision (Brooks, 2005). Chapter 11 considers the role of social services within social movements and movement organizations, by looking at the example of the Black Panthers and Young Lords, beginning in the 1960s.

Formed nearly 50 years ago, the Black Panther Party aimed to meet some of its most vital goals of its community through services, including education, child care, food, and literacy programs. Of the group's Ten Point Platform, four elements involved service issues, such as housing. A fifth included self-determination, a core ethical principle for social workers. In addition, the platform called for employment and an end to police brutality. "We want land, bread, housing, education, clothing, justice, and peace," the group demanded (History Matters, n.d.).

Black Panther Community Survival Programs

From 1966 to 1974, the Black Panther Party helped bridge the gap between direct action and direct services for its communities by organizing community survival programs. Some included ambulance services, breakfast programs, benefits counseling, busing for prisons, education, dental programs, food, and free clothing.

Community programs provided health, education, and criminal justice–based services without support from government grants. The point was to help regular people meet their own needs on their own terms (Abron, 1998; Self, 2003; Sonnie & Tracy, 2011). Starting in East Oakland, California, Panther volunteers provided a range of social programs including breakfast for school children and free ambulance services, as well as sickle cell anemia research. These programs were designed to provide basic survival supplies so that those in poor neighborhoods in Oakland were able to eat healthy meals in a supportive environment. The programs highlighted the gap between community needs and government-provided services programs such as Head Start. Vast hunger still existed in areas, not reached by Title I–funded Head Start programs. Yet beyond addressing immediate material needs, these programs also provided examples of Black self-determination. Grocery giveaways and sickle cell testing drew huge crowds. The food and child-care programs provided an ongoing public presence for the group, solidifying their reputation in the community (Self, 2003, pp. 231–232). For the Black Panthers, the very gesture of providing desperately needed services served as a model of direct action emulated around the country (Sonnie & Tracy, 2011).

Do-It-Yourself Direct Action With the Young Lords

One of the groups inspired by the Black Panthers and their survival programs was the Young Lords, a Chicago- and New York–based direct action group. The group admired the Panthers' approach to providing direct services so those in their communities could survive. Much of the work of the Young Lords was about a do-it-yourself community-building ethic (Duncombe, 1997). If part of the city was not working, the group sought to do-it-themselves, rather than wait for permission. One of the most famous direct action campaigns organized by the group was its "garbage offensive" of the summer of 1969 (Melendez, 2003, pp. 88–111). "When East Harlem residents identified uncollected garbage as a major problem, the Young Lords, joined by the community, began sweeping the streets and stacking the garbage up on the corners," explains Richie Perez, who played a vital role in this campaign with the Young Lords. He describes the offensive: "When the Sanitation Department continued to ignore the situation, we burned the garbage in the streets, blocking major traffic arteries used by commuters to leave Manhattan for suburbia. When the police came and tried to arrest people, fighting broke out. Afterwards, garbage started getting picked up regularly" (Perez, 2000).

Bronx-based organizer Panama Alba recalls another example of a Young Lords campaign organized around direct action. The story involves the theft of an X-ray truck (Melendez, 2003). "There was an X-ray truck, run by the Health Department, which was parked right on First Avenue on the Upper East Side," Alba recalls.

It was there to provide community services, but it wasn't doing so. On the other hand, we had a program of healthcare for our people, who were not receiving adequate health care. So there was a Young Lords initiative that was put together with members of the Health Revolutionary Unity Movement and a group of doctors based primarily in Lincoln Hospital called the Lincoln Collective. We had a TB epidemic, and we used to go out on Saturdays and do TB testing, community testing around things such as the determination of lead paint poisoning. And that was years before they ever made a law that would address that. So we approached the Health Department and said, "Listen, you have an X-ray truck out there with nobody using it. Bring it to a place where you have more access and we could bring people." When they blew us off, a team of people went and hijacked the truck. As one was stealing the truck, a couple of guys were in the back with the technicians, being very cognizant that this could look like it was kidnapping, but working at convincing them that they should stay and service the people. Meanwhile, the people have been called to the front of the Young Lords Office, so when the truck arrives, there are hundreds of people there ready to get TB tests.

Through the group's flair for the dramatic as well as recognition of the need for services, they were able to frame the confrontation as a story about an inefficient, insensitive bureaucracy and a resourceful community. The Young Lords contacted the media, as well as much of the community, igniting a widespread response. "The cops, everybody—high drama!" recalled Alba. "High drama, but the fact was that there was so much community there that they didn't arrest anybody."

Through such gestures, the group helped create a new affirmative storyline for its community. The story—the living example—was an important part of the activism. Alba recalls the story of a member of Fuerzas Armadas de Liberacion Nacional (FALN), locked in Bellevue Hospital and held in a room with bars over the windows. Yet he was somehow able to escape by crawling out a window. "The fact that this guy would do this and get away was high drama," noted Alba. "There were no pictures, but you can just imagine how this guy cut his way through bars and then lowered himself out the window with ace bandages. They captured people's imaginations there . . . it had that effect."

The Young Lords helped bridge the gap between direct action and direct services most profoundly with their Lincoln Hospital Campaign. If the Young Lords had a high point, it was the daylong occupation of Lincoln Hospital in the Bronx on July 17, 1970. The action was born of years of community members experiencing poor treatment as they attempted to access health care services. The poor, in particular, suffered in the hospitals in New York. "At the time, the hospitals were basically laboratories for medical schools," noted Panama Alba, explaining the reasoning behind the action. "At that time, you had a relationship between Albert Einstein [College of Medicine] and Lincoln. And there were two problems, one was exploitation and two was a very bad dynamic between the doctors and the patients. Doctors were recruited from Latin America and India because they were Latinos or people of color. But they were from their countries' elite classes, and looked at the world from a totally different place."

Alba had a particular confrontation with a doctor when he tried to help a friend who had waited for three days to see a doctor at the hospital. Alba went to see the doctor, who called a security guard when Alba sought answers for the delay. The guard happened to be a friend from the Young Lords. After Alba told the guard what happened, he recalls:

> The guard says, "Doctor, I think you owe this man an apology." And [the doctor] looks at him and says, "I don't apologize to patients." So that was his response. He was an Indian Muslim. In India, the caste system is not something that we can even comprehend here. But it's a super-duper class system. And this is the kind of guy who is brought in to treat people in a poor deprived community. Imagine the kinds of problems that were not being seen—until there were doctors there that actually spoke people's language.

The Young Lords pushed to have grievance tables at the hospital staffed by people who spoke Spanish. But still the problems continued. "When Carmen Rodriguez died during a brutal second-trimester abortion at Lincoln, we fought back," recalled Alba. "At the time, you couldn't challenge doctors, so we pushed to open up complaint tables for patients and the hospital heard us." Her death provided the catalyst for action.

"The Lords, the Panthers, hospital workers (organized in the Health Revolutionary Unity Movement), and community people (organized as the Think Lincoln Committee) set up 'patient-worker complaint tables' in Lincoln and other hospitals," Richie Perez (2000) elaborated. "Hundreds of grievances were recorded; but the hospital administration refused to address them. The old Lincoln Hospital was in a building that had been condemned and was severely understaffed. After a list of demands and mass demonstrations were also ignored, the Lords occupied the hospital in the middle of the night" (Perez, 2000).

In the early morning hours of July 17, 1970, members of the Young Lords entered Lincoln Hospital, some through the windows, some through the doors. "We took over the hospital," Alba explains. "The group encountered little to no resistance from the hospital workers and, according to accounts, the patients welcomed them. Once inside, they set up a table where people could be heard." The group's list of demands included calls for Spanish-language translation for services; an acupuncture services/detox program (funded by the city in 1971); and a patient's bill of rights. And the staff heard their concerns.

"The next morning the media publicized the occupation and the issues that led to it. After hundreds of angry police surrounded the hospital, the Lords slipped out; and only two people were arrested," recalled Richie Perez (2000).

Most of the group's demands would later become common practices and policy in New York state. "This was before the advent of patients' rights, and the majority of doctors treating low income residents did not recognize health as a right. But regarded it as a privilege," notes Melendez (2003, p. 171), who participated in the action. "We were trying to replace that demeaning system with one based on respect for human dignity" (p. 171).

"The hospital changed," Alba recalls. "They realized they needed to treat poor people, not just train their doctors on us or use us as research objects." For Alba, just forcing the hand of the hospital administrators so they would pay attention to grievances was a victory that came out of that action. "And even today, thirty-some odd years later, when you walk into a hospital, you read on a wall a patient bill of rights. That came about because of those takeovers. Before the takeover there was no place for patients and grievances." After the action, the rules of the game changed; the power balance was altered. That carries on to today. That direct change came about in part because activists had advanced a winnable, workable solution (Melendez, 2003, pp. 1–2, 14).

Common Causes

Countless groups joined the struggle of the era. Throughout this period, young work-ing-class White activists found common cause with Black Power and civil rights activ-ists, linking a fight against racism with class based-struggle, as well as women's rights. Collaborating with community groups from California to Chicago to the South Bronx, they organized across the country, engaging the poor, providing social services, feed-ing those in need, and engaging in conversations about power with marginalized White people helping them to see links between their conditions and systems of oppression. They helped cultivate a brand of feminism relevant to poor women's lives. In Chicago, they formed Join Community Union, the Young Patriots, and Rising Up Angry; in Philadelphia's Kensington, they formed the October 4th Organization, and in the Bronx, the White Lightning. Collectively they became a sort of family tree in support of each other's work, as well as the larger challenges of creating a White working-class consciousness.

Facing poverty head on, they supported radical social services, organizing com-munity clinics, occupying hospitals, collaborating with settlements, providing needed support for their own communities. The Young Patriots challenged the middle-class left to take the realities of poverty seriously, while the White Lightning made sure that a majority of the organizers in their group were from the communities they were orga-nizing. "These groups found that poor and working-class people rarely have the luxury of separating their experiences into single issues," note Amy Sonnie and James Tracey (2011, p. 170). "Their survival meant juggling multiple concerns at once: unsafe hous-ing conditions, late welfare checks, the draft, domestic violence and women's oppres-sion, labor grievances, child care, drug addiction, factory closures, the war, racism" (Sonnie & Tracey, 2011, p. 170). Addressing these concerns involved a distinct model of multi-issue organizing.

Over the years, many with the Black Panthers and the Young Lords stayed engaged in organizing with issues around community health, criminal justice, and autonomy. Many of these forces combined in the campaign to stop the U.S. Navy from bombing Vieques in Puerto Rico. Combining legal advocacy, direct action, media, research, coa-lition building, and a little play, activists pushed. Celebrities such as Jennifer Lopez and Ricky Martin joined the cause as did Robert Kennedy and the Reverent Al Sharpton, who would end up spending 90 days in jail after a civil disobedience action. And by 2003, activists with roots reaching back to the Young Lords party of the early 1970s could declare success when the U.S. Navy announced its withdrawal from Vieques. "The announcement signaled a glowing victory for the antimilitary movement" (Gautney, 2010, p. 175). Direct action provided the spark that ignited the victory.

12

From Critique to Coexistence With Capital

The Woodlawn Organization and the Dilemmas of Community Development

Of course, the Young Lords was not the only anti-poverty group of the era to use direct action to push its agenda. Many groups did. Some of the most famous were the Woodlawn Organization (TWO) and the National Welfare Rights Organizations (NWRO)—two groups that chose different paths. This chapter highlights the struggle between social movement and service orientations within community organizations. The Woodlawn Organization straddled between community development and organization in order to develop its own social and economic capital. Born of the civil rights movement, it formed a community development corporation as many anti-poverty groups did, and managed to sustain its influence over decades, while the NWRO remained true to its mission of causing disruption to incite change and did not last.

In *Poor People's Movements*, Frances Fox Piven and Richard Cloward (1977, p. 34) suggest that formal organizations rarely achieve the lasting reforms social movements achieve. What human services organizations can do is provide services, using disruptive tactics to support those in need (Brooks, 2005). This was certainly the case with the National Welfare Rights Organization, which successful bridged the gap between direct action and direct services. Throughout this movement, social workers collaborated with the movement in multiple ways, helping applicants receive the services and benefits they were legally entitled to (Reisch & Andrews, 2002). "But we were going to pursue those administrative remedies with occupations of welfare centers," noted Frances Fox Piven, who was an active in the organization. "And we did. So it was a kind of riotous strategy to force administrative compliance" (Shepard, 2008).

NWRO was certainly not alone in using outlandish tactics to fight for the poor. A product of the unrest of the 1960s, TWO established a distinct approach to organizing one of the poorest congressional districts in the United States in its South Side neighborhood in Chicago. By the mid-1960s, much of the middle class had moved out, leaving the poorest to remain in the Woodlawn (Wilson, 1997). The University of Chicago set its eyes on the community as land it could absorb. In response, neighborhood members Bishop Arthur Brazier and Leon Finney started organizing, pulling neighbors together to build the Woodlawn Organization. The group connected with legendary organizer Saul Alinski, building power through issue campaigns. Over time, the group fought off the University of Chicago's encroachment into the neighborhood. Its founders marched with Martin Luther King Jr. It mobilized thousands of members, busing them to city hall to register to vote in a show of power by TWO.

When the City of Chicago started backpedaling from promises made to the Woodlawn Organization in Chicago, Saul Alinski suggested the group use a little creative direct action to communicate their feelings. In this case, he proposed a "shit-in" at O'Hare International Airport in Chicago. Members of the group planned to occupy all the bathrooms, and to flush simultaneously, causing no small bit of chaos at the airport. When the mayor got word of the action, he acceded to most of the group's demands (Pyles, 2009). Woodlawn had power and now was using it to advance its goal of "Black Self Determination" (Hercules & Orenstein, 1999).

By the 1970s, TWO began to work more within the system, and took on 501(C)(3) status (for formal non-profit organizations), which restricted the group's advocacy work. Unsurprisingly, TWO toned down its more controversial tactics. Some suggested the organization had betrayed its mission to speak out for the poorest in the community (Fish, 1973, 2005; Ramirez, 2010; Wilson, 1997), but throughout this period, the organization struggled to stem ongoing deterioration and neglect by forming a community development corporation. It provided social services as well as remaining engaged in community economic development programs. The organization moved from confrontation to detente with city hall, while helping rebuild the Woodlawn.

Improve, Don't Move

In 1997, I interviewed the organization's founder, Bishop Arthur Brazier, at the time the Pentecostal pastor of the Apostolic Church of God in the Woodlawn. Over a nearly half century of service, he built a congregation of some twenty thousand people, who heeded his calls to stay in the neighborhood. Before his death in 2010 at the age of 89, Brazier was considered one of the most influential organizers in the United States. "I feel proud and happy that we didn't just sit around and wring our hands about these problems," Brazier told the *Chicago Tribune* in 2008. "We were able to see beyond the four walls of the church and we did something" (Ramirez, 2010). During our interview, we talked about his approach to organizing, engaging those in his community to gain power, identifying an issue, and staying on mission to fight for the poor. "Improve, Don't Move" would become a neighborhood slogan from South Chicago to the South Bronx.

"The idea of being involved with work in the Woodlawn had its genesis in my concern about how I as a Christian Pastor could become involved in the civil rights movement," Brazier explained. "I came into Woodlawn as the pastor of this church, the Apostolic Church of God, in 1960, just at the beginning of the 1960s when the Civil Rights Movement was at its height, beginning to take off."

Throughout the 1960s, Brazier marched with King, supporting the Civil Rights Movement, organizing around the core needs of those in his neighborhood. "There were serious problems here in the Woodlawn Community," noted Brazier. "First and foremost was the effort by the University of Chicago to expand into Woodlawn. And there was some great concern that the University would take over probably half if not more of the community. Many of the people who lived in the Woodlawn at that time had been victims of urban renewal in other communities. Many of these were home owners who had purchased homes in the neighborhood and they feared that they were going to have to move again. And this community, using the arm of the Woodlawn Organization, which had just been formed at that time, successfully resisted that effort by the university to come beyond 61st street."

As a student of organizing, for Brazier the story of the TWO is a narrative about organizing around specific issues.

> There were three other major issues that caused my concern—slum landlords, who were milking their buildings, not paying any taxes, not putting any money back into the communities, and taking all the rent while people got substandard accommodations. Secondly, there were some unscrupulous merchants that we felt needed to be dealt with. And thirdly, and I think the most important was the school bus segregation. At that time the Board of Education said schools were not segregated, but anyone living in Chicago knew de facto segregation was the way of life. Black schools were on the double and triple shift. Classes were being held in assembly halls, things of that nature, while at the same time there were unutilized schools in white neighborhoods. We believe that rather than have Black children on the double shift, they should be allowed to transfer to schools where there were empty classrooms. This was seriously opposed. The superintendent, at the time, put in portable classrooms in playgrounds where Black schools were located. We dubbed those portable classrooms, Willis Wagons, and used them as symbols to oppose school segregation.

Following the transgressive lessons of social justice gospel (Goss, 1993), Brazier framed his theology and organizing in terms of speaking out for the poor. "From a religious point of view, a lot of people ask me the question why was I, a preacher, involved in these things? My view was that there were people that were suffering because of injustice. And I thought that the parable that Jesus gave in relationship to the Good Samaritan was a clear indication that the church ought to be involved in alleviating human suffering." With this message in mind, Brazier got involved in community activity.

Brazier worked with Saul Alinski. "Woodlawn got the power and now they were using it and now they were making deals," noted Alinski (quoted in Hercules & Orenstein, 1999). Brazier said,

> I worked very closely with Alinski, for years. I didn't see the people who we were oppos- ing as enemies. I saw us opposing certain objectives to certain kinds of systems that I thought needed to be changed. I think that Saul Alinski and the Industrial Areas Foundation did a very, very excellent job of community organizing. I don't think that you go out and look for enemies. I think what you do is you identify a series of injustices. I never did look at the University of Chicago as enemy. I looked upon something that they were doing as something that was not beneficial to this community. And I didn't look upon slum landlords as enemies. I looked upon slum landlords as an injustice that had to be dealt with. As a Christian I do not want to identify anybody as an enemy.

So, instead of identifying a target as subhuman, Brazier took a different approach. "I don't think it's fair and it's not something that I want to get involved in. That creates a lot of animosity in your thinking."

People organize around issues, noted Brazier, in a nod to the framework for this book. "It's my view that organizing does not happen by snapping your fingers. People do not organize just for the sake of organizing. Unions do not organize just for the sake of organizing. You organize for a reason. The reason is you are trying to deal with some injustices that are happening. And you want to deal with that. You deal with that better if you organized as a group rather than trying to deal with it on an individual basis."

Brazier likened organizing to a conversation. "People live in an area who want to organize to preserve that community should do so in order to be a part of the democratic process," he explained. "And the best way to be a part of the democratic process is to organize groups. That's the reason why you have block clubs and social clubs, unions, fraternities, sororities, people organizing together for a common goal." What organizing is not is about is saying a space belongs to one group or another. "I don't think you should have someone say 'this is my turf and I'm going to organize my turf,'" noted Brazier.

Rather than fixate on what was missing from the Woodlawn, Brazier focused on community assets and strengths of the community. This approach helped influence a paradigm shift in community development strategies, organized around capacities rather than limitations (Kretzmann & McKnight, 1993). "You give folks who are moving up the ladder an opportunity to live in this community, in Woodlawn." For many years in the Woodlawn, those who had started to succeed moved out (Wilson, 1997). "Why should they always move to the suburbs? Why shouldn't they live in this community? I am com- mitted to mixed income communities, where people who are poor can live, people who are middle class, people who are in the middle can live, people who are on welfare, peo- ple who are making $80–90,000.00 a year can live—all in the same community."

At the time of the interview, I was volunteering in a case management program in the Woodlawn. The point of such direct services and outreach was to help engage marginal- ized people in community life. For Brazier, this included organizing. "I think political participation is important. I think it's extremely important," noted Brazier. Through his preaching and organizing, Brazier invited those in the neighborhood into a regenerative narrative of community. "I do think that what we might call testimonies, anecdotes, do give a lot of courage to a lot of people because the people see what other people have done, and they know it can be done. So they play a role."

One of the most famous early chapters of the Woodlawn Organization took place as the group engaged gang members from the Blackstone Rangers. "The goal was to get them back into some sort of education or training," noted Brazier. "But the main idea was getting jobs. That was a big component, back into some sort of a school setting, in which the gang members were part of the teaching. They'd all dropped out of school. Mistakes were made in part of the program. And part of it was we did not have enough professional staff. We relied too much on gang members and gang leaders." For Brazier, the point of TWO was simple. "We were more concerned with whether we were really fulfilling our role as a community organization. Were we really reducing slum landlordism? Were we really effective at reducing school segregation?"

In 1966, Brazier took part in Martin Luther King's and the Southern Non Violent Coordinating Committee Chicago Campaign. "It was a wonderful experience. I think it did a lot of good for this city. It certainly unleashed a lot of racist attitudes that were here dormant, but I think Dr. Martin Luther King's stay here was good for the city. It was good for everybody." The reaction in Chicago was far different than in the South. "It was different because here there was no official reaction. There were reactions in neighborhoods. But that official reaction from the police, the mayor, that never occurred. They were much more sophisticated. Southerners looked on Blacks as inferior, to be controlled. Northerners looked upon blacks with a different perspective. We don't want to live with ya. We don't want ya too close, but we think you ought to have equal rights."

Toward the end of the interview, Brazier reflected on his legacy within the neighborhood.

> When I look back, I think a tremendous amount of work has been done here in the Woodlawn by organizations like TWO. I would hate to think of what this community would have look[ed] like if there had not been a Woodlawn Organization. I think that the Woodlawn Organization was like a holding pattern trying to keep this neighborhood together, organized until the community fortunes changed. I think this community now has bottomed out and is on its way back up. And in [the next] the five to ten years you will not be able to recognize the Woodlawn of the 1970s. I think it will be a mixed income community. I think you will see stores here. I think there will be people purchasing homes. I believe you will still have people that are on welfare. You will have buildings that will be single occupancy buildings and you will have homes that will cost 200,000 and homes that cost under 100,000. I think they'll all be living together. I think there will be people who need subsidized rent and people who do not. I think that is a good viable community.

From direct action to community development, TWO played a distinct role in the history of organizing. Through Brazier's narrative, we have considered approaches to strengths-based community assessments, conflicts between development and social action, and approaches to community development. The history of links between direct action and direct services takes countless turns. By the 1980s, a new cohort of organizers used similar creative tactics to support community survival when faced with a different sort of health crisis.

13

ACT UP to the World

Direct Action to Direct Services

On Wednesday, April 25, 2012, the AIDS Coalition to Unleash Power (ACT UP), celebrated its 25th Anniversary with a trip to Wall Street—and forged a connection with the Occupy Movement. Social workers and street activists, health care advocates and anarchists joined the celebration and street action. AIDS activists had long supported multiple approaches to engagement, including services.

The linkage between ACT UP and Occupy was not insubstantial. Both ignited movements by targeting Wall Street. In doing so, they joined a storied critique. "Wall Street owns the country," noted Populist Mary Elizabeth Lease in 1890. "It is no longer government of the people, by the people, and for the people, but government of Wall Street, by Wall Street, for Wall Street" (Lease, 1890/2004, p. 226). ACT UP and Occupy understood that Wall Street plays by its own rules, favoring its own interests.

For members of ACT UP, as we've seen, direct action has always gotten the goods. An earlier trip to Wall Street was evidence of that. On the 14th of September, 1989, seven members of ACT UP chained themselves to the balcony of the New York Stock Exchange,

"AIDS Is Not History" die-in at the New York Public Library, Fall 2013.

Source: Photo by author

Keith Cylar speaking at the tenth anniversary action of the AIDS Coalition to Unleash Power.

Source: Photo courtesy of Housing Works

where they hung a banner declaring, "SELL WELLCOME," a reference to the venerable pharmaceutical company Burroughs Wellcome, the maker of AZT, the only promising AIDS drug available at the time. Their message was clear: Wall Street was controlling the health care needs of people living with HIV/AIDS in the same ways it has long controlled the U.S. economy. Within three days, the drug company dropped the price of the drug by a third. It was ACT UP's third major demonstration on Wall Street. Their first, in 1987, targeted "Business, big business, and business as usual," connecting campaigns to move drugs into bodies with a system of drug patents, privatization, and a global economy favoring profits over people. Their brand of street action, combining creative tactics with thoughtful media work, clear goals, and a tactical frivolity, would fuel a resurgence of both direct action and Situationist-style street pranks and protest that dated back to the sixties, connecting them in history to the Young Lords and TWO; Gay Liberation, Women's Health, No-Nukes, Anti-Apartheid, and other global justice movements.

Keith Cylar carried a sign with the words "Free AZT" to the 1989 ACT UP Wall Street zap on Wall Street. At the action, Cylar pointed out that Wall Street had made

ACT UP AIDS is not history.

Source: Photo by author

enough money with AZT. His argument was simple. The federal government helped pay for the research to develop AZT. When they charged Medicare and Medicaid for the drug, the U.S. government was paying for it twice. While Burroughs Wellcome argued the research costs were theirs alone, federal research from the National Institutes of Health (NIH) helped support the process. The government was paying twice. Burroughs Welcome's approach was one of a long history of examples of Wall Street privatizing profits generated through public-private partnerships. This sort of thing was the reason Occupy Wall Street was born.

Much of the power and potency of ACT UP was used to challenge the roots of AIDS drug profiteering, as well as the systems of racism, sexism, and homophobia that fuel the epidemic. Activist struggles to challenge these forces make ACT UP an unparalleled experience in social movement history. Watching these activists in action, one witnesses a group transforming social stigma through public education, research, and direct action. To fight the neglect and oppression of people with HIV/AIDS, a group of activists has built on the lessons and tactics of a generation of direct action groups. Through ACT UP, activists linked the struggles from women's communities and communities of color to fight a system built on inequalities in health. Members of ACT UP have always been clear how much they learned from the women's movement in this struggle.

Thinking about this movement and the passions it helped ignite, screams reverberate through the past into our current moment:

"We die, they do nothing!"

"We'll never be silent again, ACT UP!"

"Ten years, one billion dollars, one drug," screamed hundreds outside of the offices of the National Institutes of Health offices in Bethesda, Maryland, during ACT UP's storm the NIH action of 1990. "Storm the NIH," rapped Tony Malliaris. "Storm the NIH for the sick, Storm the NIH—for the poor." Reflecting on the action, Mark Harrington would note, "Direct action can be more effective than ten years of lobbyists." Each action expanded a dialog. With each zap, ACT UP helped pull power away from the experts and put it in the hands of those most impacted by the epidemic, those contending with the inequalities of Wall Street controlling their health.

I came into ACT UP three years later in 1993. There I witnessed both the despair of years without treatment for the virus, which killed hundreds of the clients I came to know during my years as a social worker in San Francisco. If I did not hear about their passing at work, I saw it reading the obits in the *Bay Area Reporter*. Coping with those losses, ACT UP allowed us to laugh and take action, to care and to mourn. It also connected collective grief with global movements, linking the AIDS struggle with anti-apartheid and gay liberation movements, as well as neighborhood politics. For me, perhaps ACT UP's most important lesson was that we could and should have some fun while fighting the carnage. One could cry or scream—all these expressions were legitimate. In other words, it was OK to be who you are, not who anyone else thought you should be. You could revel in the collective pleasure of watching friends build community, dance all night, grieve for those whose health was eroding, and celebrate the Lazarus-like phenomenon of watching people regain their health with the advent of highly active antiretroviral therapy, a treatment that actually worked, 15 years into the epidemic. Many credited ACT UP with pushing to make this happen.

Yet even with HAART (highly active antiretroviral therapy), HIV was not over. "It's not over 'til it's over for everyone," Housing Works, an AIDS service and direct action organization born of ACT UP's housing committee, reminded everyone. Over the next 15 years, wave after wave of new AIDS activist groups were born, many, such as SexPanic! Fed Up Queers, CitiWide Harm Reduction, Healthgap, Treatment Action Group, New York City AIDS Housing Network, and VOCAL, born directly from ACT UP. Moving to New York in the late 1990s, I saw ACT UP dovetail with fights over HIV prevention, harm reduction, social services, crumbling safety provisions for the poor, and struggles over access to medications all over the world (Shepard & Hayduk, 2002).

"AIDS opened up a lot of cans of worms," noted Gay Liberation Front veteran and longtime ACT UP supporter Bob Kohler before his death. Cleve Jones (2001), founder of the Names Quilt, would point out that AIDS is spread by sexism, racism, homophobia, and even capitalism itself. In response, ACT UP joined with multiple movements aimed at fighting these systems of power, including those willing to provide social services.

Social Services and Global Social Movements in AIDS Activism

Countless ACT UP veterans bridged the gap between direct action and direct services by extending their activism with ACT UP into social services. The provision of survival supplies was viewed as a rightful component of AIDS activism.

"More often actions were planned right at a meeting," noted ACT UP veteran Andy Velez. "And there were occasions when a meeting was shut down and we simply marched out and got up to Gracie Mansion and had a demonstration right then and there."

Direct action would get the goods over and over. Velez referred to a specific moment when the group helped connect direct action and services. "A social worker told us at a Monday meeting that there was a mother who had a young child who weighed 44 lbs and was unable to get her office to approve nutritional food supplements for him. Immediately, a group formed and within a day or two, they had gotten a photograph of the manager of that office. Three days later, we were picketing outside that office with the manager's face on the posters. And the kid got his supplements."

At the International AIDS Conference in Washington, D.C., in 2012, several service providers chained themselves to the fence surrounding the White House, pushing for the administration to do more around HIV. One of those providers was Eustacia Smith.

"When I left the church, I started getting involved with different things in the Gay and Lesbian Community Center," notes Smith. "I would always pass through the ACT UP meeting and hear about stuff they were doing. And that's partly what drew my interest to it." There, Smith met elder activists in the group such as Maxine Wolfe, Ann Northrop, and CJ Crain. "There was a lot of influence from the women's movement, a lot of strong women in ACT UP that carried a lot of weight." These women helped instill the lesson of speaking truth to power, that regular people had the responsibility to let the government know that people were simply not going to participate in systems that furthered injustice.

Throughout this time, Smith worked as a housing provider for people with AIDS. Here her activism overlapped with service provision. "That happens in the AIDS world probably a lot more than in other parts of social work," noted Smith. "I've definitely done activism around stuff that directly affects my clients here," Smith continued, referring to issues related to HIV/AIDS Services Administration (HASA) and the Human Resources Administration (HRA).

She joined a group of service providers called the HASA Watch, who served as watchdogs, making sure the city fulfilled its obligation to place people with HIV/AIDS into housing. "I participated in two direct actions, civil disobedience, around HRA," noted Smith. "One of them was around HASA not housing people under the time-frame that's in the law required to house people under. But then there was also a direct action that happened that was organized by a combination of Housing Works and New York City AIDS Housing Network."

At the peak of the campaign, a group of people locked themselves into the offices at HRA as clients waited for services. "Twice we went there," recalled Smith. Once inside, the group asked where people with HIV/AIDS could sleep because the city was not providing the housing it was obliged to provide under local law. "We all brought pillows and we went into the lobby, and we chained ourselves together and to the lobby and had a sleep over." Their sleepover would last another two hours before Smith and company were arrested. While Charles King was being hand-cuffed, the *New York Times* called him and he explained to the reporter that he was being arrested because the city was failing to follow the law.

Throughout this period, Smith and company saw the struggle to get AIDS drugs and treatment into the bodies of people around the world as a global issue. To move this issue forward, a small affinity group targeted the U.S. Trade Representative for threatening sanctions against South Africa for making generic AIDS drugs for people with HIV/AIDS. "I was frequently scared before doing a lot of actions," recalled Smith. "But I'd say probably the scariest one was the United States Trade Representative office takeover, which was part of the whole campaign around access to medicine." The week of before the World Trade Organization meetings in Seattle in 1999 the group took over the office of the U.S. Trade Representative. Smith explained:

> It was a scarier action in terms of it was a bit harder core. One, it was scary because it was a federal building. You're going into a building that in and of itself means a little more security. We had two teams. We had a team come up from Philadelphia and then we had the Fed Up Queers New York team. The Philadelphia team scaled up into the balcony and chained themselves to the balcony. The New York team's job was to go inside into the offices, and the way we did it was we just had someone pretend to faint to create a little bit of a distraction for the security guards, and then the rest of us just ran through the metal detectors.

Shortly after the action, the United States dropped its threat of trade sanctions.

Over time, ACT UP spawned groups such as Healthgap, which sought to bridge a gap in access to medicines around the world. It also inspired groups such as Treatment Action Campaign (TAC) in South Africa, which borrowed from ACT UP's direct action approach. Organized by HIV-positive South African activist Zachie Achmont, TAC helped the international movement for treatment and access for people living with HIV/AIDS in South Africa. TAC took the stigma of HIV/AIDS head on, shifting debate about the disease from deviance to one of human rights and access to treatment. Both HIV-positive and -negative members wore T-shirts with the words, "HIV POSITIVE" to increase visibility for people with HIV/AIDS and reduce social isolation among those with the disease in South Africa. Antiapartheid icon and international human rights hero Nelson Mandela, then South African president, even wore one of the HIV POSITIVE shirts. The former South African president's advocacy for the group also helped solidify the links between the antiapartheid struggle and the campaign for treatment access as human rights movements. For many, the stakes were equally high. When limited treatment for people with HIV/AIDS became available in South Africa, Achmont drew international headlines for refusing to take medication until it was available to everyone. In doing so, Achmont put his health at risk to make a larger point about medical apartheid in South Africa. And conditions began to change. "Making health care more accessible to South Africa's poor is now a constitutional duty facing the government," a TAC press release stated in 2001. "Our constitution says that: Everyone has the right to have access to health care services." Yet, the government was not TAC's only target. When the government did respond to activist pressure and focus on treatment for the masses in South Africa, it did so in a fashion that put it at odds with multinational pharmaceutical companies. When it sought to import generic AIDS drugs from abroad, the Mandela administration brought on the ire of the Pharmaceutical Manufacturer's Association (PMA), which threatened to sue the Mandela administration. Activists the world over cried foul, as the global treatment access movement dovetailed with the burgeoning global justice movement, and solidarity protests followed. The PMA dropped the suit in April of 2001, after a global protest the previous month. By 2003, TAC successfully pushed its own government to back a plan to distribute and expand access to antiretroviral medications for people with HIV/AIDS. Today, TAC, like ACT UP, is considered one of the most innovative and effective social movement groups of the last decade (Sawyer, 2004; Shepard & Hayduk, 2002; R. A. Smith & Siplon, 2006; Treatment Action Campaign, 2001).

14

Affinity Group to Movement Organization

Housing Works

The overlapping nature of social action and services takes any number of forms (Rothman, 1995). Countless service groups spun off from ACT UP/New York, including Housing Works, CitiWide Harm Reduction, and the Lower East Side Harm Reduction Center. This chapter highlights the story of a new model of social movement organization, Housing Works. In the years after it moved from an affinity group within ACT UP into an organization unto itself, Housing Works helped build community through a combination of direct services and successful policy advocacy on the city, state, and national levels (Schubert & Hombs, 1995). Over and over it argued that housing quite literally works; it saves lives, helps stabilize communities, and functions as HIV prevention. Combining research, direct action, legal advocacy, and services, Housing Works has forged a distinct model of services.

Staffers with Housing Works employ a number of direct strategies to advance

Keith Cylar leading the parade.

Source: Photo courtesy of Housing Works

the cause of service provision. Sometimes it helps arouse the attention of previously inattentive politicians involved in budget negotiation; in other cases, it helps move a housing application from the welfare department. Throughout my years as a social worker and housing provider, I valued Housing Works' capacity to push the slow moving city bureaucracy to respect the lives of people with HIV/AIDS, no matter how poor or marginalized. They had a Social Justice squad, which would go to the welfare centers and chain themselves up and not leave until the welfare workers did their job and moved the housing applications. This relentless and dogged determination actually got people housed. Here, housing provision and direct action overlapped effectively (Shepard, 2008). Housing Works builds on a vast legacy of antipoverty activism, most notably the National Welfare Rights Organization (NWRO).

"One of our arguments was that those direct material services are really important," noted Frances Fox Piven, recalling the NWRO. "Another one of our arguments was that no matter whether there is a movement out there or not social workers should do whatever they can, which may include defying the authorities in the agencies in which they work, to get those services to the people that need them. In welfare rights there were a lot of social workers who actually worked with the movement. And made the case managers who worked in centers as well as the managers who were social workers come alive again" (Shepard, 2008).

"What has always been most compelling to me about doing AIDS work is that HIV tracks along all the fault lines of political economy and culture of the planet," noted Jeanne Bergman. "All health issues generally do but AIDS does especially because of its connection specifically to drugs and sex and sex work. And because it kills, it is sort of super-heated in a way that some other public health issues are not. But the intersection with poverty, with homelessness, the access to care that privileged people got, the denial of the most basic human needs that poor people got, all of this made the work so challenging and important."

Housing Works undertook a task similar to groups like the Black Panthers and the NWRO, while creating its own distinct model of an antipoverty organization. Comparing Housing Works with this movement is telling. From the late 1960s through early 1970s, the National Welfare Rights Organization (NWRO) sought to create a new kind of public welfare system that did not stigmatize those who received public aid (Piven & Cloward, 1977). It did this through a strategy that began with fierce legal advocacy and ended with a wide range of disruptive tactics, including direct action. Throughout the 1990s and to the present, Housing Works, the nation's most militant AIDS service organization, pushed for a different kind of public welfare and for a consciousness about the lives of homeless people with HIV/AIDS whose diagnoses were complicated by histories of chemical dependence, mental illness, and poverty. Like NWRO, Housing Works' strategy included fierce legal advocacy and a wide range of disruptive tactics. Both organizations struggled with a dwindling welfare state, a conservative backlash, and reconciling the provision of service with advocacy. Eight years after its formation, the NWRO met its demise. In contrast, 15 years after its formation, Housing Works reached a budget of over $41 million and is still going strong (Dwyer, 2005b).

Housing and the AIDS Pandemic

From the earliest days of the U.S. AIDS pandemic, the crisis wound itself into the web of poverty in America. During these years, the AIDS epidemic threatened many of the same socially vulnerable populations that had organized with and benefited from the work of the NWRO. By the mid-1980s, about 25% of people with HIV/AIDS in the United States were African American, and 57% of all children with HIV/AIDS were Black (Cohen, 1999). Today, according to the Centers for Disease Control (2014), "African Americans are the racial/ethnic group most affected by HIV. The rate of new HIV infection in African Americans is 8 times that of whites based on population size." So, advocates screamed, fought, faced arrest, and created a safety net for poor people with HIV/AIDS (Siplon, 2002).

In the 1980s in New York City, Keith Cylar worked as a discharge planner in a hospital. "There was a gridlock in the hospital system," noted Cylar.

Housing Works banner drop at World AIDS Day 2012.

Source: Photo by author

> For me working in the hospital: I couldn't get people out of the hospital because they didn't have a place to live. We'd get them with whatever brought them in; often they wouldn't have a place to live. They'd stay in the hospitals and they'd pick up another thing and then they'd die. They were keeping people out on hospital gurneys in the hallways. That was when people were not being fed, bathed or touched. It was horrendous. You can't imagine what it was like to be Black, gay, a drug user, transgender, and dying from AIDS. (Shepard, 2002b, p. 355)

Housing Works assumed a leadership role, recognizing that the demographics of the AIDS pandemic would continue to shift toward underserved high-risk groups such as low-income women and people of color, many without housing. "I knew a couple of people in the neighborhood who were homeless," explained Eric Sawyer (2004), who lived in Harlem, and helped found the group. Cylar recalled,

> I just started reading a lot about it and, because of the connection with drug use, started learning that there's this whole other AIDS plague, tied to drug use, that is very prevalent in homeless communities, and it's a whole area where there are no services.
> So housing all of a sudden became this issue. ACT UP recognized it and formed this Housing Committee. I got involved in the Housing Committee when they came to the Majority Action Committee to do a presentation. . . . There was this guy there, Charles King. We started working together. (Shepard, 2002b, p. 356)

At the time, Charles King was working with attorney Ginny Shubert. The two saw the injustices experienced by homeless people and those at risk or infected with HIV.

"We were seeing people die because they were sharing needles and there was a complete lack of education and understanding. The epidemic was spreading really rampantly, and also a result of the sex exchange, particularly women who were very vulnerable," noted Shubert. "And then to add insult to injury, people who weren't clinically using couldn't get placement in housing. So we had a lot of funny ideas like keeping urine samples in the refrigerator so that people could use them to get placed in housing. That was really it; you had to have 30 days of clean urine in order to get into AIDS housing."

Keith Cylar, Ginny Shubert, Charles King, and Eric Sawyer started organizing, combining legal advocacy with direct action, and eventually founded Housing Works. If nobody else is going to do this, they decided, Housing Works would. So the group started organizing to make the system work for people with HIV/AIDS. Along the way, they would change the rules of the game for people with HIV/AIDS (Sawyer, 2004).

"I was always the one trying to use the legal system to create the change," noted Shubert. "Yes, we wanted to demonstrate that you could do it. There was this whole debate during that period whether homelessness is a housing issue or individual blame. I don't know if you remember there was an article by Pete Hamill and it was all about people are homeless because they're fucked up." Faced with this, Housing Works litigated, organized, and helped create a counter-narrative that challenged the stigmas related to HIV, drug use, and homelessness. "The greatest thing about ACT UP is that there was a sense of self pride, there was no shame, there was no apology, there was pride and there was fun and people dressed up and blew whistles," explained Shubert. "It's just trying to force other people to embrace everyone in the community."

Many in the group reveled in the joyous disposition. Between Keith Cylar's spirit of play as well as expertise in social services, Charles's and Ginny's legal knowledge, and Sawyer's understanding of the housing market, the group brought many potent elements together to push their campaign for housing for people with HIV/AIDS. And they had a lot of fun doing it. Jeanne Bergman, who worked at Housing Works in the 1990s, recalled joyous moments with the group sometimes just driving home from a trip to Albany after lobbying. All these elements combined to create a distinct model of activism and service provision. "I think that they did a brilliant job of using the activist mobilization within New York to build community and to change the way [people saw] people living with HIV and homeless people," explained Bergman. The core component of Housing Works' approach to service provision was to find out what was going on the lives of clients, to hear their stories, to take them seriously, and learn from them. Their programs were born of these conversations. The result was a distinct brand of empowerment-based service provision (Cowger, 1994; Hasenfeld, 1987; Lindhorst & Eckert, 2003).

"One of my favorite things from the early days was a client group called AIDA, Anger into Direct Action," noted Shubert. "That was a great group of people—Wayne Phillips, Phyllis Sharpe, really early warriors, all dead now. We sold T-shirts at Gay Pride and we went out to San Francisco for the AIDS Conference."

Through such actions, Housing Works clients found a voice as advocates. "There was a particularly fun action that we did at one point," noted Shubert. "We made these posters for the subway, the square subway posters, and it said 'Dinkins Lies, People Die.' It was when the Dinkins administration instituted discretional shelter for people with HIV and we went to the subways and replaced the existing ads with these posters. That was fun. There was a kind of spirit; you know just telling the truth. It was always fun." Through such gestures, Housing Works helped people coping with something extremely heavy—life on the street with HIV. These first years of Housing Works in the early 1990s were before protease inhibitors and combination therapy, so people were still dying fast. Yet, the esprit de corps of Housing Works helped people work with each other despite the heavy stakes. The gallows humor helped the group move from

Housing Works co-founder Charles King on World AIDS Day 2012.

Source: Photo by author

anger to action, even when things got difficult. "It has been also really sad and really hard. Especially when the city went after us," recalled Shubert.

Charles King describes the ways the group reveled in defying authority as they used direct action. "We organized this action," he recalled. "Eric Sawyer actually drove the truck where we brought a bunch of desks and chairs and phones into the middle of Church Street in front of HRA and handcuffed ourselves to them. I loved the chant. The chant was probably one of the best that we ever created. It was, and I laugh as I say it: 'The check is in the desk and the desk is in the mail!'" And the city agency responded.

Over and over, direct action moved direct services. "Our HPD [Housing Preservation and Development] action was another amazing one," recalled King. "On Gold Street they have revolving doors. We went around on a Sunday night and picked up a bunch of abandoned furniture on the Lower East Side and Monday morning took it down to Gold Street [and] stuffed the revolving doors with furniture trying to deliver it to furnish housing for people living with AIDS." The action also served as a form of a blockade.

> What was actually cool about it was we had been pestering the commissioner who had sworn that no HPD units were going to go to people with AIDS. He was very conservative. So we had been pestering him and we did that action. That very afternoon he issued a press release announcing that he'd established a commission to study whether or not they could identify housing for people with AIDS. That was in June. We waited until late August, early September, right before the Dinkins/Koch primary. We sent the commissioner a fax saying we had another load of furniture to furnish housing for people with AIDS. "Where would you like it delivered?" That afternoon he issued a press release announcing that they had identified 60 units of housing for people with AIDS. Of course, they were going to turn the units over, 20 units per year,

over the course of three years. They were going to do the pilot project to see if people with AIDS could live in their housing.

Over time, the group came to recognize that what was needed was a movement to push back against this government inaction. Housing Works would help create that movement for poor people with HIV/AIDS. Doing so, the agency is perhaps most famous for its tradition of street activism and pioneering services (Dwyer, 2005b; Shepard, 2009). The challenge for professionals who collaborated with grassroots groups, such as those in Housing Works, was to serve as mediators between movements and funders, constituents and resources, policy targets and policymakers (K. Moore & Young 2002).

Building on the legacy of aggressive HIV/AIDS advocacy advanced by the AIDS Coalition to Unleash Power (ACT UP), the community-building spirit of the settlement houses, and the community economic development movement, Housing Works imagined itself as a different type of anti-poverty organization (Shepard, 2008; Stoecker, 1996). Over time, the group ran thrift stores, as well as created housing and job training for clients. These ventures helped the organization generate income for its programs as well as "employment opportunities for its clients" (Shepard, 2002b, p. 352). By focusing on organizing and advocacy while using tools of community economic development to take control of its own resources, Housing Works provided support for a newer trend in social movement organization that suggests that radical beliefs are often quite consistent with professionalization in activism and service provision (Reeser & Epstein, 1990).

The organization's mission remained to reach the most vulnerable and underserved among those affected by the AIDS epidemic in New York City—homeless people of color whose HIV diagnoses are complicated by a history of chronic mental illness and/ or chemical dependence. Since its founding in 1990, Housing Works has had to strike a balance between social service and a social movement orientation.

By cultivating group solidarity among mostly homeless low-income people of color and linking their needs with those of other stigmatized groups, Housing Works advanced both socioeconomic and ethical agendas with their often colorful, flamboyant actions and beliefs that everyone deserves a place to call home. Here, Housing Works valued the importance of a messy, queer sort of collective identity among its clients and the movements in which it operated. By acknowledging the emotional and expressive needs of social actors, Housing Works helped those it organized create meaning in their lives through community building, creative direct action, housing, work, and an often joyous, even playful pursuit of happiness and democratic political engagement (Shepard, 2009).

Housing Works has strived to maintain its position as a radical advocacy organization that combines activism and services despite the conventional view that professionalization and organizational development undermine acts of group solidarity and advocacy. As Piven and Cloward (1977, p. xxi) argue, "it is not possible to compel concessions from elites that can be used as resources to sustain oppositional organizations over time." Yet Housing Works' life course reflects a different experience; it has aggressively and successfully attacked government, bureaucracies, and even agencies that provided funds for the organization. Moreover, it survived and thrived despite attacks by Mayor Giuliani and his efforts to defund the organization (Dwyer, 2005b; Ferrell, 2001). Rather than cave in, Housing Works stayed true to its mission (K. Moore & Young, 2002).

The group made use of a wide range of tools, including research, aggressive legal and service advocacy, direct action, pranks, street theatrics, and media savvy to successfully demand services for socially vulnerable populations. Here, the group effectively staked the claim that active drug users, sex workers, and homeless people all deserve a place to sleep and eat, as well as the right to earn a paycheck (Shepard, 2008). Housing is health care and prevention, backing up their claim with substantial research that forced governments and funders to take notice (Aidala & Lee, 2000; Schubert & Hombs, 1995). And quickly, the group was recognized for being smart, visionary advocates.

"The strategy was to push, push, push," Keith Cylar said in describing the approach of the early Housing Works years. "It wasn't different than the general ACT UP strategy about inclusion. But it was always to get those populations also included. . . . People of color were so far off the Richter scale." This meant creating an organization in which aggressive advocacy for unpopular causes coincided with the group's unique institutional needs. "Housing Works started when, after demonstrating, fighting, and working in the AIDS community, the people that I cared the most about were the people least likely to get served," Cylar elaborated. "And so we decided we had to do it ourselves" (Shepard, 2002b, p. 356). Over the next two decades, it would remain true to its ethos, even as the organization straddled between direct action and direct services. The Housing Works story highlights the utility of a smart group's capacity to remain flexible, highlight a workable alternative harm reduction program, compile research to support its claims, and use direct action to advance its goal of providing life-saving direct services for those on the margins. Throughout the years, the group built on the work of a number of social movements, including an effort to reduce harm, the subject of the subsequent chapter.

15

Harm Reduction and Human Services

Experiments in Syringe Exchange

❝**H**uman service professionals respect the integrity and welfare of the client at all times. Each client is treated with respect, acceptance and dignity," reads the Human Services Code of Conduct (National Organization for Human Services [NOHS], 1996). Under "The Human Service Professional's Responsibility to Clients," Statement 13 notes, "Human service professionals act as advocates in addressing unmet client and community needs" (NOHS, 1996). These calls for "dignity" and consideration of "unmet client and community needs" are fundamentally consistent with the harm reduction approach to practice used in a range of practice settings around the country. Through a wide array of nonprescriptive approaches to public health, policy, and services, harm reduction advocates have brought the unmet needs of a range of socially vulnerable, hard-to-engage client populations into policy and treatment circles.

This chapter builds on ideas from the stories of the Young Lords and Housing Works to consider the use of direct action to create a new modality of service provision called harm reduction. Tracing the development of the harm reduction movement in New York, we will see how these direct action groups borrowed from the work of the international harm reduction movement to influence U.S. AIDS policy and practice. We'll focus on the work of ACT UP's syringe exchange committee and its effort to legalize the practice, followed by narratives of innovative harm reduction organizations CitiWide Harm Reduction, Washington Heights CORNER Project, and NYCAHN, now called VOCAL.

From the War on Drugs to Harm Reduction

As we noted in Chapter 2, under the Nixon administration policy emphasis shifted to crime control, rather than welfare provision or prevention. Nixon's "War on Drugs," rather than providing services to alleviate poverty (a major predicate of drug abuse), the new emphasis was on criminalizing drug use (Shepard, 2007b). The draconian Rockefeller drug laws of the 1970s were a prime example of this approach.

Faced with increased attacks on social movements under the new administration, a number of groups sought to protect their communities. The Black Panthers organized survival programs to provide material support for their community in Oakland, California (Abron, 1998; Self, 2003; Sonnie & Tracy, 2011). The Young Lords organized a number of forward thinking, audacious acts of direct action aimed at cultivating a more responsive system of public health for poor people and social outsiders (Melendez, 2003). The group called for a public health program that actually favored health over social controls. The Lincoln detox and acupuncture program would become a model for treatment for people coping with heroin addiction. Harm reduction advocates a decade later would look to the model of self-determination for social outsiders.

Throughout the early years of the AIDS epidemic, AIDS activists grappled with questions about the appropriate approach to HIV prevention. While some suggested HIV prevention should include a temperance era, abstinence approach that called for strict prohibitions of sexual contact (Gusfield, 1986), others called for a more humanistic approach. "You must celebrate gay sex in your writing and give men support," Dr. Joseph Sonnabend counseled Richard Berkowitz and Michael Callen as the three worked on a HIV prevention pamphlet in New York in the early 1980s (Berkowitz, 2003, p. 121). Berkowitz and Callen recognized that condemning promiscuity would not work. Prohibition is often more dangerous than acknowledgment, careful expression, and prevention. Instead, Berkowitz and Callen would build on the lessons of gay liberation to draft "How to Have Sex in an Epidemic." The result was a revolution allowing for personal and political protection and cover for both sex and the liberation movement, which dismantled the shackles around it. The tract outlined core principles of HIV prevention built around reduction of risks:

- Get informed about high- and low-risk activities
- Be honest about needs, desires, and risks
- Meet a person where they are at
- Practices, not places spread HIV
- Provide safer sex information, as well as the tools necessary to achieve it

Faced with the prohibitionist logic of conservatives, HIV prevention activists built their own movement to challenge the moralists, and a harm reduction movement was born. The roots of this movement are located in any number of directions.

Many involved in syringe exchange look to England's Merseyside model developed in 1988. Its core principles suggest the following: (1) HIV prevention takes priority over drug treatment. (2) Abstinence is not a realistic or feasible goal. (3) Create "safety nets" to reduce harm. (4) Provide user-friendly services that attract users; reduce barriers to care. (5) Provide for the whole person (Elovich, 2002; Springer, n.d., 1991).

The Canadian approach to harm reduction built on a similar set of intervention approaches used to reduce drug-related harm. This model includes the following assumptions: (1) Drug use is a given. (2) The user is treated with dignity as a normal human being and is expected to behave as such. (3) Harm reduction is the first step to reduce drug use. (4) Respect and dignity engage many who are outside of care (Elovich, 2002; Springer, n.d., 1991).

Building on these practical approaches to public health, the U.S. Harm Reduction Coalition formed to address the needs of drug users in the United States. The Harm Reduction Coalition (n.d.) defines the practice as a set of interventions that seek to "reduce the negative consequences of drug use, incorporating a spectrum of strategies from safer use, to managed use, to abstinence." Thus, "Harm reduction is a public health approach that aims to reduce drug-related harm experienced by individuals and communities, without necessarily reducing the consumption of drugs." To do so, harm reduction strategies meet users "where they are at," addressing conditions of use along with the use itself. Harm reduction emphasizes a pragmatic, nonjudgmental approach aimed at collaboration and partnership rather than repression and incarceration. Provider and service participant work to identify high-risk behaviors and reduce these behaviors (Elovich, 2002; Springer, n.d.).

Part of the utility of harm reduction is its capacity to bridge the divide between direct action and direct services. From San Francisco to New York, the passion of direct action spawned this movement. Some of this approach involved fighting against policies that restricted client needs or harm reduction programs. It also meant fighting to create space for innovative, less paternalistic programming. "[S]ometimes you have to use direct action to muscle your way in to get the funding," explains Kate Barnhart, an ACT UP veteran who has taken her activism to providing services for homeless queer youth. She continues: "If you don't fight for a piece of the budget, you're not going to get one. Even if you're just asking for a crumb you still have to fight."

Barnhart alludes to the point that harm reduction groups are often organized around direct client needs, with little extra resources for other forms of lobbying. But more than advocacy, the direct action Barnhart refers to involves gestures of freedom, some of which are not deemed legal. Gandhi was famous for leading his followers to make salt, even if it meant facing arrest, in order to force a change in laws. A range of movements, including the U.S. civil rights and AIDS movements, which spawned harm reduction, have borrowed from this approach. Statement 10 of "The Human Service Professional's Responsibility to Clients" in the Human Service Code of Ethics states, "Human service professionals are aware of local, state, and federal laws. They advocate for change in regulations and statutes when such legislation conflicts with ethical guidelines and/or client rights" (NOHS, 1996). Much of the harm reduction movement builds on this ethical commitment to client rights. Statement 10 of the Human Services Code of Ethics concludes, "Where laws are harmful to individuals, groups or communities, human service professionals consider the conflict between the values of obeying the law and the values of serving people and may decide to initiate social action" (NOHS, 1996). Such social action includes a wide array of approaches to action, including lobbying, others involving mobilization of bodies, and even civil disobedience.

Experiments in Syringe Exchange

New York–based groups, including ACT UP, Housing Works, Moving Equipment, and CitiWide Harm Reduction, were born of an approach to public health aimed at meeting unmet needs. Building on the knowledge of users, ACT UP saw syringe exchange as a lifesaving intervention. The group members were willing to face arrest, committing civil disobedience to give away clean syringes to users (Elovich, n.d.; Springer, n.d., 1991). These experiments are worth exploring.

ACT UP member Richard Elovich carries syringes at the Days of Desperation ACT UP demonstrations, January 22, 1991. "Dead addicts don't recover," other signs declared, highlighting the need to engage users in whichever way possible.

Source: Photo by Allan Clear

Members of ACT UP fashioned their late-1980s underground syringe exchange as the group's longest running civil disobedience. At the time, 60% of intravenous drug users were HIV positive. With no other reasonable alternative in sight, ACT UP member Greg Bordowitz started an underground syringe exchange. ACT UP member Brian Weil stumbled into a network of drug users in single room occupancy (SRO) hotels in upper Manhattan and the Bronx and built a program around their needs. A former intern at CitiWide got fed up with seeing the clients at her first social work job without access to syringe exchange, so she started one. Sean Barry wanted participants in New York City AIDS Housing Network (NYCAHN, now VOCAL) to feel comfortable using their syringe exchange program, yet police arrested them for carrying syringes—so his group helped pass a syringe decriminalization law. Each built linkages across issues in order to address unmet needs. This innovation is worth exploring.

Syringe exchange programs in New York grew from the work of the ACT UP syringe exchange group. "Now, because I wasn't a needle user, I wasn't involved with the stigma around needles," noted Greg Bordowitz (2002, p. 36), a central organizer in this committee in an interview for the ACT UP Oral History Project. "I didn't have this charged relationship to them, and I wasn't afraid that necessarily distributing them was condoning drug use. I was sensitive to the idea, and always thought . . . that needle exchange was

VOCAL Clean Needles Save Lives.

Source: Used with permission of VOCAL New York

never sufficient. We should always be fighting for more treatment slots and much more funding for treatment . . . needle exchange was just part of it" (p. 36).

Bordowitz, Richard Elovich, Rod Sorge, Donald Grove, and Allan Clear and others in the committee aimed to build common cause with activists and service providers from the South Bronx and Brooklyn as well as downtown Manhattan. "I thought it should be a place where drug users would feel comfortable coming. There were a lot of issues for drug users that weren't being addressed" (Bordowitz, 2002, p. 35).

"What we saw at the Lower East Side is people who came frequently to syringe exchange, also came frequently to use other stuff," noted Donald Grove, who was also involved with the ACT UP Syringe exchange for the next two decades.

"ACT UP organized it," noted Donald Grove in our interview. "And it took ACT UP three votes on the floor before ACT UP was going to get behind it. The resistance came from people in recovery, with some this was enabling. Greg Bordowitz had the best sound bite—he said of intravenous drug users, 'This is a population created by force of law. This is an epidemic created by force of law.' I just thought that was beautiful. That was why I was drawn to syringe exchange. It was beautifully put." Much of the anxiety stemmed from a "fear of addicts," noted Greg Bordowitz (2002, p. 36). "There was enough stigma. It was enough that this was a gay group during the AIDS crisis—do we have to bring in addicts too?"

"I was always really into the idea that if you had privilege then you could use it in this way," noted Bordowitz. "So we were willing to pass out needles because we had nothing to lose. But the other groups who were involved weren't ready to go that step. They didn't want to be trumped by ACT UP, or it could have backfired. There was a lot of resistance. . . . We listened to those groups. We were still arguing. It was still legitimate to argue for a needle exchange, but no one was willing to go that step to actually hand out needles. It wouldn't be for three years that we in ACT UP would do that" (p. 38).

It took three years but the committee successfully put the HIV prevention needs of drug users on ACT UP's agenda. To do so, Bordowitz, Elovich, and company started providing clean needles to users on the Lower East Side. Another group took them out to single room occupancy hotels in Brooklyn. "We would ask for needles back, but we rarely ever got them and we would still give clean needles out—with bleach kits, and condoms, and education material in Spanish and English" (p. 40). The effort was largely symbolic. The group recognized they needed to push the point for everyone to see for the city to support it. The police knew what they were doing. So ACT UP helped organize an action.

On the West Coast, syringe exchange supporters had already found ways to help this radical DIY public health approach find support. Global justice activist Starhawk recalled her involvement with San Francisco's Prevention Point as one of the high points of her long career as an activist:

> One of the actions I've been involved in where I can say every time we did it, "Ok, this is saving someone's life," was the needle exchange program that was done in the 1990s in San Francisco by Prevention Point. There were a number of my close friends who were more involved in setting it up, who also worked in the field of urban health and planning and sociology and they'd been doing studies, surveys on drug use and AIDS. And they felt like a needle exchange would be one way of addressing the spread to the drug-using population. And of course, that was entirely illegal in California. So we decided to do it as a direct action. It worked beautifully. The first week when we went out and did it we thought we were going to get arrested. And we exchanged about eighteen needles and we didn't get arrested. Then we started going out every week. And it just grew and grew. We kept not getting arrested. And within a few months we were exchanging hundreds and then thousands of needles every day. And finally, after about three months, the *San Francisco Chronicle* ran a story on us. And they interviewed the police chief who said, "Yeah, we know they are out there, but they are doing something that needs to be done." And so it turned into a social service program. And eventually we were able to get the mayor to declare a state of public health emergency and do an end-run around the state laws and fund and legalize the programs.

The route to legalization was not nearly as a smooth on the East Coast. "We thought we would get arrested and we would take the case to court. But no one was going to arrest us, because the police actually didn't think it was a bad idea," recalled Greg Bordowitz (2002, p. 41). "So we had to tell the press. So I think Richard called someone up at *Newsday* who he had been talking to, who had been following the issue. Some reporter, I forget her name, she came out to an SRO in Brooklyn that we went to, where we were passing out needles" (p. 41). Elovich called the paper and explained what they were doing, saying they were going to be at the corner of Delancey and Essex on a certain day and they were going to be passing out syringes. It was a well-coordinated effort. And as soon as he called the paper, the police started calling. Elovich promised there wouldn't be any needles on them, bodily, that there would have a sharps container for the syringes and no one was carrying needles (Bordowitz, 2002, pp. 42–43).

"We thought that in this instance, since it was ten people getting arrested, and it was really all about getting the press—saying, 'There's a group of ten people down on Delancey and Essex handing out sterile needles,'" recalled Bordowitz. "It wasn't really about the arrest. It was about the court case. So we all walked into the vans. They searched us. It was over in like ten minutes—lots of press, lots of pictures. We handed over our sharps container, our few token containers of clean needles. Ten of us walked into the police vans, and that was it. Then we were in court for like a year" (p. 43).

In court, nine of ten of them were represented by an attorney; Richard Elovich represented himself as a former user. Elovich had only recently come out as an injection drug user. But this experience helped the group navigate both treatment circles and the court. Navigating the process, Elovich came to recognize that he had a voice and experience that ran contrary to the opinion of those in authority. He had come out during a session at 103rd Street, to the Academy of Medicine, where Anthony Fauci, of the National Institutes of Health, was speaking. "I asked Fauci, or someone asked Fauci why there weren't injection-drug users enrolled in AIDS clinical trials," recalled Elovich (2007, p. 37) in an interview with the ACT UP Oral History Project. "And Fauci said, because they're part of a noncompliant population. And I had, been [at the methadone clinic] there every day for two years. So it brought me home. When I heard Fauci say that, I just became enraged, and hopefully in a more measured tone said, there's no such thing as a noncompliant population. I'm part of that population. Again, that was the first time I came out as an IDU" (Elovich, 2007, p. 37). The experience prepared Elovich to defend himself in court.

ACT UP had successfully used the necessity defense years before. "And we had already had a precedent," noted Elovich (2007, p. 51).

> Seven of us got arrested at the Stock Exchange; for disrupting the Stock Exchange so that no one could hear the bell, and the Stock Exchange was delayed, I think, for a half an hour. And when we went in front of a judge, our ACT UP lawyer offered the Clayton Motion. And the Clayton Motion essentially is the medical necessity; that this shouldn't even be a case. But it's basically the medical necessity defense; that you're doing something, you're breaking the law, but you're really not harming the community as such, because you're doing a greater good. And we just managed to get a really cool judge—Bruner—who was with us from the beginning. And he basically said, the Stock Exchange does not constitute a community. And what we were doing was life-saving; the AZT, lowering the price. So we got off. It was dismissed, on the Clayton Motion. (Elovich, 2007, p. 51)

The group was very prepared for court. "What you have to prove, first in the Clayton Motion, and then, certainly, through a medical necessity defense, is, even if it's irrational; . . . if you totally believe that what you've done is for the greater good, you can get off on medical necessity," explained Elovich (2007, p. 51). "It was presented almost like a play—they figured out what everyone's role needed to be. Steve Joseph's role was to tell the history of medical necessity defense. And he used the story of John Snow in London and the cholera thing—trespassing in your neighbor's yard and stealing their water, in order to put another neighbor's house fire out. And we had each of these experts tell their part of the story that contributed to what was a pretty persuasive case" (Elovich, 2007, p. 53).

"The other things we were able to say back then were that my zip code of the Lower East Side has more drug users than the entire country of Britain," noted Donald Grove. "So in places where they had syringe exchange—and Britain's syringe exchange had been very half assed—they still managed to keep control and do it better."

"We won on the grounds of necessity . . . [W]e were arguing that we were committing a wrong, breaking the law, to prevent a greater wrong. That greater wrong was not providing needles and treatment to drug users. We won. That's the Holy Grail of activists, to win a necessity defense. That's what we won" (Bordowitz, 2002, pp. 44–45).

"What we risked by being arrested with needles in our possession was a misdemeanor crime that carried up to a year in jail as its consequence. Now most people who get arrested with needles on them don't spend a year in jail. It's something that cops were using. It's like they were harassing a homeless person, or if they arrested a homeless person and that homeless person had a needle in his or her pocket they could put that person in jail overnight, or whatever, or give them jail time" (Bordowitz, 2002, pp. 45–46).

The group succeeded in winning a syringe exchange, but not the legalization of carrying syringes per se. The police could still arrest people carrying syringes. "Our demand was for there to be needle exchange. So they didn't legalize needles. To my knowledge needles are still considered paraphernalia, which would carry a charge if the police or the city decided to press one against people," noted Bordowitz (2002). "What was allowed to go into law was an exception that allowed for people who were doing authorized needle exchange work to carry needles" (pp. 45–46).

As a result of the decision, needle exchange programs were legalized, sanctioned, and funded by the New York Department of Health. Rod Sorge helped the Lower East Side Syringe Exchange get off the ground with the help of Allan Clear (Bordowitz, 2002, p. 46). Other syringe exchange programs began in Brooklyn and the Bronx.

Gradually, syringe exchange moved from the ACT UP syringe exchange to something the state sought to control. "The state said, OK, if the programs operated in this way, then they can provide drug injectors with sterile syringes on a one-for-one basis: you bring me ten used syringes and I'll give you ten new ones," explained Grove. He continued:

> It's a one-for-one exchange sort of system. In 1992 syringe exchange became legal, and there were some ACT UP syringe exchanges which became legal programs and then there were also some community based organizations which had also endeavored to create syringe exchange, and they also became legal programs. It was never all just ACT UP. And I had never heard of the expression harm reduction before, and had never really thought about anything except the idea that I don't want to get AIDS or HIV. And that was the approach I took to syringe exchange at that time. Over time, harm reduction was actually written into state laws and policies for the new programs.
>
> And essentially what that means is a low threshold model recognizing that we're working with a population which has strong reasons to be furtive about what they're doing. So the programs are anonymous, the programs have flexible hours. We do a lot of things to try and make syringe exchange as available as possible to the people who need it most urgently.
>
> As soon as the state announced that there was money, I do not know who within the needle exchange committee of ACT UP did the carving up. Bronx Harlem (NYHRE) will be one; the Lower East Side will be one and the Brooklyn program is going to be handed to this not-for-profit. That carving up began and there were big scandals right away. NYRE immediately applied for private money. The not-for-profit skullduggery began immediately. And it was being committed by some of the saints of direct action harm reduction.

The program immediately reduced the spread of HIV/AIDS, yet not without complications. The police harassed those attending the programs and ignored health department regulations, as the war on drugs conflicted with harm reduction models.

Syringe exchange represented a radical experiment in public health. "It was the most radical program for a long long time because you could just show and start making something happen," mused Donald Grove.

As the movement became formalized, compromises followed. Each syringe exchange was forced to track and restrict access to a point that seemed to contradict the very spirit of the programs. "That's what one for one is all about is punishing," explained Donald Grove. "That we need to put in some sort of a corrective. You can't have all the needles you need to use to have a sterile syringe for each injection. . . . What it creates is obligation. It's morally instructive." In response, Donald Grove continued to work supporting data evaluation efforts of formal exchanges while facilitating underground syringe exchange as a form of direct action with others from the group Moving Equipment. The inside-outside radical public health approach of harm reduction continued as programs created innovations, looking to the lessons of the street and those with different forms of knowledge and expertise.

In the years since ACT UP's civil disobedience, programs expanded and harm reduction came to be recognized as a successful public health intervention that does not increase drug use (Des Jarlais et al., 1996). Over and over, comprehensive approaches including frank discourse on sexuality, family planning, and harm reduction were found to be far more effective than abstinence-only approaches toward sex and drug use education (Collins, Alagiri, & Summers, 2002). All the while, different programs grew, creating services by and for those most impacted by HIV, homelessness, drug use, and social stigma.

Part of the vitality of the practice stems from an emphasis on the needs and knowledge of those in the streets. "Harm Reduction research tends to start from the idea that the people most affected by something know a lot about the circumstances surrounding the problem," explained Naomi Braine (2010), a sociologist at Brooklyn College, "that people act in an environment and primarily out of some individualized set of characteristics, that people are not passive or helpless no matter how marginalized, and that experts may be part of the solution but never all of it." Rather, the harm reduction movement fosters "active collaboration with communities and activists, and enables us to bridge the worlds of policy makers and affected communities," explains Braine. This action research approach "helps communities and advocates understand what works and why, build on 'street knowledge'—ideally, combining the strengths of community members with those of [the] highly educated." Examples of such collaboration include syringe exchange research that shaped local and state level ordinances; overdose prevention; and support for sex workers, drug users, and others not seen as active agents in their own health. Much of this innovation was born of the practice and praxis of creative activists.

CitiWide Harm Reduction

CitiWide Harm Reduction began as an underground needle exchange organized by former ACT UP (AIDS Coalition to Unleash Power) member Brian Weil, a New York artist, in 1994 (R. Smith, 1996). CitiWide began formal operations in 1995 with the support of La Resurrection United Methodist Church, providing services in a setting few service providers had reached out to: single room occupancy hotels (SROs) throughout the South Bronx and Upper Manhattan (Lyon, 2001). Under Weil's leadership, CitiWide brought services directly to sites where the need for needle exchange was greatest. The hallmark of the program was outreach to people with or at risk of HIV living in SRO hotels, which served as emergency housing for homeless people with HIV/AIDS. "It was a really good idea. It was absolutely the way it should be," recalled Donald Grove.

CitiWide Harm Reduction was part of the second generation of needle exchanges in New York City; along with Housing Works, it assumed that the demographics of the AIDS pandemic would continue to shift as low-income women and people of color remained an underserved HIV/AIDS high-risk group. The agency was also New York City's first syringe exchange to go to SRO hotels. The highly chaotic, poverty ridden context of the SRO hotel environment contributed to high-risk behaviors. In addition to serving as a focal point for extensive sex work transactions, components of the black market economy, such as drug-dealing and loan-sharking targeting residents at the site, takes place at SROs. Here, women, men who have sex with men (MSM), and transgender individuals in the SROs are impacted by risks including violence. In this dangerous and transient environment fear, isolation, and lack of information create barriers to residents' obtaining social, mental, and physical health services, including access to HIV treatments. The CitiWide Harm Reduction outreach model integrated low threshold harm reduction outreach with home delivered social and medical services. Its strength was a low threshold manner for engaging with those in SRO hotels, meeting participants "where they are at" with their drug use, providing easy access to services to those engaged in outreach, as well as survival supplies such as needles and toiletries to those in SRO hotels. Once trust was established, participants were connected to health care services in their rooms or social services at CitiWide's drop-in center (Heller & Shepard, 2001; Shepard, 2007a).

"The whole approach of CitiWide is different than at other programs," explained Grove. "It's like 'I have something I actually want you to have. So I have to go out and find you.' That is not other programs."

By bringing HIV prevention and care services to people at their homes and in a respectful, nonjudgmental fashion, staff establish trusting relationships with residents at the hotels. Here, staff establish a comfort level for participants who may be wary or distrusting or uncomfortable with service providers after negative experiences or interactions in the past (Heller & Shepard, 2001; Shepard, 2007a).

Harm Reduction and Clinical Practice

A few words about these relationships can be informative. "The truth is, treatment for me wasn't really about drugs. It was really about me connecting with people and, just putting' my life back together," noted Richard Elovich (2007, p. 23) in his interview with the ACT UP Oral History Project. To reach clients the programs had to hit the streets, connect, create trust, and build relationships with those in need. In this way, the work of this program was very consistent with the relational school of psychoanalysis. Steven A. Mitchell helped initiate this framework as a supervising and training analyst at the William A. White Institute in Manhattan. Founded by Clara Thompson and Eric Fromm with Harry Stack Sullivan, the White Institute emphasized the interplay between the individuals and their social environment. It combined Fromm's view of psychoanalysis as a means to relieve basic human suffering and Sullivan's emphasis on active collaboration between therapist and patient. Mitchell's (1988) central thesis was that personal relationships and human interaction help determine the nature of human health and functioning. Much of the sidewalk psychotherapy of harm reduction builds on a disposition that grounds the practice in relationship building (Marlatt, 2002; Shepard, 2007a; Springer, n.d., 1991).

University of Chicago's William Borden (2009) argues a relational paradigm centers engagement within "the dyadic, reciprocal nature of the helping process and view of the practitioner as a participant-observer, emphasizing the importance of suggestive elements and mutuality in formulations of therapeutic interaction" (p. 7). In this way, treatment and healing are seen to take place between client and provider. Here, social problems and challenges of living are located within a matrix between self, family, community, and social environment, rather within the isolated individual.

"What matters is what works," William Borden paraphrases American philosopher William James. "[T]he practitioner determines the validity of clinical formulations on the basis of their effectiveness in a particular situation" (2009, p. 9). This pragmatic approach stems from an emphasis on flexibility and acknowledgment of diverse approaches to practice. The patient is considered an expert on his or her own story. Such a view involves an implicit rejection of paternalist motives in which practitioners all too often seek to alter the lives of the poor by improving their moral worth and behavior. "Pluralist orientations attempt to foster dialogue across the divergent perspectives that shape the field, working to broaden ways of seeing and understanding as practitioners explore what is the matter and what carries the potential to help," Borden writes with a nod toward Brazilian educator Paolo Freire's conception of dialogue as a form of democratic engagement (Borden, 2009, p. 9). The point of a dialog is that it requires a breakdown in social hierarchies, as both parties actively work together. In this way, power is shared in a collaborative dialogue.

The utility of this approach is it brings honesty into the nexus of the clinical relationship, which allows for healing, personal development, and growth (Borden, 2009; Mitchell, 1988). Rather than "the big lie" in which providers and clients each share half truths about drug use and other less socially controversial yet common behaviors, harm reductionists emphasize frank acknowledgment of desire, which helps move the relationship and the treatment forward. Such a model emphasizes client strengths, rather than viewing people as difficulties or the totalities of their problems (Saleeby, 1996). Kate Barnhart talks about the kinds of social capital that grow from building relationships in this way. "[Y]ou have to find it in yourself to be able to connect with everybody on a human level—like every single person. You can't just see somebody as a bundle of their problems. And it's OK to share human moments with them or laugh. I often will make jokes, like puns, and it just creates a relationship that then I can use.

It's a sense of capital, like relationship capital. I'm gaining points with you that then I can spend when I need to tell you something difficult, like, I really think you need to be in rehab."

Given the social isolation, stigma, and shame experienced by individuals residing in the SRO hotels targeted by outreach, and the frequently chaotic and unsafe environment of the SRO hotel setting, it is essential that those engaging in harm reduction outreach build trust with this community to support and promote use of the services offered at programs such as CitiWide (Shepard, 2007a). The outreach model involved lowering a threshold for care so those living in SRO hotels could actually make use of these services, and allowing participants to maintain control of their decision to use services and on their own terms. From a direct action–based underground syringe exchange program to an established service provider, CitiWide has continued to grow and evolve along with those involved with it.

Washington Heights CORNER Project

"Social work is really about social justice," explains Jamie Favaro, the executive director and founder of Washington Heights CORNER Project (WHCP). As a graduate student at Columbia School of Social Work, Favaro interned at CitiWide Harm Reduction, where I served as her field advisor. After graduating from school, Favaro built on the work of harm reduction innovators such as Brian Weil and Daliah Heller at CitiWide, who helped push the limit of what harm reduction could be. She helped the Washington Heights CORNER Project in November 2005 as a volunteer endeavor rooted in harm reduction and aimed at eliminating high-risk practices of the Washington Heights drug using community.

At the 2008 New York City Anarchist Book Fair, she participated in a panel on mutual aid and radical social work. There she told the story of founding the Washington Heights CORNER Project.

> I started my work as a social worker for the George Washington Bridge Outreach Program, which serves basically homeless individuals living in and around the Port Authority bus terminal. A lot of those people had been living in the park areas and under the highway systems in Washington Heights. And I found just very quickly that a lot of these people are intravenous drug users with no access to any type of education on basic harm reduction resources. People were shooting up with toilet water out of toilets at the Port Authority bus terminal. People were picking up syringes out of the parks. And there's something very wrong there. So basically what I started doing was going to a syringe exchange downtown—Lower East Side Harm Reduction was down there—and getting syringes and harm reduction resources from their syringe exchange, and doing syringe exchange out of my office, which was completely illegal.
>
> It was kind of one of those points where no one was doing it, and we were working with homeless people and you can spend 50 cents at the pharmacy to buy a syringe or you could buy a beer for 50 cents at the bodega right next door. So like, a beer? Or,

a new syringe? You have one in your pocket—you have used it 10 times, but I'd much rather have a beer. So it was one of those types of situations.

In November 2005, I started going out regularly after work, at night, and standing on the street corner and doing a high level volume of exchange with the clients that I knew through my day job. And it was awesome. I had no rules; however, I was always keeping data on what we were doing. There was a lot of integrity to the work and there was no kind of restrictions. We weren't being funded in any way. It was just kind of doing what needed to be done.

And I think this experience that I had is really unique.

Favaro has worked to maintain the egalitarian spirit of harm reduction while helping transform her underground exchange into a state funded nonprofit organization. To do so involved contending with the complex challenges of funding (Incite! 2007). "A lot of work goes into getting a syringe exchange program started. And I found that through doing that, who I was as an activist and my work really changed," confessed Favaro. Through the years, the Corner Project has worked in collaboration with the Intravenous Drug Users Health Alliance to make its case for city funding, while procuring Department of Health funding from the state of New York with support of the American Foundation of AIDS Research. Through this support as well as collaboration with an active board of directors as well as Young Professionals Board, the project grew. "Our office is flush with new programming, interns, and volunteers," notes Favaro (2010). In addition to outreach, the program expanded to include "an on-site Medical Clinic where program participants receive free Medical consultations, basic treatment, vaccinations, and targeted referrals. The Medical Clinic, spearheaded by the Columbia University Harm Reduction Outreach Network (CUHRON) has

September 17, 2013: members of VOCAL, Housing Works, Washington Heights CORNER Project, Treatment Action Group, ACT UP, and Harm Reduction Coalition got arrested together while fighting for a Robin Hood financial transaction tax.

Source: Photo by author

been a long-held dream for us at WHCP and we are thrilled it is now a reality" (Favaro, 2010).

Today, the WHCP is one of 19 syringe exchange programs in New York City. Like CitiWide, the Corner Project offers a continuum of essential services, including social services, HIV and hepatitis C testing, support, and case referrals to other area providers. Here, many of those lost to other providers are able to connect and find support. Gaining housing and medical services is vital for such clients, notes Corner Project program director Taeko Frost, "but the most important thing is that [clients have] a place to come to, be with other people, and talk. Many people think of syringe exchanges as dark, depressing places, but we actually spend a lot of time laughing" (amfAR, 2010). And perhaps that is the program's key to success.

From **NYCAHN** to **VOCAL**

As the narratives profiling WHCP and CitiWide Harm Reduction highlight, syringe exchange is most vital when it connects hard-to-reach populations with a continuum of services to address the bio-psycho-social needs of each client. Some of these services include housing and health care; others include syringe exchange and basic survival services. Perhaps most important than any of these, such programming is vital when it helps often invisible populations of the homeless, of drug users, or sex workers connect with their own sense of collective power. This is what Voice of Community Activists and Leaders (VOCAL), formerly NYCAHN, does. Like Housing Works and the National Welfare Rights Organization before it, VOCAL uses community organizing and policy advocacy to remind the city of the legally obliged policies it is failing to deliver. It also provides basic services, including syringe exchange, through the state expanded syringe access program. The final narrative of this chapter highlights the efforts of VOCAL to address the unmet needs of those in their communities in Brooklyn.

Over and over in social work school, students are told not to engage in direct action, particularly if programs are using direct services. Former New York Mayor Rudy Giuliani specifically targeted Housing Works for its advocacy, but the program managed to demonstrate that the City retaliated against it for its advocacy, and eventually won a large settlement from the city (Dwyer, 2005b). VOCAL has shown a similar willingness to use direct action while providing basic services for housing and funding for health care.

This spirit was certainly in play during the From NY City AIDS Housing Human Rights Watch of the early 2000s. This campaign was organized around a shared belief that housing is a human right (Stedile, 2003; Van Kleunen, 1994). In New York City, where gentrification has put housing costs beyond the reach of many working people, the need for shelter is no different. Here, the AIDS crisis compounded the problem as people who were once able to house themselves fell ill, lost their jobs, faced eviction, and entered the homeless popula-

The VOCAL crew and Deborah Glick of the N.Y. State Assembly, lobbying and using direct action to get the goods. Such efforts helped VOCAL succeed.

Source: Used with permission of VOCAL New York

tion (Shepard, 2002c). "Housing is an AIDS Issue, Housing Equals Health," became a slogan for AIDS housing activists. They linked the co-epidemics of homelessness and AIDS into a struggle to house homeless people with AIDS.

To guarantee a right to shelter for homeless people with HIV/AIDS, housing activists fought for the creation of the New York City Department of AIDS Services and Income Support (DASIS) in the city Human Resources Administration (later renamed HIV/AIDS Services Administration [HASA]). They also fought for a law passed in 1997, referred to as Local Law 49, that guaranteed people with HIV/AIDS the legal right to be housed by the city within a day of a housing placement request. Unfortunately, the spirit of the law would not find full expression for another 5 years.

In a campaign reminiscent of the 1960s National Welfare Rights Organization campaigns (Piven & Cloward, 1977), NYCAHN spent well over 2 years monitoring the city's compliance with this local law. The core organizing principle remained the demand that the City of New York obey its own law. By the end of 2001, the city was compelled to do just that—some 4 years after the local law's passage. The campaign involved extensive legal research into the workings of the public welfare bureaucracy and the tenacity to make it work; it included the willingness to push through winter nights, hot summer days, and every other day for over a year; finally, activists drew attention to the cause through a media strategy that highlighted the city's failure to implement Local Law 49. They had to build support with caseworkers and with policymakers. Finally, they had to make use of highly creative forms of direct action. By 2001, the city began complying with the local law. Thanks to the diligent work of organizers to combine a willingness to communicate around a problem, mobilize around an issue, and apply this mobilization to a long-term legal strategy, organizers were able to succeed. "Once you get one win, you want more," noted Kohler. "Once you got a water-cooler and doors then you keep going. And it shows you, we got that."

Born of NYCAHN and its close ties to housing providers and organizers across the city, VOCAL/NYCAHN has built a distinct model of organizing.

> While we engage in advocacy, at the core of what we are doing is developing new leaders and trying to change who has power rather than only changing a policy. . . . We also believe that in order to address the root causes of problems that become policy issues, we begin by asking our members what they want changed, and then creating campaigns around those issues. Since we have a base of people who are setting the agenda, we are multi-issue. However, all of our members share the common identity of living with AIDS or being affected by AIDS. . . . We ask membership dues from our members even though they are poor. . . . We are constantly recruiting members and we do this by door knocking in buildings where low-income people living with HIV/AIDS are sent, going around to local welfare centers where low-income people living with AIDS receive their entitlements and talking to people about the organization and what they want to see changed in the world. (VOCAL/NYCAHN, n.d.)

Like other harm reduction groups, VOCAL connects direct action and direct services. Its executive director, Sean Barry, described in an interview how the group is able to reconcile these forces. "First, it begins with people's lived experiences in issues which directly improve their lives," notes Barry. "We're rooted in what can directly improve someone's life. We have a whole issue identification process and survey members about what they're most interested in. What do you want to get active around? How it would benefit them. We provide drug user health services—syringe exchange, overdose prevention, we prescribe naloxone, which reverses overdoses, hepatitis C education and counseling, a great unmet health services need, buprenorphine, etc. But we don't just stop there."

For VOCAL, harm reduction is a practical point around which to organize as well as engage people in their communities. Much begins with dialogue as part of a non-judgmental conversation. "When someone OD's, it's a moment to ask where are they with their health," notes Barry. "Is there something they want to do different? Do they want to get to a different place in their life, where they are better able to manage their use or maybe stop for a year or transition to less harmful drugs?"

As it evolves, VOCAL builds on the tradition of Housing Works and a legacy of housing activism. "We recognize that HIV has always been about more than individual behavioral decisions," explains Barry in our interview.

> And we know certain communities are at higher risk because they are engaged in activities that other communities that are at lower risk are engaged in, because of structural factors—the homelessness, unequal access to health care, mass incarceration, discriminatory policies such as access only until marriage, schools which stigmatize queer youth. There is a whole series of policies which are deeply homophobic. There is no HIV specific response which is going to end the epidemic. We need to build linkages across issues that are really the structural risks that are what's actually driving sexual risk for the epidemic. For example, we know mass incarceration drives the epidemic in a number of ways. HIV disproportionately affects people who are incarcerated compared with people who are not incarcerated. It disrupts families, relationships, safer sex. The health care provided inside of jails is abominable, leading to higher viral loads and lower CD4 counts. . . . Universal prohibition on condom use, on syringe access. . . . So prison is the driving force of HIV. And sometimes this is when we get frustrated with the model that stops at direct services. For example, the notion of viewing prisons as a public health opportunity—there is nothing about prisons which is a public health opportunity. The best public health measure is to reduce the prison population.

On this point, Barry is not alone (Cloward & Piven, 1975; Kingsbury, 2011).

Instead of seeing AIDS or harm reduction as an isolated policy need, VOCAL has joined Occupy and ACT UP and other movements that look beyond AIDS and housing, supporting a multi-issue movement against neoliberalism. "We don't want to constantly be on the defensive and just reacting to all the attacks on people with AIDS," argues Barry. "We realize we are having a hard time preserving, not even creating housing for people with AIDS because of a financial crisis that was precipitated by deregulation and too much corporate control. That lead to the economic recession and that then dropped revenue available for public programs. Our members can clearly connect that. You can see it in the neighborhood. HIV remains a central identity around what we organize. But our members are not just community leaders as people living with HIV. They are community leaders around being queer, or people of color, or women, and people who are formerly incarcerated. HIV may be the most difficult thing they are managing but they realize that that's not the only issue in their lives."

Many of the organizers profiled in this book move from identifying issues to direct action through the organizing framework described in Part II of this book. This certainly includes VOCAL, which has had a number of wins in New York city and state AIDS services and policy. For Barry, this begins with the winnable win Alinski described. "It's a big part of our base building process," notes Barry. "When we are agitating people between where they are at now and where they want to be and there is just enough tension and optimism to move people to action. And we've got a track record of it actually it happening and moving people from where we're at now to where we want to be and victories."

Over the years, both NYCAHN and now VOCAL have created significant wins for their communities. "In 1994, I had spent a lot of time documenting all this police harassment of police arrest," noted Donald Grove. "I went to ACT UP and called for a demonstration against the 9th Precinct. There were people coming to ACT UP because they had heard this was going on." The problem persisted for years until VOCAL pushed it. "Each of our campaigns has particularly different strategies, which is testament to the flexibility we take to each of these," noted Barry. "And with the vocal issue that was something that we defined as a smaller leadership campaign. We identified people being picked up for syringe possession even when they are not breaking the law, even when they had a card saying it was ok to carry it. It was a problem. Everybody knew it throughout the city." At CitiWide Harm Reduction, for example, police used to arrest people just for walking into the program. "One of the coordinators used to say the law only matters when you get in front of a judge. The police just want any charge," noted Barry.

Still, VOCAL members identified police harassment as an important issue for them. "We identify an issue," Barry continues, walking through the campaign.

Talk to members and leaders and ask who want to be involved. Pull them together and say what do we need to get this issue on the radar? That can go in a lot of directions. The direction they took it in is we gotta document the problem. I am usually skeptical. I usually think information alone is not enough to convince people in power to do the right thing, necessary but not sufficient. But we did show the scandal that the state has high rates of arrest, the primary charge was syringe possession, even though it's effectively decriminalized. I remember we took that data to the governor's Division of Criminal Justice, and said what are you guys going to do about this? And also took it to the heads of the Health and Codes Committees and said you guys have had modest bills that would address this over the past sessions that always die in committee. This issue hasn't gone away. We need to address this. So, our members went to the targets in the state and just agitated them through traditional lobbying tactics. Being picked up, put through the system, doing the bullpen detox for 36 hours, getting sick from withdrawal.

Still, VOCAL stayed focused and pushed this specific issue, lobbying daily. "The arrests shouldn't even be happening in the first place," Barry continued.

There are a surprising number of actual convictions. So our members agitated and then organized the legislature and the governor's office. It was drug users going to the Governor's criminal justice people saying we gotta meet and figure out how we are going to fix this. So, they got everybody together, showed how it was affecting their lives, and they brought the data from the state and then they brought a list of demands for what they wanted to see in legislation that went beyond what had been introduced in prior sessions. And they got the governor to introduce a program bill. The governor introduced the legislation into the legislature. The primary sponsors were the chairs of criminal justice and the health committees in both chambers and they passed it with Republican support. After 20 years, NY's Penal Code now permits possession of new and used syringes.

Asked how the group was able to break through all the arguments against syringe exchange, Barry noted, "One of the most fundamental factors was just the persistence. VOCAL combined organizing with research on a report the group co-authored with the Urban Justice Center titled 'Stuck in the System'" (VOCAL/NYCAHN, 2009). It documented how police harassment of users for syringe possession undermines public health.

In subsequent years, the group continued to support movements, such as Occupy, while pushing their own agenda around issues such as the 30% rent cap. It was an issue they had worked on for years.

Barry noted,

We wanted him [Sheldon "Shelly" Silver, the Speaker of the New York State Assembly] to allow a vote on the 30% rent cap bill. We wanted this to come up for a vote. And we had tried everything. And I think community organizing. People identify different lineages for community organizing. Everybody agrees it been around for decades. For me a big lesson is that you need to be flexible in your tactics and your strategy. Any practice that has been around that long begins to ossify to a certain extent. And you lose the innovation. The dogma sets in. And everybody just keeps doing the same thing even as you say we need to do something different. And I think one of our strengths is we really have been flexible.

We tried everything. We did lobby visits with the staff. We did more polite rallies. We went to his [Sheldon Silver, the Speaker of the New York Assembly's] house at 9 AM. We went to community leaders in his community and explained why we needed him to take action and appealed for them to become allies. But I think the non dogmatic approach we worked was really effective and has become one of the most important components of our strategy. And there is no guarantee that anything will work. There was concern by campaign leaders that if we did this we could permanently alienate Sheldon Silver. And nobody really knew the answer to that. And we took a risk because we were at a desperate moment at that time and thankfully it paid off. And if it didn't we would have gone back to the drawing board. And I think another factor is only people who are directly affected working around an issue are so fundamental for their lives. You know a bunch of lobbying organizations are not going to push that hard. And they are not going to be as creative with strategy as people whose lives are on the line. And there is this retrenchment and this withdrawal.

Yet, VOCAL never stopped pushing this issue identified by their leaders, even after a version of it passed in 2010 before it was vetoed by then-governor David Paterson. Four years later, the group garnered the support of the new governor. In February 2014, the governor announced in a press statement that he would support the 30% rent cap.

Governor Cuomo and Mayor de Blasio Announce Affordable Housing Protection for Low-Income New Yorkers Living with HIV/AIDS

30 Percent Income Cap Added to New York City Rental Assistance Program for People Living with HIV/AIDS

Action Protects More Than 10,000 Vulnerable New Yorkers from Homelessness

Governor Andrew M. Cuomo and Mayor Bill de Blasio today announced a new affordable housing protection for low-income New Yorkers living with HIV/AIDS. With today's announcement, New Yorkers who are permanently disabled by HIV/AIDS and receive rental assistance will pay no more than 30 percent of their income toward their rent. Without this protection, more than 10,000 New Yorkers living with HIV/AIDS are denied affordable housing and required to pay upwards of 70 percent of their disability income toward their rent.

"This action will ensure that thousands of New Yorkers living with HIV/AIDS will no longer be forced to choose between paying their rent or paying for food and other essential costs of living," Governor Cuomo said. "By implementing a 30 percent income cap for low-income renters with HIV/AIDS, we are protecting New Yorkers in need and making our communities stronger, healthier, and more compassionate for all."

Mayor de Blasio said, "I'm very proud to work with Governor Cuomo to provide some measure of security to people struggling with the debilitating effects of HIV-AIDS. And we come to the table ready to shoulder two-thirds of this program's costs because we are committed to lifting up the most vulnerable among us. This is the mark of a compassionate city."

Senator Brad Hoylman said, "Governor Cuomo and Mayor de Blasio deserves our highest praise for their decision to extend the affordable housing rent contribution cap to low-income people in the State's HIV/AIDS rental assistance program. Their decision will prevent homelessness and dramatically improve the health and well-being of more than 10,000 vulnerable New Yorkers with HIV/AIDS. The Governor and the Mayor's decision is also extremely smart budget and public health policy because it will reduce emergency shelter and healthcare costs and the rates of HIV transmission associated with unstable housing."

Assemblyman Robert J. Rodriguez said, "Much praise is due to Governor Cuomo for supporting our legislation and prioritizing affordable housing protections for more than 10,000 low-income New Yorkers living with AIDS. The 30% Rent Cap is a smart policy that will keep people stably housed and better positioned to stay healthy." . . .

Currently, the primary housing program for low-income New Yorkers living with HIV/AIDS is tenant-based rental assistance. As with other state housing programs for people with disabilities, residents with income from disability benefits are expected to contribute a portion of those benefits toward their rent. Unlike all other state disability housing programs and federally funded housing assistance, however, New York's HIV/AIDS rental assistance program did not include a 30 percent cap on the tenant's required rent contribution.

Right now, many people living with HIV/AIDS in emergency shelters and supportive housing could live independently but cannot afford to move out because they would pay substantially more in rent in the rental assistance program. By creating this affordable housing protection, the State can better target the limited number of supportive housing beds for those who need them most.

Studies show homelessness and housing instability are significant public health issues that increase the risks of HIV acquisition and transmission and adversely affect the health of people living with HIV. The conditions that lead to homelessness for some individuals, coupled with the numerous challenges of being homeless, result in a substantially higher risk of HIV acquisition. People who are homeless or unstably housed have HIV/AIDS infection rates that are three to nine times higher than individuals with stable housing.

Dan Teitz, executive director of the AIDS Community Research Initiative of America said, "This affordable housing initiative pays for itself by keeping people in their apartments and out of costly shelters. It improves HIV health outcomes and is associated with better access and adherence to medication."

Sean Barry, executive director of Vocal New York said, "This action furthers Governor Cuomo's and Mayor de Blasio's mission of reducing spending and creating a healthier, stronger, more fiscally responsible New York by preventing unnecessary healthcare expenses, including emergency room visits and hospital stays, which are associated with homelessness and unstable housing."

Source: https://www.governor.ny.gov/press/02132014-affordable-housing-protection

From syringe decriminalization to the 30% rent cap, VOCAL creates wins. It is a model for a new kind of poor person's movement buttressed by the years of work by those in harm reduction. Policy is fluid, like much of modern life. What we gain can be taken away. Organizers remain vigilant. All the while, harm reduction has established itself as a best practice in community organization, social services, and approaches to public health. Still, it must grapple with some of the limitations of current models of care.

AIDS, Inc.

Today, AIDS is big money, a source of research funding, grants, conferences, and jobs; in short, people with AIDS are a huge market. Within this, syringe exchange programs exist as a radical extension of health care. Some exchanges stand on their own; others function as part of AIDS service organizations. Each faces its own kind of challenges. AIDS organizations increasingly struggle to maintain their relevance to the communities they once served as they become bureaucratized, a part of the AIDS Industry, or "AIDS Inc.," as AIDS activists dub them (Shepard, 1997b).

For some critics, the funded programs created a new form of paternalism. ACT UP veteran Bill Dobbs concurs. "Advocacy has to be done by people not on a payroll," he argues. Rather than struggle for their own survival, as most human services organizations tend to do, groups of activists, of volunteers, ask bigger questions, create pressure, and navigate outside of the realm of funding (Douglas, 2007; Incite!, 2007). While AIDS Inc. still exists, so do groups that function outside out of it. Their efforts and critiques are the subject of the next chapter.

16

The Perils of
the Nonprofit
Industrial Complex

Over time, countless movements have found themselves compromised by funding arrangements. It all starts innocently enough: a community group identifies a need in the community, cobbles together a needs assessment, and seeks funding to solve the problem. When the funding arrives, those seeking support are so relieved they often dismiss the fine print, the stipulations. Yet, over time, these restrictions can become onerous. A community group's character is curtailed, controlled, or it falls off mission (McCarthy & Zald, 1973). This happens over and over. Piven and Cloward warned about this early as 1977. Organizers call this phenomenon the nonprofit industrial complex (Incite!, 2007).

Others suggest it is just part of capitalism. "As neoliberalism posits individuals as self-managed 'autonomous' citizens—consumers, it also . . . renders illegitimate forms of life that cannot or will not be converted into its framework," argues Heather Gautney (2010, p. 176). "In this regard, it depoliticizes social life into a series of individual pursuits and cost-benefit analyses, rather than toward ideas of the good life as collectively defined."

Yet, many look to a different route, asking questions about whether they even want funding for their programs, especially if control or co-optation are likely to follow. Others look to alternative solutions, born of a do-it-yourself spirit of engaging bodies and connecting communities through music and autonomous spaces. This antiauthoritarian spirit has spurred countless projects and programs. Let's consider some of the questions programs can and do ask about funding and development, and examine some Marxist and Weberian critiques of capital and the nonprofit industrial complex.

The "Iron Cage"

In *The Protestant Ethic and the Spirit of Capitalism*, Max Weber coined the phrase *iron cage of despair*, suggesting many workers find themselves trapped in this struggle for survival. Certainly, this describes the life of many nonprofits.

Today, many social services are delivered around a model of service in which the government or private foundations subcontract tasks and services to nonprofit organizations. This can lead to a paternalistic worldview wherein those in need of services are given hoops to jump through. Over time, Donald Grove has seen service provision and syringe exchange become more and more of a business with an attitude: "It's like 'The reason you are putting yourself at risk of exposure to HIV is you have not gotten the pamphlet from my organization yet,'" muses Grove. "The not-for-profit thing is poverty pimping. I have something you need and I'm not going to give it to you unless you come to me in a certain way. And that's what most of the programs are doing."

Still, most nonprofits provide services that are prioritized by their community. This environment is increasingly competitive. In order for funders to find service providers, they release a call for proposals, typically announced at bidders conferences attended by nonprofits competing for limited resources. These conferences are often crowded and stressful. To be awarded the funds to provide services, organizations are forced to argue they have the best capacity to engage in the highest number of service priorities identified for the least cost. Organizations often find themselves working harder to meet contract requirements than they do for those whom their organizations are charged to care. Organizational theorists call this "mission slip" (Meyer & Roman, 1977). Critics describe it as a symptom of the nonprofit industrial complex (Incite!, 2007).

At the 2008 New York City Anarchist Bookfair, Jamie Favaro (2008) talked about the challenges of moving her grassroots syringe exchange through the process of organizational development that would allow it to gain resources necessary to do what she thought was necessary.

> As we were getting the syringe exchange started, everything started to revolve around funding—who's going to fund us? And I found that the funding streams and the stress on getting funded really changed the work that I was able to do. I found myself increasingly stressed about deliverables, about my relationships with our funders. And I started to really resent funding. Because when you get funded, you're a lot more accountable to the funder than to the actual community that you're serving. It's all about what they want. When you get funding, you're expected to do certain things with your funding.

Over and over, funding transforms grassroots groups into formalized organizations that feel less connected to their communities. This was particularly the case with AIDS service organizations born to help the sick when the AIDS crisis began 30 years ago. During the late 1980s and early 1990s, Eric Rofes was the executive director of Shanti Project, a group providing care for people with HIV/AIDS in San Francisco.

He was painfully aware of how much AIDS services were losing connection with the communities that birthed them, and he spoke about this in multiple forums, including during his 1989 testimony at the National AIDS Commission. "They were doing hearings in San Francisco," he explained. "It was at a point when we were feeling like the gay piece of it was becoming kind of bureaucratized and mainstreamed away from authentic gay male subcultures. At that time I was the new executive director of an AIDS group." Rofes gave his testimony first in a suit and then in leather. "I got flack for it because people thought it was disrespectful and unprofessional. This was when I was thinking AIDS groups were still community-based. I later learned how wrong I was. But I was trying to bring an organization closer to grassroots gay male cultures at a time when it was a tension within AIDS organizing, about whether that was appropriate or not." The experience spurred Rofes to move away from AIDS services into a closer connection with social movements. Looking back, Rofes noted:

> Many organizations were great examples of authentic communities that by the 1990s were inauthentic communities. I think that's an important distinction to make. Because there are moments within community organizing where authentic community forms around people coming together in crisis, and being there for each other for that growth. And then there are times when people are trying to emulate or recapture that moment. My experience, at least with some organizations, is that they are really not there for you when push comes to shove; they are around only in rhetoric or representation.

Reverend Brazier talked about the positive and negative impacts of money on organizations. "It [money] hurt the Woodlawn Organization. It hurt in the sense that we went through all those investigations. But TWO is still flourishing, thirty years later. Like any organization or business if you take on more than you can handle, it does hurt you."

In other cases, funding has the effect of discouraging participation in advocacy efforts, which are seen as inconsistent with the funds allotted to organizations to provide basic services. "That's part of why a lot of social service agencies don't do activism," noted social worker and AIDS activist Eustacia Smith. "There is a huge fear that you're not going to get funding if you participate in activism. And that's a reality to a large extent."

When I worked managing a Housing Opportunities for People with AIDS (HOPWA) grant for CitiWide Harm Reduction in the mid-2000s and participated in a direct action over budget cuts for AIDS services, our executive director received a phone call asking whether her deputy director (myself) was off getting arrested with HUD money. The funder reminded her that I was funded under HOPWA to work in this agency. There was a tacit threat in the funder's message. Eustacia Smith elaborates: "That's a reality, that people can risk losing their funding. But sometimes organizations take that to an extreme and they become so fearful that they don't push as much as they could."

In other cases, funding helps dictate what kinds of services are provided. "I was on a panel this morning, and they were talking about how Human Rights Campaign doesn't want the Trans inclusiveness," noted Jamie Favaro, referring to the New York Employment Discrimination Act. "That it's all about funding. So it's, how do we do the work that we need to do when the funding dictates the work that we do? That's an ongoing question and a struggle that I have working on the street."

A Virus in the System

"Society is toxic and it's making everyone sick!" declared a group of San Francisco performers, therapists, and activists in 2010 after a beloved neighborhood health clinic was closed. They suggested the clinic's downfall was part of a larger trend. "The non-profit and public health sectors have already been contaminated, and the infection is spreading," noted these activists from the group Gay Shame, dubbing themselves Mary (2010). "The closure of New Leaf LGBTQ counseling center is just one symptom in the Social Identity Crisis Kontamination (SICK). New Leaf offered mental health and substance abuse services for low income queer and trans folks for the last 35 years. The top-down model of the non-profit proves itself unsustainable again and again" (Mary, 2010).

In front of the clinic, members of Gay Shame (n.d.) arrived dressed in white lab coats. "The US Department of Mental Security declares a STATE OF MENTAL EMERGENCY, and issues an EMERGENCY KUARANTINE," they announced. "It is the INSTITUTIONS that are INFECTED. The main source of the infection: the Department of Public Health. The threat remains in effect" (Gay Shame, n.d.).

The "state of mental emergency" was actually a bit of street theater, designed to highlight Gay Shame's disenchantment with nonprofit professionalized systems of service provision. "Sick of the limits of your life being dictated by doctor's degrees, 501(c)3s, and 5150s? Society is suffering from a serious 'disorder.'" GAY SHAME invites you to relocate the diagnoses off our bodies and minds and onto the structure of the system: "Do you recognize these symptoms?" they asked. "Medicalization of life; criminalization of illness; alienation, trauma, despair—Growth of the prison-military-medical-non-profit-industrial complex YES?!?! Your health is in imminent danger, Take action!" Critiquing medical models of care, Gay Shame suggested:

> Psychiatric diagnoses (like Gender Identity Disorder) isolate and medicalize people, hiding and naturalizing the structural violence that produces ill health. Our minds and bodies become the sites of disorders and the targets of regulatory prescriptions, while the greater system remains untreated. Issues that are social, political, and economic in nature become individual psychiatric disorders (like trauma from police brutality), while differences in people's ways of being in the world are criminalized and punished (people w/ mental health "disorders" are institutionalized in jails, prisons, and psych hospitals). To receive care at New Leaf, one had to participate in the medical systems that demonize anything outside of the status quo. Our larger social context is a pathology driven by profit and criminalization, seeking to quarantine us. This action is a culmination of our many experiences negotiating with mental health institutions, both on the inside and outside, as people who provide and who receive, as people who attempt and refuse, to access mental health care in the sick system. We'd like to envision mental health support systems that do not pathologize us, that relocate the site of the disorder onto society and actually eradicate the social, political, and economic violence that makes us "sick." (Mary, 2010)

Beyond Psychic Prisons

Part of the appeal of anti-authoritarian organizing is its open rejection of administrative social controls in favor of a politics of freedom and direct democracy. Through such activism, regular people carve out alternatives to social spaces based on domination and hierarchy (Pyles, 2009, p. 37).

Unfortunately, many human service organizations are anything but empowering, as Gay Shame points out. Many favor social controls rather than liberation and human relatedness. Others come to resemble Gareth Morgan's (2006) image of organization as "psychic prison." "As we examine the bureaucratic form of organization, we should be alert to the hidden meaning of close regulation and supervision of human activity, the relentless planning and scheduling of work, and the emphasis on productivity, rule following, discipline, duty, and obedience," notes Morgan (2006, p. 209). "The bureaucracy is a mechanistic form of organization, but an anal one too. . . . [S]ome people are able to work in this kind of organization more effectively than others. If bureaucracies are anal phenomena encouraging an anal style of life, then such organizations will probably operate most smoothly when employees fit the anal character type" (p. 209).

Faced with some of the complicated questions involving managing organizations, many have come to wonder if funding or building an organization is even worth it? Early in the days of the Settlements, Jane Addams (1910) warned that social workers should avoid building organizations or a profession that resembled a business model. All too often the organizations we create emulate the systems we hope to avoid. Sociologist Max Weber worried that under capitalism impersonal relations replace the personal, while means and ends are inverted in a race to accumulate capital. Here gain becomes an end in itself, no longer just a means to satisfy material needs. Humans have created systems of management designed to control rather than foster freedom. The result is a voluntary loss of autonomy to a system of our own creation (Löwy, 2006).

Over and over, human service organizations follow management models that resemble the machinated aspects of work Frederick Taylor outlined in *The Principles of Scientific Management* in 1911. These principles, known as Taylorism, include developing a "science" for every job, carefully selecting workers with the right abilities for the job, and training these workers to do the job and planning their work. Many of these features are found in human services organizations, where managers often seem more fixated on funding than quality of care. Ideally, funding is a means to provide quality services so clients live happy lives and achieve health. Yet when an assessment is 30 pages long and must be completed four times a year, it becomes about funding, not services. Over and over, social workers are forced to prioritize functions, as means and ends are inverted.

Probably the most articulate critic of capitalism is Karl Marx, whose theories have long served as resources for understanding a world in which workers are isolated from their work, their labors exploited, and efforts minimized (Knickmeyer, 1972). "It is not necessary to be a revolutionary, communist, or socialist to appreciate the ideas and contributions of Marx," explains Loretta Pyles (2009, p. 30). "These ideas have been very relevant for union organizers throughout the world for over a century and likely will continue to be relevant in the future" (p. 30).

Marx's critique of capitalism is organized around seven fundamental themes:

1. **Exploitation:** that injustice takes shape in any number of forms, including through the persistence of sweatshops, child labor, environmental degradation, racism, sexism, and other forms of oppression.

2. **The loss of liberty due to alienation:** as humans remain isolated from their labor, communities, and selves.

3. **Venal quantification:** in which the exchange of goods and services consumes all qualitative meaning or experience; numbers and accounting overtake poetry or stories.

4. **Having replaces being:** as consumer citizenship, shopping, replaces democratic living, as money devalues other experiences and associations.

5. **Irrationality:** the periodic crises, notably the market crash in 1929 and the fiscal meltdown in 2008, that seem to jolt the capitalist system by exposing its irrationality, or "absurdity" as Marx explains. "Irrational exuberance" was the phrase Alan Greenspan used during the latest boom.

6. **Modern barbarism:** in which capitalism and its inevitable wars and inequalities are seen as the final step in human history; from asylums to poorhouses to jails, modern forms of barbarism are many, repeating age-old patterns of brutality.

7. **One step up, two steps backward:** as the expansion and or imperialism of capitalism takes shape through wars, structural adjustment plans, and inevitable domination or displacement of colonized peoples, vis-à-vis the primitive accumulation of capital. Look no further than housing foreclosures for an example of this phenomenon (Harvey, 2010; Klein & Levy, 2002; Löwy, 2006; Ollman, 1977; Sites, 2003; Talen, 2003).

"The forcible expropriation of agricultural populations from their land and homes, accomplished through forms of bloody discipline and state action had enormous and long lasting impacts that deeply influence the geopolitics of particular areas in different ways," notes Stephen Shukaitis (2009, p. 34). "These enclosures occurred, the social relations embodied in them, had long-term consequences extending through and suspended within the world as we know it today." Deprived of self-sustenance, outsiders are turned into "vagabonds, and then whipped, branded, tortured by laws grotesquely terrible, into the discipline necessary for the wage system" (p. 34). Sadly, this process has not stopped or slowed since the days of Marx. "One could say that primitive accumulation, which isn't very primitive at all, continues to exist suspended within and underpinning the continuing reproduction of capitalist social relations," concludes Shukaitis (p. 35).

This is also the system that produces human services organizations, as well as non-governmental organizations (NGOs), to address the unemployment, homelessness, and mental illness that are a very part of life within capitalism. The critiques of NGOs are many (J. Davis, 2002). David Harvey (2010) notes there are now vast numbers of NGOs that play a role rarely seen before the mid-1970s. They tend to be supported by both public and private funds to address a range of social and environmental needs. While some espouse progressive politics, many borrow from features of neoliberal economics, including privatization of services (Buffett, 2013; Harvey, 2010). There are many talented, caring people involved, yet Harvey (2010) suggests "their work is at best ameliorative." Still he grudgingly acknowledges that "in certain arenas, such as women's rights, health care and environmental preservation, they can reasonably claim to have made major contributions to human betterment." Like nonprofits, NGOs are restricted by their funding. "So even though, in supporting local empowerment, they help open up spaces where alternatives become possible . . . they do nothing to prevent the re-absorption of these alternatives into the dominant capitalist practice," charges Harvey. Still, many play vital roles in movements, such as the World Social Forum (Gautney, 2010).

Others have come to question the utility of government grants for research (Thyer, 2011).

"Money should be spent trying out concepts that shatter current structures and systems that have turned much of the world into one vast market," writes Peter Buffett (2013) in an editorial dubbed "The Charitable-Industrial Complex," in the *New York Times*. "As long as most folks are patting themselves on the back for charitable acts, we've got a perpetual poverty machine. It's an old story; we really need a new one."

And new stories are emerging. There are alternatives—including anarchist, autonomist, and grassroots organizations (AGROs), which reject outside funding in favor of grassroots means (Gautney, 2010). What distinguishes such approaches is their emphasis on community and capacity. These organizations serve as a testament to the creative alternatives to NGOs. Their expressive approach is a topic for the next chapter.

17

DIY Politics and World-Making

Mutual Aid, Anarchism, and Alternative Solutions

Many are drawn to an anti-authoritarian organizing ethos after witnessing the hyper-controls of large organizations up close. After watching the Nicaraguan Revolution of 1978–1979, anthropologist Luis Fernandez (2012) concluded that the revolution had replaced one oppressive structure with another. So he turned to anarchism. "The classical anarchist thought began to help me explain that if you are not careful with certain human organizations, they tend to reproduce hierarchical relationships that end up reproducing these tendencies for human control" (Fernandez, 2012).

Anarchist, autonomist, and grassroots organizations (AGROs) have fashioned countless approaches to community organization. Some involve anti-authoritarian impulses toward freedom extending into approaches to public health, urban development and social services. Others are born of a do-it-yourself spirit that says build what you can with what you have. Through such activities, social capital expands, supporting alternate models of mutual aid. Chapter 17 considers this search for new models of organization, service provision, and community development.

Do-It-Yourself to Create Counterpower

"The idea of just going out and doing it, or as it is popularly expressed in the underground, the do-it-yourself ethic," notes Stephen Duncombe (1997, p. 117). "Doing it yourself is at once a critique of the dominant mode of passive consumer culture and something far more important: the active creation of an alternative culture. DiY is not just complaining about what is, but actually doing something different" (p. 117). During the last four decades, anti-authoritarian organizers, anarchists, and queers have found their way into countless social and cultural movements with the spirit Duncombe describes. Through DIY culture, punks, poets, organizers, junkies, and community gardeners have built their own projects, groups, structures, and forums, using counter-power to fashion spaces and counter-institutions of their own design (Gautney, 2010). Along the way, they have literally created a world of their own creation within the shell of the old.

"By counter-power I understand the capacity by social actors to challenge and eventually change the power relations institutionalized in society," notes social movement scholar Manuel Castells (2007). "In all known societies, counter-power exists under different forms and with variable intensity, as one of the few natural laws of society, verified throughout history, asserts that wherever is domination, there is resistance to domination, be it political, cultural, economic, psychological, or otherwise."

This is very much an act of doing something. Rather than succumbing to despair, it helps social actors find a route to fashion a better world by building alternatives. "The DIY movement is about using anything you can get your hands on to shape your own cultural identity, your own version of whatever you think is missing in mainstream culture," writes Amy Spencer (2005, p. 11). "[T]he enduring appeal of this movement is that anyone can be an artist or a creator." Drawn into the action, those involved help create alternates, ideas, and projects with whatever tools they have. Much of this takes shape within a public commons—of music venues and meeting spaces—of the movement's own creation. Participants tend to follow a gut instinct "to create a new cultural form and transmit it to others" (Spencer, 2005, p. 14). Here, use is valued over commercial exchange, as participants play with new social realities, creating a space for life, reflection, art, and pleasure (Holtzman, Hughes, & van Meter, 2004).

Efforts to create a new world have taken place in many venues and DIY cultural projects. Building on movements extending back to Dada and Emma Goldman's anarchism, queer groups and punks have helped create spaces that blur social boundaries. Take organizer and musician Bonfire Madigan. Influenced by the Riot Grrrl movement, Madigan starting playing music and putting out records when she was a teenager. "Riot Grrrl is a cultural movement which is still happening really, in that it's a feminist based, DIY movement of empowering young women to take our lives into our own hands and sharing this with the world," explains Madigan. "I like to think it always had an anarcho-feminist bent and our heroines were people like Emma Goldman and Lucy Parsons. We held up images of Pippi Longstocking and Girl Power Now." Born as social organizing, the project took off from a spirit of creative direct action. "We organized big sticker making parties, where we had Girls Fight Back, with little girls with big fangs, we put them on the buses or at the hangout centers where the punk bands were. We saw no images of women empowered to participate in creating or defining our lives."

Riot Grrrl was an expressive critique of repressive social mores. This ethos churned through the mix of passion, bodies, sweat, play, violence, and pathos of the punk scene. "Punk," writes Stephen Duncombe (n.d.), "was not just a music; it was an attitude, an ethic, and a sense of community." Punk's organizing an extension of DiY culture. "This value put on self-sufficiency came largely from necessity . . . DIY . . . is an ideal that transcends immediate need. It's an ethic that guides the punk outlook on the world, encompassing not only the logistics of a music scene, but also artistic creation and political action." Here, music, poetry, and cultural production serve as a basis for a community of resistance. "The scene is a place where punks can practice DIY most intimately, in constructing a community by and for themselves that offers up a system of values, aspirations, and behaviors in rebellion against those of the mainstream society." It builds on cultural movements dating back decades. "The scene gives the support and reinforcement necessary to stand up and against the daily onslaught of the hegemonic culture. It's a safe space to experiment with new ways of being and doing." Here, those involved find support to experiment with new practices in living. "It's a place to reinvent yourself," Duncombe (n.d.) explains.

Spreading from Queens to Cairo, London to Long Beach, the punk scene found its way into spaces for organizing around the world. Take Positive Force, a Washington, D.C., based "party activist collective" that Mark Andersen helped to cofound in 1985. "We organize benefit and free concerts, art shows, film screenings, protests, and educational events while also doing direct work with people in need," explains Andersen. The group believes in building a community in which regular people support social change efforts. "People who want to fundamentally alter that system will not tend to have the majority of the money or the majority of the guns," explains Andersen. Yet what they do have is "power and that is people. And that's really, really important. But how do you get these people reasonably coordinated and together? Well, you've got to be creative. You've got to figure out the way to draw people together. The divisive power of money and buying people off is immense. And of course the fear factor of the repressive force of the apparatus that defends that system is also immense. We need people and to get the people we need to be really creative." For Positive Force, creativity is a mechanism that challenges isolation; it churns through the group's work, transforming alienation into community projects. A few such projects include support for grocery delivery to elders, volunteer work at the syringe exchange, and support for sex workers.

In their own way, each punk show, zine, poem, film, zap, piece of art, gesture of direct action, and form of guerilla media helps spread the word and create solidarity. For Bonfire Madigan, punk shows were spaces where movements she cared about—from Riot Grrrl to Home Alive—found expression. Home Alive was a Seattle-based antiviolence organization that helped teach women self-defense. At each show, they would set up teach-ins. People would get up onstage and show women in attendance how to do "eye, knees, groin, throat, where to hit if you're being attacked," Madigan explains. Their work served as an optimistic, performative response to a world of violence. "Then there'd be girls on drums pounding along to this whole audience, in between band sets, on how to do self-defense as you get home that night." Rather than dictate, participants were invited to participate. And everyone learned from each other. In this way, cultural resistance is an ideal framework to make visceral breakthroughs possible (Kahn, 1995). "People tell me that I compose the kind of music that makes them want to raise their fist and weep and shake their butt all at the same time," confesses Madigan proudly. "And I think how often do we have the opportunity to bring all that emotional, cerebral and tangible reality into our interacting in our lives?" Here, everyday life becomes an arena for social change. With each show or piece of art, DIY culture helps those involved think about another way of seeing the world. But it is not by telling people what to think or hitting somebody over the head. "I also always have materials that are handmade, fanzines and music and homemade or handmade accessories and stuff," notes Madigan. At her shows, people connect with each other through self-made art, zines, and creative gestures. "It becomes a new shared culture," explains Madigan. "I call my work sometimes post-apocalyptic self-help music with this mantra of share or die. That's why I get so angry and frustrated with capitalism, it's robbed me of my ability to know how to cooperate and trust and love sharing." Madigan's work connects with a systematic critique and social movement. "It created whole new networks of allies," notes Madigan. "More so than ever I see young gay men joining forces with feminists, calling themselves feminists. And I can only feel safer and more empowered to define my own life knowing there's people who want to see me and feminism have an opportunity to thrive." Over the years, the culture has evolved and changed. "More women are safer, have the ability to reach out, are fighting for things like reproductive rights. And also more young women are creating their own small businesses, making their own clothing and lives and ideas."

Anarchism, Mutual Aid, and Communities of Support

A foundation of DIY culture is the practice of anarchism. "[A]narchists work toward two general goals. First they want to dismantle oppressive, hierarchical institutions. Second, they want to replace those institutions with organic, horizontal, and cooperative versions based on autonomy, solidarity, voluntary association, mutual aid and direct action," notes anthropologist Luis Fernandez (2008, p. 53). "[A]utonomy, voluntary association, and mutual aid [are] central values" (p. 52). Through mutual aid, anarchism takes shape as a practice in care, exchanging resources and solidarity, information, support, even comfort, and understanding. People give what they can and get what they need. When a group comes together to push for a change, when social outsiders come together to share or explore ideas and new ways of living—these are all forms of mutual aid (Steinberg, 2004).

In an era of a dwindling welfare state with social safety net provisions crumbling (Saini, 2009), the benefits of mutual aid and support networks could not be more important. Examples of such models are many. Clients at a syringe exchange share a place to stay. Such mutual aid networks helped keep many alive and off the streets, where they inevitably would have been swept up by police and sent to the de facto poor person's housing provider: city jail. In San Francisco, when people lost lovers to the AIDS crisis, neighborhood members formed a group called the Mary Widowers. This mutual aid group helps widowers cope with their losses, find new spaces for care, work, love, art, and fun (Shepard, 1997b). Mutual aid helps people survive.

Syringe exchange activist Donald Grove helped organize an underground syringe exchange program called Moving Equipment. "It was about creating a basis of mutual self-support from which we could do this other stuff." And much of that support was born of an ethos of care among social outsiders. "User organizing, people want it to be about political campaigns and stuff like that but what I see is that users are already organized in a hostile environment about just providing basic survival needs. To say that is not enough is to demand that everything and all political models act and look like the dominant political model." Sometimes self-care is enough.

Survival projects such as this build on direct action, a direct care continuum born of an impulse to take solutions into one's own hands. "Direct action, or taking action based on one's beliefs," Luis Fernandez (2008, p. 53) suggests, "means solving the problem concretely and directly confronting authority if necessary." Rather than appealing to the state to change a policy (Graeber, 2009), anarchist direct action is framed around creating solutions—serving free meals to the hungry, planting a community garden in a vacant lot, or squatting an abandoned building for those without anywhere else to stay. The point is to create a solution within one's own means, via creativity and a do-it-yourself spirit of cooperation, and care.

For Donald Grove, much of this takes shape as an impulse to support his community. "Moving Equipment was really this very positive, supportive environment. Within that framework we were able to get a select amount of work done." Countless movements and cultures have built on these traditions of mutual aid and community care (Graeber, 2009). After all, mutual aid is a practice that has existed for ages, note members of the Occupy Wall Street May Day Mutual Aid Cluster. In essence, mutual aid is an exchange of resources and services in a way that is both voluntary and mutually beneficial to those involved. From this perspective, everyone has something to offer and share. Instead of relying on the state, groups like this rely on one another. "We want to demonstrate that mutual aid is a viable alternative to capitalism," explain the May Day Cluster. "Actions of mutual aid prove that scarcity is manufactured by capitalist structures that commodify everything from the environment to human life in order to build individual wealth, whereby mutual aid seeks to build community. Value is placed on a large spectrum, not just on monetary or material goods. Relationship and community building within the structures of mutual aid are of the highest value."

Social welfare scholar Loretta Pyles (2009) witnessed the innovation born of necessity after Hurricane Katrina and the flooding of New Orleans in August 2005. With the Lower Ninth Ward, loaded with dilapidated houses, seemingly abandoned by government relief efforts, regular people took action, providing resources where there was little else, and neighbors shared resources with each other. Through such exchanges, those involved created new spaces, networks, and collectives (Crow, 2011; Pyles, 2009, p. 36). Such tradition hearkens back to the Black Panther food and survival programs of the late 1960s and early 1970s, which included medical services, free breakfast for kids, clothing, education, and prison support, discussed in Chapter 11. Such efforts are important because they emphasize empowerment of marginalized people and a social change agenda aimed at dislocating mechanisms of power that place an undue burden on the poor. Here social services are seen as one tool to provide essential supplies to those in need, yet not an end in itself. Instead, they are seen as a first step in a process that emphasizes social change by challenging causes of oppression, exploitation, and degradation (Pyles, 2009, p. 8). Part of the appeal of anti-authoritarian organizing to such practices is its open rejection of administrative social controls in favor of a politics of freedom, the creation of new social relations, and direct democracy. In this way, activists cultivate alternatives to spaces based on domination and hierarchy (p. 37).

Donald Grove offers another example. "In 1997 at the San Diego needle exchange conference, there was a group called the Sex Workers of Toronto (SWOT). They were brilliant. They said look, 'our goal is to take care of each other. We don't have a political agenda. We're sex workers. And we're shooting drugs. And our thing is to make sure we have a place to live. And we do it for each other.'"

As Madigan explains:

> I think that they ultimately all work together. I have to look at literally every day of my life as an art project. If I want to wear two different shoes that day I want to know that I'm going to be in the culture of life where I'm not going to be thrown in some crazy house or something . . . to me it's almost [an] act of resistance, playful. . . . We can be whole new human beings. We get to decide. Whose reality is this? We can perform out the lives we want to see right now we don't have to wait for some other world, or room, or reality, it's right here—take advantage.

A Politics of Freedom

Today, countless movements have come to think of other ways of looking at mental illness and reality. Rather than take more medications that fill the coffers of pharmaceutical companies, groups such as Mind Freedom call for alternatives for people being labeled as having psychiatric disabilities. For example, the Icarus Project is a project that Madigan supports. They call for

> a new culture and language that resonates with our actual experiences of "mental illness" rather than trying to fit our lives into a conventional framework. We are a network of people living with and/or affected by experiences that are often diagnosed and labeled as psychiatric conditions. We believe these experiences are mad gifts needing cultivation and care, rather than diseases or disorders. By joining together as individuals and as a community, the intertwined threads of madness, creativity, and collaboration can inspire hope and transformation in an oppressive and damaged world. Participation in The Icarus Project helps us overcome alienation and tap into the true potential that lies between brilliance and madness. (Icarus Project, 2006)

Looking beyond deficits-based psychiatric models that emphasize diagnosis of pathologies over human agency, the Icarus Project (2006) seeks "new space and freedom for extreme states of consciousness." Instead of more psychic prisons, "[w]e call for more options in understanding and treating emotional distress, and we advocate for everyone, regardless of income, to have access to these choices." This call is consistent with research that recognizes that those with mental illness benefit from participation in making decisions about their own lives (Lindhorst & Eckert, 2003).

The Icarus Project is very much a product of the DIY spirit, which translates art into ideas and actions. "All of us with a relationship to the punk scene brought something to it and took something from it," note Duncombe and Tremblay (2011, p. 17). Out of this movement grew "punk-influenced political gestures like Reclaim the Streets (n.d.), Food Not Bombs, and the Icarus Project or even the mass globalization protests, which applied punk style, strategy and infrastructure to other forms of organization" (p. 17). These cultural movements help blur lines between audience and performer; instead of looking for a leader, everyone could become involved and create solutions. This was the spirit of community members planting gardens in rubble heaps, squatting buildings, and giving out food even when they could not afford it; they helped occupy Wall Street when they did not know what else to do with inequality. Countless projects and mutual aid groups have taken shape within a similar vein over the years.

Social movements of the last five decades—from the Beats to Punk, civil rights to gay liberation—help serve as inspiration for social organizing. Personal freedom, autonomy, and self-determination serve as abiding principles for these movements (Fernandez, 2008). Over the years, these movements gained vitality through an embrace of the insurrectionary power of pleasure and connection. Throughout the Gay Liberation Movement, gay people met and cruised (Shepard, 1997b). Part of going to a protest was meeting friends. Take New York organizer Tim Doody. "It mixes cruising and public sex," he mused, describing his model of activism. He continued:

> Queeruption is a great example of that, of people creating a space and doing it themselves, coming up with all these different activities, putting out workshops on things like survival shoplifting to trans activism. There was definitely a pleasure politics in there. One of the most amazing things for me in Queeruption, in addition to seeing all these colors of hair, the colors of the rainbow, all these spikes, was meeting a guy and going down to the old concrete slab in Dumbo and playing old Ani DiFranco songs. That was totally part of resistance. When we're not in the streets fighting, this is what we like to be doing.

This creativity can also serve as a life force. Mark Andersen tapped into this energy to help his group collaborate and share spaces with other communities. "It created a space first with our communal house. Well, actually first with our meetings at the Washington Peace Center. And then with our communal house," explained Andersen. "Positive Force exists 20 years after it started and this whole time it's all volunteer, no one's ever gotten paid to do anything with Positive Force, somehow it all worked together—the music, the special community in D.C., the ideas behind it. Positive Force was never a narrowly ideological group; in a sense it functioned as a support group and as a necessity had to have fairly flexible, if clearly radical, politics."

Over time, Andersen helped link the efforts of Positive Force and services groups, providing services to the elderly, building bridges across communities in the city.

> Positive Force has come to volunteer and through that they've been able to tie an essentially largely White suburban punk community to a by and large very low income, inner city African-American community and create spaces where people can

start to build relationships across these kinds of boundaries. The aspect of building relationships or building family of some sort is so important. And naturally within that the playful element comes down, because all of a sudden this is not just simply, OK, we're here for this instrumental purpose of getting from A to Z. We're here because that's how human beings are meant to be. They're meant to be social creatures. When they get together they find joy in the encounter of another person.

For Andersen, networks of care are born through these connections. "We can create these contexts where we can get to know each other and kind of build community and family, where the incredible potential that human beings carry within them becomes possible to be realized." Through these connections, Andersen and company created a punk space in the senior center. Such gestures connect individuals with larger movements; they "remind us that resistance always lies just below the surface, waiting to rise when least expected," notes Fernandez (2008, p. 172). Here, cultural groups, such as Positive Force, built on the lessons of punk and DIY culture to create new cultures of resistance out of a wide range of movements with influences, such as anarchism, dating back decades (Graeber, 2009).

A Short History of Anarchism

The roots of anarchism can be traced to Europe in the mid-1800s. The anti-statist, anti-authoritarianism of Mikhail Bakunin's work was hugely influential for the movement. Flashpoints include the 19th-century Haymarket Riot, when labor activists were shot down in Chicago, Emma Goldman's struggles against efforts to control the body and imagination, and the Spanish Civil War as anarchists fought fascists (Gautney, 2010).

During the Spanish Civil War, women played a particularly important role in both the anarchist and resistance movements. The Free Women, or *Mujeres Libres*, aimed to end the subjugation of women to men, ignorance, and capital, insisting social revolution should not be postponed. Bridging the gap between direct action and direct services, these Free Women provided free education, child care and health care. And the movement spread, influencing the new government. Frederico Montseny led efforts to provide health care, even abortion services, as Minister of Health in the republican government. At its peak, over 30,000 were part of this federation of women (Ackelsberg, 2001).

The efforts of the anarchist Mujeres Libres very much anticipated the women's movement. "The activists of [the] 1960s were critical not only of capitalism, but also the patriarchal state and all forms of authority, over regulation, and social control," notes Heather Gautney (2010, p. 113). Throughout the period, "[f]eminists of all stripes founded their own abortion clinics, shelters for rape, and victims of domestic violence, and formed consciousness raising groups to deal with issues specifically related to patriarchy and its manifestations in the lives of women," Gautney continues (2010, p. 122) "[T]hey also gave birth to punk, which resisted the cultural consensus of the conservative 1980s" (p. 113).

Here, groups such as Mark Andersen's Positive Force helped bridge the gaps between cultural resistance, direct action, and organizing. "One of my basic ground rules as an organizer is you start with your community that you are part of," notes Andersen. "It's just logical. You have a certain credibility and knowledge there that enables you to be successful in doing this. Now, clearly the organizing ultimately has to go beyond subcultural niches, you also have to build alliances with other communities. And also, help to foster that same organizing and empowerment there." In this way, the practice of anarchism takes shape as an interaction between organizing, resistance movements such as punk, services, and connection among community members. Such a practice is often described in terms of a set of prefigurative practices and approaches to living, shared by organizers whether they "identify as anarchists" or not, suggests Heather Gautney (2010, p. 112). Elements of this "anarchist praxis" include "decentralized organization, voluntary association, mutual aid, direct action, and a general rejection of the idea that a movement's goals could justify authoritarian methods for achieving them" (p. 112). And there is good reason for this.

The game of politics often leaves people cold or embittered (Duncombe, 2007; H. Zinn, 2002). So organizers in the anarchist tradition suggest the way we get there matters—it's got to be fun to organize. Emma Goldman is associated with a famous quote (which she did not actually say): "If I can't dance, it's not my revolution." Many look to a more a more free flowing, rambunctious ludic approach (Shepard, 2011). Take French social theorist Henri Lefebvre. After being expelled from the French communist party, Lefebvre developed an increasingly festive, exuberant, even playful Marxist urbanism. Asked if he had become an anarchist, he is known to have replied, "I'm a Marxist, of course . . . so that one day we can all become anarchists" (quoted in Merrifield, 2002, p. 72). This playful disposition resonates throughout anti-authoritarian organizing circles.

Rejecting the coercive approaches to organizing seen in NGOs or state party politics, anarchist-inspired organizing tends to dedicate its energies toward "movement building and challenging illegitimate forms of authority that deflect power away from everyday people," notes Heather Gautney (2010, p. 112). "Many autonomists and anarchists believe that radical change and ultimately, freedom and the good life, can be discovered through direct action (protests, but also 'squatting') and the development of cooperative projects and counter cultural communities, and not through the realization of a predetermined revolutionary movement or participation in electoral processes abstracted from the conditions of everyday life" (p. 112). This sentiment is better understood as a set of practices than as any one social or political movement.

Graffiti in the streets of Paris in 1968 called for "all power to the imagination!" This message inspired generations of anarchists. Hopes and dreams help us realize it here, hence the concept of "imaginal machines." For anti-authoritarian thinker Stevphen Shukaitis (2009, p. 13), "imaginal machines" "are composed by the affective states they animate, reflecting the capacities to affect and be affected by the worlds that are contained within them. They activate a cartography of thought" (p. 13). Such mechanics propel regular people to dream. "Themes of imagination, creativity and desire run throughout the radical left movements," explains Shukaitis (pp. 13–14). Such thinking ties together projects ranging from Mujeres Libres to today's Critical

Mass bike rides. "[T]hey exist within a secret drift of history that runs from medieval heresies to bohemian dreams of the Big Rock Candy Mountain in the 1930s. It is a drift that connects Surrealism with migrant workers, the IWW with Dadaism, and back again" (p. 14). Often neglected, these ambitions "find channels of influence in collective dreams and a pervasive yearning for freedom" (p. 14).

In order to contend with these hopes for a better life, many anarchists turn to the concepts of everyday life and autonomy. Why everyday life? It is a way to stay clear of fixating on the spectacular moments of history at the expense of so many more enticing moments. Many could not make it to Paris in 1968 or Seattle in 1999. Yet they still took part in their own delirious struggles for jobs, play spaces, and autonomous communities. "Following the ideas of the Situationists and many related currents of thought, the idea is to refuse to fetishize particular dramatic, visible moments of transformation" (Shukaitis, p. 15). The struggle is for freedom and autonomy in the everyday rather than a totality. Here, "autonomy broadly refers to forms of struggle and politics that are not determined by the institutions of the official left (unions, political parties, etc.)" (Shukaitis, p. 17). At its core, such a politics steers clear of party politics; it functions as "a rejection of the mediation of struggles by institutional forms" (p. 17). Instead, autonomous organizing projects tend to be characterized by "self-organization . . . non-hierarchical organization, horizontal communication and relationships" (p. 17). The concept of autonomy is particularly appealing for those favoring a politics of freedom and self-determination. While it is hard to imagine anyone opposing such politics, many of the professional left as well as the right tend to oppose such organizational practices.

Those who support such practices face any number of obstacles: first and foremost, the world of work and neoliberal economic forces, which seems to have rigged the game. "Questions around how the nightmare of capitalism began, how the horrors of capitalist accumulation were set in motion, are in many ways a logical starting point for a consideration of the existing state of affairs and how to escape from it," notes Shukaitis (p. 33). "We begin, from a scream of terror formed in the realization that the daily horrors and suffering around the world are not props in some B-movie but are all too real" (p. 33). The point of organizing is reminding us there is still room for agency. "It is possible to find not fear, but hope, in the apocalypse: to turn the process of the subsumption against itself and to create a new basis for radical politics from the reclaiming of the flesh of zombified struggles," Shukaitis follows (p. 49). It is up to us to move beyond the B movie, the same old script. There are many stories out there. "The everyday life of revolution—the ceaseless movement of the radical imagination is premised not only upon creating and embodying new desires for liberation," notes Shukaitis, "but also working from the social energies unleashed all around us, and redirecting their course" (p. 49).

Through such efforts, anarchists revel in the joy in resistance. There are zaps, temporary autonomous zones and spaces for the imagination to conjure other realities. Sometimes they begin with dancing in the streets. This is a space for a full, authentic expression of self. There are moments for music, ritual, time out of time, and even the sublime. There are beaches beneath the streets. We create them every day we ride our bikes in groups, share music, create that alternate world within our daydreams, as the imaginal machines churn forward in between graffiti, radical marching bands, punk shows, and jazz musician Sun Ra's symphonies of sound. Through such escapades, the city really does become a work of art. While the struggle is anything but simple or linear, there is room for agency. Imaginal machines help remind us that we are not passive spectators of history. There are other ways of living. It is up to us to recreate them and set out a path toward different kinds of stories.

Anarchist Social Services

Although the anarchist movement is traditionally viewed as anti-statist, today many "acknowledge that states can play an important role in providing social welfare services and protections against the detrimental effects of unregulated capitalism" (Gautney, 2010, p. 126). As the stories of Positive Force, the ACT UP Syringe Exchange, Moving Equipment, and even the Mujeres Libres remind us, anarchists have long been involved with anti-authoritarian, radical social services (Ackelsberg, 2001; Crow, 2011; Gilbert, 2005a, 2005b). "While anarchists concede that states are often times more well-equipped than grassroots movements to ensure a sound infrastructure and social welfare for ordinary people," Heather Gautney is quick to note, "they are critical of the system of coercion that undergirds state authority, which for them ultimately limits its potential to serve as an agent of liberatory change" (Gautney, 2010, p. 127).

Many strive to create alternate programs in spaces such as abandoned buildings, warehouses, that serve as social centers (Holtzman et al., 2004). "Social centers involve a diverse array of social subjectivities," notes Gautney (2010, p. 130). These spaces serve as outlets for social networking, art, organizing, bike repair, community meetings, and even radical social services. "[A] common thread among contemporary social centers is their desire and effort to take back what neoliberalism has taken away" (Gautney, 2010, p. 130). To this end, "social centers tend to offer [an] assortment of vital services, including housing and documentation services for immigrants and homeless people, condom distribution for prostitutes, daycare or housing for homeless children, counseling and care giving for battered women, and many others" (p. 130). People are starting them from Barcelona to Bushwick in Brooklyn. A group of students in my community organizing classes started one in an abandoned building in 2013, generating support from a local church and the community.

Perhaps the most famous example of anarchist-inspired social services is Food Not Bombs (FNB), a group that has distributed free food, even in the face of multiple objections from state authorities. "FNB chapters are indeed diverse, and they do not employ formal leaderships or central apparatuses," explains Gautney (2010, p. 131). "They recover food that would otherwise be thrown out and serve fresh, vegetarian meals to hungry people free of charge" (p. 130). Food Not Bombs started as a direct action food distribution program in 1980 by anti-nuclear activists in Boston. Today, it has autonomous chapters throughout the world. "Most of the time, they would be supporting people at actions," San Francisco activist Starhawk explained. "But for quite a long time in San Francisco, they would be serving food right in front of City Hall, where the homeless people hang out. And they literally got beaten up by the cops every week." Police would pull activists out of the Civic Center area and arrest them feeding the poor. In 1987 alone, 725 volunteers associated with the group were arrested for giving away food without a permit (Vitale & McHenry, 1994). "It was encouragement," Starhawk explains. "It was an embarrassment to the city that the area around City Hall was full of homeless people. They were going to get them out of there and clean up that area."

Yet, the group has stayed the course and grown. Today, Food Not Bombs is one of any number of anarchist survival service programs. Poor people in cities around the world took part in the Occupy movements, organizing spaces, providing food for each other and the movement.

When looking at the threads between direct action, anarchism, queer organizing, DIY politics, and social services, it is easy to wonder what they have to do with each other. Yet, they share a great deal of common ground, including most importantly an impulse toward freedom. Theoretically, social services are driven by a similar impulse toward helping people be free and healthy. Do formal social services accomplish this? Not always.

Anarchism actually supports social services in many ways. One, it's an anti-authoritarian ethos. From Emma Goldman to queer theory to anarcho-feminism, an abiding anti-authoritarian disposition that says "get the state off my back, we can do this ourselves" propels anarchism. Social workers could borrow this thinking in terms of rejecting certain intrusive models of care. The second point is mutual aid; people supporting each other. It's a principle in social work and anarchism. The third involves the idea of a prefigurative politics. Anarchism really says that we should build the world we want to live in within our organizing. Yet, all too often that doesn't happen in service provision. All too often people do not feel free when they receive services. Finally, a democratic, bottom-up principle propels anarchism. Those who have a need organize themselves. Such a principle is very much consistent with empowerment-based schemas of care that suggest clients benefit from input into treatment decisions (Cowger, 1994; Lindhorst & Eckert, 2003). This is a do-it-yourself politics.

So, why are there so few examples of anarchist-inspired social services? There are some age-old conflicts and competing impulses. While services start off with this impulse toward supporting client health and freedom, many quickly find themselves caught in a familiar bind as they try to assess the worthy versus unworthy poor. There's a dichotomy between providing services to help people not be poor, and controlling those with illnesses or suffering from poverty. If someone is hungry and goes to a soup kitchen but they have to say a prayer before they may eat a meal, this kind of experience has more to do with social control than freedom of bodies and support for self-determination. Over and over again, service providers are caught in a conflict between supporting those in need and controlling them, between helping people get better and tracking people, between organizing around individual needs and looking at root causes, between one-on-one counseling and challenging broader issues.

So what do alternative models look like? A few principles are worth reviewing. First, alternative models involve not taking money that's going to control service provision. A second is, they're flexible; consumers who need service can get services the way they need them. It's a bottom-up model, so consumers drive the organizing, building the service model. Third, the emphasis is on staying on mission rather than chasing whatever funding trends take programs in new directions. Fourth, there's an explicit rejection of social controls and prohibitions around funding. And finally, such groups move away from the idea that direct action is an alternative to service provision. For many, direct action is a kind of freedom. In terms of providing services, it gets the goods. Countless organizations continue to use direct action to help people get the services they need and find their own voices.

As this chapter highlights, examples of anti-authoritarian mutual aid network social services support abound. The free health clinics from the San Francisco Haight-Ashbury to Berlin (Danto, 2005), the Rock Dove Collective, Sylvia Rivera Law Project, Common Ground Collective, and New Alternatives for LGBT Youth that build communities around mutual aid and support services—all are groups that are very much interested in what their consumers are saying.

These anti-authoritarian efforts overlap in a large scale multi-issue organizing project. Rather than favor one identity or another, much of this organizing is practiced intersectionally, between movements and organizational cultures. As these movements churn forward, such activism offers a route toward a richer, more democratic, and meaningful experience of living for everyone.

18

Multi-Issue Organizing

From the Women's Movement to Struggles for Global Justice

[T]here are so many amazing heroes in the world. And because for centuries and centuries and centuries, men have written history, we don't even know about all of the women change makers out there.... One of our jobs as women change makers, which you are by showing up today, is to tell each other stories and recognize the impact that all women have on the world.

—Ilyse Hogue (Bravo, 2007)

Over the last five decades, the women's movement has become intimately connected with broad-based universalizing discourses based on human rights and multi-issue organizing. This brand of organizing is represented by both innovative organizing repertoires and the willingness by cohort after cohort of women to take leadership roles in broad-based campaigns for social change. Notable examples of women's leadership can be found in the civil rights, gay liberation, transgender, reproductive rights, AIDS, Harm Reduction, Global Justice, and Occupy Movements. A closer look at contributions of women to organizing efforts provides a richer, fuller, more complete understanding of the field and practice. These contributions and their support for multi-issue organizing project is the subject of this chapter.

Community organizing has been a continual activity on the political landscape in the United States since the 1960s. While a handful of women have been celebrated for their contributions, many more have been the backbone of community organizing activities during this time. In fact, many informally suggest that if there are no women in the room, organizing work is doomed to fail. While Barbara Epstein (2001) has argued that the women's movement has become a demobilized idea, not a movement, its principles are woven into a wide range of organizing campaigns and movements. These principles include direct democracy, prefigurative community building, and consensus-based organizing. The point of these

Time's Up! Woman and Trans Dance Ride 2013.

Source: Photo by Mickey Z

principles is that the body of a movement is as important as the head; democracy should be bottom up, not top down. The process should be fair, transparent, and accountable.

In order for marginalized groups to have an impact, they must benefit from fresh organizational repertoires (Clemens, 1993). Sociologist Elizabeth Clemens (1997) notes that women involved in campaigns for social change have long understood that "the ability to organize determined whose voices would be heard" (p. 43). The challenge is to figure out how innovations or community organization can actually result in desired changes. Fact and organizational form inform such dilemmas. The organizing principles in question—direct democracy, consensus-based decision making, and prefigurative, and multi-issue organizing—represent just a small handful of innovative organizational approaches that have come to inject vitality into social action (Clemens, 1997, p. 49). Throughout the years activists have sought to infuse such principles into a wide range of campaigns.

The case narratives discussed in the following pages involve both innovative organizing repertoires and willingness by cohort after cohort of women to take leadership roles in broad-based campaigns for social change. Many extend beyond identity-based movements into campaigns involving multiple complicated targets. "There's an understanding that many issues are tied up together," notes Laura McSpedon, a student anti-sweatshop organizer at Georgetown University, and "that to separate culture and identity and race and gender from class and the concerns of working people is artificial, and divides us in unproductive ways" (Shepard & Hayduk, 2002, p. 18). In order to formulate a broad-based feminist model for multi-issue organizing, these leaders advance the understanding that power interfaces with multiple forms of oppression.

"Oppression is like a large tree with many branches. Each branch being a part of the whole. They cannot be separated; they draw from each other," Lois Hart, one of the Gay Liberation Front (GLF) founders, explained during the group's heyday in 1969 (Teal, 1971/1995, p. 88). On the thirtieth anniversary of Gay Liberation Front in 1999, I started reading about the group and the vision of multi-issue organizing that inspired many of the women and men in the more militant branch of the movement. To better understand this complicated history, I conducted long interviews (McCracken, 1988) with those involved with both Gay Liberation and the movements that followed. In the years that followed I continued talking with male and female organizers for social change in both New York and around the country. Many suggested I read this or that book or article, or attend a particular demonstration. Once there, I often ran into others with similar sentiments. What took shape within their stories was a series of counter-narratives that represented a kind of alternate history of organizing. The following considers examples of women's leadership in multi-issue campaigns from social work, welfare rights, civil rights, gay liberation, transgender, reproductive rights, AIDS, harm reduction, and global justice movements. It considers the ideas of feminist organizing, leadership, its history and its influence on larger movements, as well as its ongoing evolution. Let's begin with a brief history.

Women, Social Work, and Social Movements

Social welfare advocacy has long been championed by women. Jane Addams (1910) led organizing campaigns for housing, child welfare, and labor laws as a leader within the settlement house movement. Bertha Cappen Reynolds (1963) fought to link the struggles of social work and labor. Frances Fox Piven played a central role in founding the National Welfare Rights Movement (Piven & Cloward, 1993). And Mimi Abramovitz in 1996 helped organize women on public assistance to become advocates. Through her 2002–2003 "Community Leadership" class, Hunter College social work students helped draft public welfare rules calling for greater access to education for those on public assistance, which found support in the New York City Council (Arenson, 2003).

Unfortunately, the social work field has not always valued these contributions. Jane Addams's influence on the field waned when she spoke up against World War I (Elshtain, 2001). Reynolds was terminated from her position at the Smith School of Psychiatric Social Work in 1938 after disputes over her efforts to link social work with trade union advocacy and a Marxist critique (Reisch & Andrews, 2002). Similarly, Piven left social work education when Columbia University failed to promote her after her public role in the student sit-ins at the university during the late 1960s (Miller, 2002).

Over time, their contributions to broader movements for social and economic justice have been better understood. Today, Reynolds is embraced by the National Association of Social Workers (NASW). "Social work is blessed to have as one of its early founders a person of deep and wide ranging intellect, of compassion, and of independence and integrity," the NASW Foundation (n.d.) website states. "Social work is shamed, as well, by its failure to stand up for this courageous and radical New England woman during conservative times," it now laments. Addams, Piven, and Reynolds are one part of a long history of contributions of women to human rights and multi-issue organizing. Building on their efforts, women have intimately connected their organizing efforts with broad-based universalizing discourses that support notions of change in its deepest forms (Sedgwick, 1991).

Women have long cultivated and supported multi-issue, U.S. social movements, often facing substantial opposition. Organizers such as Ella Baker and Lucy Mason struggled against the deeply embedded cultural assumptions that leadership traits and masculinity overlapped. Rejecting conventional top-down models of leadership, these women developed leadership models that favored collaboration over hierarchy, humanistic rather than sectarian instincts, and appreciation of the needs of the group, rather than doctrinaire adherence to the principles of any one charismatic leader (Glissen, 2000). Many pushed for a commitment for movement participants to value the soft and compassionate, as well as the hard and courageous, the lovers and healers as well as those willing to take risks, to appreciate the means as well as the ends, the internal process as well as the impact on the institutions movements oppose (Starhawk, 2004).

Such innovations in organization helped bring waves of new participants into movements (Clemens, 1997; Glissen, 2000). Feminist organizer Starhawk (2004) suggests that they make their movements richer in countless ways. "A movement which embraces feminist values becomes more alive, more creative—for patriarchy is inherently predictable, and boring," Starhawk contends (p. 50). "It spawns the 'tactical frivolity' of the Pink Block snake dancing through police lines to the Congress Center in Prague, and the magic of the Pagan cluster taking over Grand Central Station in New York with an impromptu spiral dance" (p. 50). These principles help organizers find their full potential "for action and compassion, for fighting for and loving. It embodies the world we want to create: a world where we can all be whole," Starhawk concludes (p. 50).

There is much to learn about the history of political organizing in general, and feminist organizing specifically. Many of the most influential organizers of the last 50 years have been women. Their influence can be traced through a series of overlapping movements dating back to the civil rights era. Yet the route they took was often highly spontaneous, creative, and intuitive from issue to issue.

From the civil rights and gay liberation movements, the birth of the AIDS Coalition to Unleash Power (ACT UP) in 1987, the Seattle World Trade Organization (WTO) protests in 1999, to the contemporary global peace and justice movements, activists have built on the lessons of the women's movement and its emphasis on consensus-based organizing (Kauffman, 2004). This radical renewal drew upon a distinct set of bottom-up organizing principles brought to the Civil Rights Movement by Ella Baker (Ransby, 2003). Over the decades, countless social movements adopted the lessons of "peoplist" organizers such as Baker (Crass, 2002).

Using many of the same organizing principles, movements that were initially considered separate from each other and larger issues of social change were all linked in a direct lineage of activism. "[T]hese movements profoundly influenced both each other and the larger radical project and, across decades of political experimentation, created the new vernacular of resistance that has been showcased in the global justice movement of today," radical historian L. A. Kauffman writes (2004, pp. 35–36).

Today, these principles can help multi-issue, multi-gender, direct democratic organizing take shape. There are few more influential organizing narratives than the story of Ella Baker.

Ella Baker and the Civil Rights Movement

While Martin Luther King Jr. is often perceived as the spiritual leader of the U.S. Civil Rights Movement, many others helped King and the movement do what it did. Notable examples include Fanny Lou Hamer, who put her life on the line to help get Black people the right to vote: Jo Ann Gibson Robinson (1987), who helped do the logistical work for the Montgomery Bus Boycott, which helped propel the civil rights movement, Rosa Parks, and many others. Perhaps no one was more important in this process than Ella Baker, who suggested that King link the movement with the work of grassroots student organizers, such as those involved with the Student Nonviolent Coordination Committee (SNCC). Baker, the longtime field secretary of the NAACP, understood that such an alliance could propel the movement forward in ways no single leader could (Payne, 1995).

Baker was deeply opposed to the charismatic model of leadership, which paid a premium for the leadership of an individual rather than a collective. Her point was that leadership was an abundant quality, best cultivated within the body of a movement, not its head. Leadership was something everyone had in them. Thus, movements were best served when organizations looked to themselves, and identified and cultivated leadership from within, rather than from the outside (Ransby, 2003).

The Ella Baker model is best understood as a framework for group centered leadership. "My basic sense of it has always been to get people to understand that in the long run, they themselves are the only protection they have against violence and injustice," Baker explained (quoted in Crass, 2002, p. 430). For Baker, activism was about the work of regular people rather than that of any one leader, however charismatic he or she might be. "People have to be made to understand that they cannot look for salvation anywhere but themselves," she noted (p. 430). The Baker model built on three core components: (1) an appreciation for bottom-up leadership development and decision making, especially with decisions that affect people's lives; (2) the reduction of hierarchy or emphasis on professionalism in leadership; and (3) a call for direct action as an antidote to fear, disempowerment, alienation, or disengagement (Crass, 2002).

In order for people to become movement leaders and put their passion into the struggle, the movements in which they worked had to reflect their individual needs. For King to learn as a follower as well as a leader, he had to trust and listen to the counsel of individuals such as Baker and Bayard Rustin, while learning to be part of a network of collective leadership (Johnson, 2001). Baker's opposition to the charismatic leadership model favored by civil rights organizations such as the NAACP and the Southern Christian Leadership Conference (SCLC), put her at odds with their male leadership (Ransby, 2003). Many of the same forces opposed Rustin's contribution, on the grounds that he was homosexual (D'Emilio, 2004). Despite the obstacles to the democratic nature of the Baker model (sexism and homophobia), both leaders had long-term impacts on their movement and those that followed.

A central theme of the Ella Baker model of organizing and community building is the recognition that *how* organizers create a new world is just as important as the society they create. The means and the ends cannot be separated. There was little point in creating a new society that replaced racial apartheid with another mechanism of oppression. The process of organizing was as important as the final results. Community building was a central piece of this model, serving both instrumental and external aims, means, and ends. It helped hold the movement together by allowing it to reach both short-term and long-term ends. At its core, the Baker model helped organizers redefine movement success in terms of social interaction and the development of healthy human relationships, not just external goals achieved, laws passed, voters registered. In so doing, the Baker model offered an outline for a different kind of freedom, which supported both individual and collective aspirations (Glissen, 2000).

Activists have come to describe such notions of building a new world within the shell of the old as "prefigurative" community organizing. This idea has been profoundly important for generations of organizers. This organizational repertoire has been adopted in movement after movement—from anti-nukes (B. Epstein, 1991), to the environment (Starhawk, 2000, 2004), to today's battles over global justice (Clemens, 1997). Organizer David Solnit's 2004 anthology on the global justice movement, *Globalize Liberation,* specifically highlights the lessons of Baker's advocacy for non-authoritarian, non-hierarchical organizing approaches (Crass, 2002). Building on her work, Solnit notes that a primary ambition of the global justice movement is to get the process right, and thereby to avoid the slow route toward authoritarianism that overwhelmed so many 20th-century social movements. Power corrupts absolutely, regardless of who is in charge. To avoid such pitfalls, many in the new movements work toward fostering a spirit of creative experimentation, in which openness and respect for difference is a given. Here activists aim to articulate and embody their new approaches to social change. "Without a creative break from these patterns," D. Solnit (2004) explains, "we doom ourselves to stagnant movements, another generation of disheartened radicals, and a world unchanged" (p. xiv). "Process counts" is a theme we owe to organizers such as Baker who helped make the idea real. After all, what happens on the streets, patterns of friendship, and the details of daily interaction are essential sources for social inquiry and engagement.

For many, Baker's life story is the active embodiment of such politics. Her lesson that the members of an oppressed group could transform the conditions of their lives was profoundly inspiring for a nascent movement taking steam during the late 1960s—gay liberation (D'Emilio, 2004; Payne, 1995). For many involved, the implicit values of equality, truth, and non-violence, which characterized the movement, could be understood as lessons for everyone. As civil rights overlapped with gay rights, the opportunities (for human liberation) and barriers (patriarchy) seemed to mirror each other (Berube, 2001).

Gay Liberation and LGBT Organizing

Out of the Civil Rights Movement, a different movement for freedom gained steam with the same spirit of defiant direct action that had characterized the civil rights years and the Baker model. In 1966, after one too many insults from the police, a group of patrons at Gene Compton's Cafeteria in San Francisco's Tenderloin district finally fought back. The patrons, mostly transgender women, street hustlers, and queer youth, responded by trashing the cafeteria and torching a police car parked outside. Following years of harassment, the Compton's riot helped radicalize the San Francisco queer community (A. Lee & Ettinger, 2006; Stryker & Kuskirk, 1996). In 1969, a similar riot outside the Stonewall Inn in New York's Greenwich Village helped push gay liberation into a national movement.

New York's Gay Liberation Front (GLF) was born in the weeks after that incident. Yet prefiguring an egalitarian community remained a challenge for the nascent LGBT movement, just as it had for the civil rights movement. GLF was structured as a radical organization that linked its struggle with those of the Black Power, women's and third world liberation movements. "What was incredible about the Gay Liberation Front . . . is that it saw itself as a multi-issue radical movement," writes Michael Bronski (2009). "It was as concerned with ending wars abroad, fighting racism and securing reproductive freedom for women as it was with fighting homophobia. Members . . . also understood that they needed, pragmatically and philosophically, to work in coalition with other movements." The goal of overcoming all forms of oppression was ambitious and the practical route was elusive. Within a matter of months of the birth of the new organization, many walked out. "When the women left, most of the energy was gone," Kohler recalled. "I felt abandoned. A lot of the energy was gone." The post-Stonewall experiment in multi-issue, anti-racist, pro-gay, pro-feminist organizing was brief, exhausting, and exhilarating. Yet it established an ambition for a movement, as well as a lasting legacy. Looking back, Karla Jay suggests, "there were neither villains, nor victors. There were no other models. So we did the best we could." The gay liberation movement and the struggle against patriarchal social arrangements it personified continued long after GLF faded into memory (Teal, 1995).

An early gay liberation group was the Street Transvestite Action Revolutionaries (STAR) (transvestite was the original group name, though the revived group used the modern "trans"). STAR was organized by transgender women Sylvia Rivera and Marsha P. Johnson, who infused gay liberation with a connection to the struggles of homeless youth and gender variant people who had little or no other voice. In the years to come, the LGBT movement would continue to grapple with the issues Rivera raised concerning the position of those on the margins. Throughout the years, transgender women, such as Rivera, developed a feminist praxis in which a struggle for personal freedom was embodied in both the most intimate aspects of their private lives and public struggles. At her death, Rivera was remembered as the "Grand Dame" of the movement (Shepard, 2004, 2012a).

While the 1970s are often characterized as a time when gay men and lesbians coexisted within separate cultural camps, in fact queer men and women worked together to achieve some of the greatest successes of the period. Lesbian Anne Kronenberg, for example, managed Harvey Milk's successful campaign to become one of the nation's first openly gay elected officials in 1977. Lesbians, including Kronenberg, played key roles in the victory over the 1978 Briggs Initiative (Proposition 6), which sought to ban homosexuals from teaching in California public schools. "The forces that we figured would be against Proposition 6 were the gay movement and sections of the women's movement, period," explained Amber Hollibaugh, a lesbian and sexual civil liberties activist who campaigned across the state of California to defeat the initiative. "We did not assume support from anywhere else because no other groups had shown support" (quoted in Hollibaugh, 1979/2000, p. 48). Hollibaugh brought a distinct understanding of the class dimensions behind the Briggs initiative, helping give voice to more moderate interests within the California body politic that were opposed to the encroachment of the religious right into public life. A brief consideration of Hollibaugh's contribution to this campaign offers useful insight into female leadership in movement organizing.

On one occasion during the campaign, Hollibaugh debated a supporter of the initiative, Reverend Blue, who suggested that maybe Hitler was right about how to treat homosexuals. "I looked out at the audience, a big audience, with a lot of his congregation. The audience's age was my parents' age, in their fifties. This meant that they were in World War II and would define themselves as antifascist." And Hollibaugh saw a wedge. I said, "Well, you know Reverend Blue, my guess would be that many of the people in this audience fought against someone that had this kind of a position in World War II, and my guess is that this audience does not support genocide" (p. 51). The audience soundly backed Hollibaugh, and the initiative was defeated later that year.

Through her involvement in the lesbian-feminist "sex wars" that followed in the late 1970s and 1980s, Hollibaugh also helped give voice to those who sought a different path toward personal and sexual freedom than had existed within previous social movements. "One of the most profound things about the Briggs Initiative is that it forced people to have to deal with sexual issues in a society that actively represses non-oppressive forms of sexual searching" Hollibaugh continued (1979/2000, p. 52). Yet with Briggs, a new generation of queer activists was able to bring questions about sexuality and freedom into the public sphere for debate. It was a unique moment for a culture that "by and large does not encourage sexual debate on controversial issues," Hollibaugh elaborated. "It doesn't do that around sexuality for women, and it certainly doesn't do that around same-sex issues" (p. 52). Hollibaugh used her experience fighting the initiative to stake out a clear pro-sex, anti-censorship argument that benefited not only queers, but people of all sexualities in the years to come.

Throughout the 1970s and 1980s, the ascent of the Christian Right became a catalyst for a generation of women who joined the women's movement as organizers. One such woman, lesbian playwright Sarah Schulman (2002), described her entry:

> My family was very homophobic. I was basically exorcized from home as a teenager. I dropped out of college . . . and I went to Europe. And I met people who were involved in helping women from Spain, which was still fascist at the time, to go to France to get abortions. So I had hands-on, front-row experience of illegal abortion and how it operated. So when I came back here in '79, the Hyde Amendment eliminated Medicaid abortion. And my friend and I just immediately went to CARASA

[Committee for Abortion Rights and Against Sterilization Abuse]—it was the day of the Hyde Amendment—and got involved in the abortion rights movement. . . . Then of course, the next year, Reagan [was] elected. That just felt like a very immediate place. (p. 134)

Yet even in CARASA, Schulman experienced some of the lingering effects of the complex relationship that existed between the women's and the LGBT movements, dating back to the early 1970s. During the early days of gay liberation, lesbians had often been misunderstood by the women's movement. American feminist Ti-Grace Atkinson contended that lesbianism was antithetical to the feminist agenda because it "involves role-playing and, more important, because it is based on the primary assumption of male oppression" (Echols, 1990, p. 212).

After inauspicious beginnings—including feminist icon Betty Friedan's fear of a "Lavender Menace"—the woman's movement gradually changed its tune (Jagose, 1996, p. 45). Slogans such as "Sisterhood is Powerful" helped feminists link women's and gay liberation. Herein activists recognized that freedom to control one's own body and to live in human dignity and self-respect were key issues for both movements. The women's health movement emphasis on women's spaces, and self-education motto "Our Bodies, Our Selves" served as both a health slogan and as a call for self-determination that mobilized a generation of feminist, LGBT, and AIDS activists (Stoller, 1998).

Nevertheless, tensions between the camps remained, as reflected in Schulman's (2002) experience with CARASA:

CARASA was the radical wing of the reproductive rights movement. In those days, there was NARAL [National Abortion Rights Action League], which was single-issue: abortion rights. [CARASA was] looking at birth control, childcare . . . that would allow a person to have some sort of autonomy. And these were a mixture of socialist feminists, the left wing of the feminist movement. Unfortunately the whole thing self-destructed in 1982 around homophobia. The lesbians in the group were increasingly out. Suddenly, we wanted to say "lesbian liberation" and talk about lesbian stuff in the context of reproductive rights and they just wouldn't do it. And it was very much old left arguments: "It will alienate the working class; it will alienate Latinos. You are trying to turn this into a lesbian organization." And we all got kicked out. And that was very upsetting. . . . I didn't do anything for four years until I came into ACT UP. (pp. 134–135)

The old obstacles of patriarchy, homophobia, and lefty rigidity were hard to shake. "Some of the things these groups had in common were an outdated concept of organizing, an unwillingness to reach outside their known constituencies, and a rigid set of politics around which everyone had to agree," Maxine Wolfe (1990), another veteran of the reproductive rights struggles of the late 1970s, explained in describing why she turned toward queer organizing with ACT UP in the following decade. "Then you couldn't question anything or you were suspect" (pp. 234–235). Clearly, there were even women within the women's movement who did not support prefigurative notions of sexual self-determination and autonomy in all their forms. Throughout the 1980s, sex wars raged between rivaling camps as the movement split over the meanings of sexual expression, pornography, and sadomasochism (Jagose, 1996). Camps parted ways. On the one hand, a cohort of liberal leaning women continued down the road of professional reform, supporting a demobilized, straight, White movement. On the other, a cohort of women, many of color and many lesbians, went on to support a range of movements around an intersecting bundle of issues. Many of these women took the lead in building a wide range of movements. They brought a distinct set of life experiences, including being social outsiders, to their organizing (Kauffman, 2004). No doubt this helped provide insights about how to help others feel included, supported, and not marginalized within their movements. The queer contribution to these efforts was recognition of the multiple axes of oppression. Its focus remained on personal freedom, liberation from oppression, and a respect for the right to pleasure (Jagose, 1996). With these principles in mind, women such as Schulman and Wolfe helped create a vital new form of queer activism.

The AIDS Coalition to Unleash Power

With ACT UP in the 1980s and 1990s, Schulman plugged into one of the best organizing experiences of her life. The organizing skills she and other women such as Maxine Wolfe brought from the women's movement were sorely lacking during ACT UP's earliest days. "They were people who had been in gay liberation politics. But that was not the mainstay," Schulman recounts (2002, pp. 134–138). "The main people in ACT UP had been apolitical, totally apolitical. So when this thing [AIDS] happened they really didn't understand a lot about how to run a meeting, how to do things." On the other hand, "a lot of women had been trained in the feminist movement this whole time and had an incredible skill," Schulman explains. "So a lot of the women rose to a position of leadership because they had organizing skills" (pp. 137–138).

They also had a very specific insight into the problem. Vito Russo, an early member of ACT UP New York with experience in gay liberation organizing, noticed the influence of women in the group right away. He argues that part of why women were so effective in ACT UP was because of their experiences with the inequalities of the health care system. The AIDS crises exposed the glaring cracks that were already in this system. Activists who had dealt with institutional inadequacies around women's health care knew what they were up against (Elgear & Hutt, 1991).

ACT UP's approach worked very well—and continues to do so this day. Part of that success was attributable to the talent of so many people and their capacity to deal with tough policy minutiae and political differences in an open way. Another aspect was the quality of prefigurative community building—of creating the world in which one wants to live as part of the organizing process, and embodying this vision. Such an ambition took shape as an affinity model, in which friendship networks helped the group thrive. "Many of the friendships within the affinity groups allowed the groups to work," explained New York harm reduction activist and ACT UP veteran Donald Grove. The non-hierarchical nature of these affinity groupings of caring friends who were invested in each other helped the groups achieve both short- and long-term goals simultaneously. The point of these affinity groups was often to take care of each other. Sarah Schulman (2002) has famously argued the first goal of a lesbian activist is to get her friend a girlfriend.

For ACT UP, the intelligence, the meetings as theater, and the sense of play often prevented the ugly side from taking over. Ann Northrop, a Vassar graduate with experience in the women's and antiwar movements, brought these lessons into her work of facilitating the large early ACT UP meetings, which sometimes included four or five hundred people. She explained:

> Well, certainly one of the reasons I felt myself comfortable in ACT UP, and at home, was that I felt that it was a room that—in spite of being so predominantly male—was very feminist oriented, and was one of the few rooms of men that I could imagine, let alone be in, where I could speak in feminist terms and principles. And that was a very important factor for me and I think for a number of other women in the room. Now there are also people who would say ultimately that didn't work. And there were wars between some of the men and the women in the room. For a long time, I think it did work and there was a hunger among a lot of the men to learn that stuff.

"I stayed in ACT UP because it is a place where I can be a lesbian, a woman, and an activist," Maxine Wolfe concurs (1990, p. 235). She describes similar experiences as Northrop. Part of ACT UP was a curiosity. "I have seen men who wanted to hide being gay behind their AIDS activism do a teach-in on lesbian and gay history, become more and more openly gay, and develop a gay liberation, and not a gay rights perspective," Wolfe notes, suggesting it was not a long step from awareness of the links between different movement histories to an expanded political consciousness. "I have seen the issues expand—a year ago no one was talking about nationalized health care" (p. 235).

The issues most certainly did expand as AIDS activism exposed multiple levels of race-, gender-, and class-based discrimination that fueled the carnage. As this activism overlapped with a global justice movement, AIDS activists looked across borders to a new set of challenges. Building on their experiences with ACT UP, a number of younger women, including Asia Russell, Julie Davids, and Sharon Ann Lynch, helped create a well-connected and well-funded global AIDS movement (Davids, 2007). Part of the success of their work involved taking the lessons of praxis they learned in ACT UP as a theory of action.

Prefigurative Politics Within the Global Justice Movement

Given the assumption that the means of organizing should not be distinguished from the ends, prefigurative models owe a great deal to anarchism and the women's movement. Egalitarian and consensus-based direct democratic approaches to social change are basic cornerstones of this work (B. Epstein, 1991). This model of joyous resistance can be summed up in Gandhi's aphorism, "We must be the change we want to see in the world," which has been so much a part of the new organizing (Hudema, 2004).

For many of today's activists, this prefigurative approach is considered an imperative. "This is how it works: someone has a vision that arises from a fierce and passionate love. To make it real, we must love every moment of what we do," Starhawk (2000, p. 59) writes, describing this model of protest: "Impermanent spirals embed themselves in asphalt, in concrete, in dust. Slowly, slowly, they eat into the foundations of the structures of power. Deep transformations take time. Regeneration from decay. *Si se puede!* It can be done."

Prefigurative community-building approaches have become increasingly popular. "Protests gain in power if they reflect the world we want to create," L. A. Kauffman (2004) elaborates. "And I, for one, want to create a world that is full of color and life and creativity and art and music and dance. It's a celebration of life against the forces of greed and death." Yet, more than this, such a form of protest advances the affirmative. One of the primary forms of such a mode of protest took shape in the street actions of the direct action group Reclaim the Streets (RTS). "RTS reclaimed more than a style of protest—they popularized a model of political action wherein the protest itself is a living, breathing and in this case, dancing, political message" activist Stephen Duncombe (2002a, p. 347) explains. He describes the application to RTS' do-it-yourself politics: "By filling the streets with people freely expressing themselves, RTS not only protests what it is against, but also creates an experimental model of the culture it is for" (p. 347).

In order to attempt to create a context in which the Baker model can best merge with prefigurative ambitions, many in the global justice movement employ an affinity group structure designed to maximize egalitarian, direct democratic organizing. This model was revitalized during the late 1960s, before its recent renaissance. Lesley J. Wood and Kelly Moore (2002) explain that the model emphasizes "intentionally nonhierarchical organizing mechanisms which date back to radical feminist, civil rights, antiracist, environmental, and anarchist movements" (p. 30). This approach is used to overcome negative aspects including sexism, racism, and machismo that often accompany the organizing process. To achieve this end, affinity groups are expected to be aware of their internal dynamics and the systems of power implicit in their interactions.

Despite these efforts, the same obstacles Baker contended with (patriarchy and male privilege) continue to be blind spots that hinder organizing efforts. Take Reclaim the Streets. The issue of male domination was a constant issue for the group. During the group's peak years, women assumed positions of leadership, and actions thrived within the emphasis on creative action. During low points, however, women were interrupted at meetings and felt marginalized and underappreciated (Shepard, 2011b).

Describing the meetings of the original English RTS, John Jordan notes, "It was never really thinking about the process. RTS meetings were the most macho, boring, dull, unembodied, unpleasurable experiences ever." Many participants had similar experiences with RTS NYC. Amanda Hickman reflected on the irony of a group that aspired to create a better world, yet had difficulty overcoming interruptions and conflict during meetings: "Are we trying to build a better world or a more abusive world, 'cause the abusive one already exists out there. We don't need to replicate it here."

The phenomenon was hardly unique to RTS. At its height, the North American global justice movement occasionally mirrored the power structures it sought to challenge. For organizer L. A. Kauffman (2004), the 2001 Quebec City Free Trade of the Americas protests represented "the apex of that tactical radicalization." While the police acted violently against the protests, Kauffman was also concerned with the dynamics within the movement. "I had a big problem with the aesthetics of the Quebec City protest, and with the aesthetic drift of the global justice movement more generally. Our side was becoming more and more militaristic," she explained. "All those people—mainly, but not exclusively, young men—dressed in black, looking all menacing and ominous, getting off on confrontations." The movement seemed to be mirroring what it was fighting—militarism and violence.

In the following years, these dynamics continued to present a complicated issue for the movement. During the spokes councils preceding the Republican National Convention protests in the summer of 2004, many women experienced a pattern of male domination of the meetings. In order to address these issues, male and female facilitators not only discussed the problem within the meetings, but with the letter titled "Movement Dynamics" posted to the Direct Action Network electronic message list (Marina, 2004). It stated, "We are saddened . . . by how some in the global justice movement are treating others in the movement . . . in spokes councils. We are all the more disturbed that most of those who have been attacked, for apparently political reasons, are women." The authors noted that sometimes such behavior is the work of provocateurs, while at other times it is lack of thought among participants. Yet, "The most important thing is to deal with this as a movement and treat one another with openness and respect." The authors asked that everyone actively think "of strategies, tactics, and structures that make the world we want possible." It concluded with a call for organizers to act on the movement's prefigurative ambitions. "Many of us in the movement believe that what we do now and how we relate to one another is the world we want to create, believing the future is created in the present."

To address these shortfalls, a number of men involved in the contemporary global justice movement have sought to create strategies by which men can contribute to activism without replicating systems of domination. For example, San Francisco community organizer Chris Crass (2002) has created a series of tips for activists called "Tools for White Guys Who Are Working for Social Change (and other people socialized in a society based on domination)." The list outlines practical steps almost anyone involved in community practice can use to make meetings more effective. The first five steps are listed below:

1. Practice noticing who's in the room at meetings—how many men, how many women, how many White people, how many people of color, is it majority heterosexual, are there out queers, what are people's class backgrounds. Don't assume to know people, but also work at being more aware.

2a. Count how many times you speak and keep track of how long you speak.

2b. Count how many times other people speak and keep track of how long . . .

3. Be conscious of how often you are actively listening to what other people are saying as opposed to just waiting your turn or thinking about what you'll say next.

4. Practice going to meetings focused on listening and learning; go to some meetings and do not speak at all.

5a. Count how many times you put ideas out to the group.

5b. Count how many times you support other people's ideas for the group.

With these points in mind, activists are expected to check themselves and their own biases. Today, a new cohort of men has actually sought to grapple with male privilege, while taking action to change imbalances of power (Tirrant, 2007). The difference between groups in which this consciousness becomes part of the organizing and those in which it does not can be profound. When it happens, organizing can become a dynamic process in which people and groups grow together. Activists access their own potential as organizers to achieve what those in power hope for but most citizens would not believe possible: self-organization in action. This philosophy assumes that leadership is a quality everyone possesses; it emphasizes a strategy of self-emancipation in which people are liberated from the need for liberators.

Activists tend to assume that how the movement organizes itself is as important as the results, but it is certainly not simple. Hundreds of activists poured into spokes council meetings to plan the day of direct action on August 31, during the 2004 Republican National Convention (RNC) in New York City. More than 1,000 people were arrested, and the actions garnered a great deal of media attention (Shepard, 2011b). Simultaneously, a small and highly effective affinity group from ACT UP was able to garner as much, if not more, sustained media attention for their carefully tailored message through a series of creative actions, including a naked protest outside the convention center (Epstein, Lemire, & Becker, 2004). Affinity groups made up of a small number of activists are typically more efficient, and often just as effective, as large numbers. Within well-coordinated affinity groups, the realization of Schulman's conception of the linkage between aim, tactic, and outcome often finds its best expression.

The issues of internal process versus external goals involve core questions about effective organizing. Queer organizing veteran Cindra Feuer helped coordinate the media for the naked action. She discussed how much the process mattered in organizing to create change. "Often I find that when you are working really well together, it doesn't matter who's calling the shots and it's usually an organic process." In such moments, Feuer explains, "I find that actions go really well when there is not too much concern for process. Like when you pay too much concern to the process and how the decisions get made, shit doesn't get done and people get upset. Feelings get hurt." And the emphasis on process can actually backfire. "I've worked in situations where I realized decisions were getting made by one person. And I just bite my tongue and I remember, the bigger picture is we want to get this done. We want this action to happen." The emphasis is on the goal, "I don't care about the process as much as I do about the end product."

Answering the question, "Are you fighting to build community or create external changes? And are these aims mutually exclusive?" Starhawk explained: "I think it depends. Ideally it's one and the same. In civil disobedience, there are two things: opposing and building. One side is stopping what you don't want from happening, and the other is building what you do want." The point of the multi-issue organizing is to merge process and outcome to emphasize the affirmative, to build the world in which activists want to live.

Creating a New Multi-Issue Politics

Strategies of action are critically important, and while the prefigurative model is taken as a guiding philosophy of organizing, no model can or should remain static. Movement organizing repertoires continue to evolve with the issues. Such a project depends on a critical praxis in which activist theory is critically outlined and practiced. Fortunately, new cohorts of social actors are standing up to take on this challenge.

Multi-issue organizing inspired much of the global justice movement's ascent. As organizer David Solnit explains:

> For me, organizing around art and culture and theater was a way to do anti-systemic organizing, or anti-capitalistic organizing. We all knew that the problems were deeper than any single issue. The conventional wisdom was, you can talk about your issues, you can make a few changes. But if you talk too much about any of the systemic issues, you alienate your constituency. That was the single-issue organizing wisdom that I was brought up with. It was very unsatisfying to me. Most of us knew things were wrong and wanted to overthrow the system. And we didn't want to just get reforms around one issue. The corporations do not have a different committee for how to destroy the ecosystem and how to disempower the communities and how to screw the workers. They act cumulatively and think more systemically than our social movements often do.
>
> Doing Art and Revolution, in the same week I'd work with forest activists and homeless groups, indigenous rights groups, striking unions. Sort of tie it all together and be able to put out radical messages. If I wore all black and clenched my fist and yelled into a microphone, people would all shut down, but if you do it with dancing puppets, if you make it fun and lose the rhetoric, then people are very open to it.

Take the work of trans activist Dean Spade. "[T]he connections between opposition to the consolidation of global capital and domestic queer and trans activism remain under discussed," Spade writes (2004, p. 34). Yet, rather than just talk about this, Spade has helped create a legal clinic, named after Trans icon Sylvia Rivera, for trans people currently facing hostile conditions in the streets of New York. Rather than create an identity-based model, Spade helped create a model for services based on the imperatives of lived experience, in all its complexities. Such a project involves recognizing that many people occupy complicated social identities informed by race, education, culture, gender, class position, and immigration status. "What I would like to see most is trans activism and trans analysis that reflects the most urgent issues in trans life and that creates dynamic responses and ideas that move us to think in new ways," Spade writes, alluding to the prefigurative ambitions of the social movements that inform both his work "and the alliances we're building to create the world we want to live in" (2004, pp. 32–33).

At the end of the day, Spade's work is informed by countless social movements, including feminism and queer activism, with its roots in the liberation of sexuality and pleasure. "I do not find it a stretch to see how interrogating the limits of monogamy fits into the queer, trans, feminist, anticapitalist, anti-oppression politics that most of my personal work and political practice is focused on" Spade (2006, p. 29) recently wrote. "[O]wning sexual pleasure and being allowed to seek it out is a radical act for everyone in our shame filled culture," Spade continues, making reference to the controversies and contributions of radical pro-sex feminists (2006 p. 34). Much of this process is about shaking off imposed identities and striking a course that recognizes the complexities of people's lives and needs. "We've done difficult things before," Spade notes. "We've struggled with internalized oppressions, we've chosen to live our lives [in] ways that our families often tell us are impossible, idealistic, or dangerous, and we get joy from creatively resisting the limits of our culture and political system," Spade concludes; they are "both external and part of our minds" (p. 38). (For more on the Sylvia Rivera Project see Shepard, 2012a.)

A new generation is taking the lead in creating a different kind of social justice politics based on a multi-issue agenda, rather than a politics of identity and inclusion. Younger activists strive to connect linkages between issues and struggles. Recognizing, for example, that issues of violence against women cannot be separated from struggles against the prison-industrial complex and police brutality, a new cohort of women is charting an activist course based on a broad human rights framework. "The focus on building autonomous power does not imply separatism," Andrea Smith (2006), of INCITE!, explains. "In fact, this model of radical women of color organizing is not simply based on a narrow politics of identity but more on a set of political practices designed to eliminate the interlocking systems of oppression." For Smith, the struggle against "heteropatriarchy, White supremacy, capitalism, and colonialism" is aimed at "liberating . . . all peoples. Unlike the demobilizing reformism of the mainstream women's movement, this organizing is about asserting power and taking responsibility for transforming the world" (p. 69). It is a goal to which many can contribute.

From Jane Addams to Ella Baker to Starhawk and Ann Northrop, women have helped reinvent postmodern political and community struggles in movements. Their legacy can be seen in movements from civil rights to global justice, trade unionism, and AIDS activism. The principle of an egalitarian mode of engagement understood as prefigurative community organizing has become a vital tool for movements for social change. Process counts, but so does outcome. In its best form, a democratic organizing process is linked with a substantive critique, as well as an effective mobilizing strategy combining research, communication, and a sense of possibility. In the examples explored in this chapter, feminists have taken the lead in multi-issue organizing campaigns and change has followed. Out of these stories a new organizing praxis is born. In the years to come, countless movements would build on this sentiment.

19

Community Building Against Inequality

Zapatistas, Occupations, and Transnational Advocacy

Each year, when I teach U.S. social policy and community health, my class and I look at root causes of illness, one of the most significant of which is poverty. We usually watch the film *Unnatural Causes*, a documentary about the ways inequalities in wealth are reflected in our health. The film explores indicators of inequality including social determinants of health among various populations, examples of excess death in low-income communities, high pre-term births among African American mothers, and overall high rates of infant mortality across the board. The U.S. rate of 7 deaths per thousand infants ranks it 34th in the world, below Cuba and Portugal (California Newsreel, 2008). The statistic is thought to be an indicator of general health of a population. Income inequality is a means to think about core barriers to community health. Throughout the class, we talk about solutions for the problem, such as the Earned Income Tax Credit and national health care. But what we all agree is really needed are movements to break down these inequalities.

This chapter considers efforts from occupations to Zapatismo to challenge inequality. Both movements identified issues—inequality and neoliberalism—that resonated. In doing so, they ignited movements the world over. This final case study in this work looks at how they did this.

The Occupy Movement

On a week in September 2011, when new statistics came out pointing to an 18-year high in poverty levels, a group of idealistic youth descended on Wall Street. Dismayed with President Obama's one-sided approach to serving the needs of bankers, and with the lack of a national policy to address increasingly severe social and economic inequalities, a new generation turned to the street to pursue their own solutions, establishing a space where they would rally, cook, create art, and participate in an open-ended experiment in democracy. Occupy Wall Street (OWS) was a call to action heard around the globe (West, 2011). Its central target: inequalities of income and wealth.

Of course, Occupy Wall Street was not the first movement to take on this issue. The French Revolution of 1789 expressed a similar aspiration. So have many subsequent movements, yet the problem has remained. In recent years, there has been an exponential increase in income inequality worldwide. Domestic inequality widened during the 1990s economic expansion, and the United States maintained its position as the leader in inequality among advanced nations. The great bulk of the wealth created in the 1990s went to the upper 5% of U.S. families. The top 5% got 43% of all income, whereas the bottom 20% got only 5% (R. Freeman, 1999).

Movements I cared about, from the burgeoning global justice movement to queer/AIDS activism, recognized that their challenges were only magnified by the problem. Eric Rofes, in a 1997 speech, noted that "What we are witnessing . . . powerful social shifts . . . causing a full-scale sex panic to break out nationwide," and that the "intense concentration of wealth" was making U.S. cities into "sites of contentious class-based battles over massive corporate land-grabs." He added, "This is the way terror and scapegoating operate in a postmodern culture."

Economic and social inequality produces countless social problems, as well as systems of blame and retribution. After all, the U.S. prison population represents 3% of the U.S. male workforce, most of whom are high-school dropouts for whom the job market has collapsed. Those without high-tech skills remain locked out of the new economy. All the while, incarceration rates have doubled, and then nearly doubled again, with disproportionate numbers of people of color locked up and subject to capital punishment. "Racially targeted mass incarceration: Not in a democracy!" declared a sign in the February 20, 2012, OWS march in New York against the prison-industrial complex. OWS would connect the dots between systems of oppression, as well as between movements.

Global capitalism, activists would contend, is mauling the public: the "commons" are being turned into private malls; genes and seeds are being altered and patented; water is being dammed, bought and sold as an increasingly scarce and valuable commodity; politicians and whole governments are routinely bribed and bent to capital's will; children are targeted and tracked at birth, fed advertisements and slogans in place of needed nourishment. With OWS, a new movement would challenge such social displacement by connecting the dots between banking practices and their social consequences.

Most importantly, OWS stayed downtown and local. It set its eyes on Wall Street and the system it supported, focusing on it for months on end. On Friday, September 16, 2011, activists held a general assembly and Critical Mass bike ride in support of the movement. The 17th began with rallies, street actions, and general assemblies. No one knew what to make of the action at first. Young people had organized it, although looking around the space that afternoon I saw many of the usual suspects, police, a few old-time libertarians, and others. With backpacks in hand, activists wandered through Zuccotti Park, later dubbed Liberty Plaza. They held a general assembly and spent the night. Many talked all night. The actions continued Sunday and so did the general assemblies. For many, this was a continuation of actions taking place from Egypt to Wisconsin and Albany, where waves of protests challenged the politics of austerity. Earlier in the year, activists from around the country had converged on Wall Street to protest budget austerity; the comparison with Cairo's Tahrir Square was widely made.

In the months following September 17, I would ride my bike to Liberty Plaza almost every day. One of my favorite activities was to peruse the painted cardboard signs on display. Sign after sign highlighted record-level inequalities in wealth (Winter, 2010). "The wealthiest 400 Americans own more than the poorest 60%. Who do politicians really care about?" On the north side of the park, many posted messages explaining why they were there. "GET MAD" read a message painted on the back of a pizza box. "Citizens United Against Greedy Bankers" read another. Many addressed the influence of money on politics. "Who Funds Our Senators? Wall Street." "Corporations Are People Too: RIP McCain Feingold." Others raged at the system itself: "Occupy Wall Street: Time to Change the System." "Kill the Corporate Worm." "The Rich Get Richer, The Poor Get Poorer, Flawed System." "Wall Street Doesn't Pay." Some recalled the generation of 1968: "Revolution Is Poetry, Poetry Is Revolution! Imagination!!!" Others called for a Velvet Revolution—type moment in which we'd tear down the wall: "Rip Down Wall Street and Make a Just Street." The central theme was that democracy is bought, sold, and controlled by Wall Street.

The driving force behind OWS was (and remains) its focus on how inequalities affect people's lives. Research from the Fiscal Policy Institute (2010) shows that the richest 1% of earners receives 35% of all income collected in New York state. In New York City, 44% of all income is collected by the top 1%. The financial services industry is once again making record profits and real estate interests have spent millions on PR and lobby campaigns to weaken rent control, undermine teachers' contract rights, and cut social services. Today, one in five New Yorkers lives in poverty. And poverty has risen to 15.1% nationally. The poverty threshold

All of Our Grievances Are Connected—the theme of Occupy's two-year anniversary march on Wall Street, September 17, 2013.

Source: Photo by author

for a family of three is $15,205. Conversely, the wealth of the top 1% is greater than that of the bottom 90% combined. With poverty numbers on the rise, the movement's declaration, "We are the 99%," seemed to resonate. "Banks got bailed out, we got sold out!" "All day, all week: Occupy Wall Street!!!!" everyone chanted as the early morning rallies made their way through New York's financial district. And more newspapers started writing about the growing inequality.

Activists would stay downtown for two months, until their eviction on the night of November 14/15, 2011. During that time, those in support of the 99% held rallies for health care and against police brutality; built solidarity with labor, immigrants, and AIDS activists; and shifted a national conversation. And policies began to change. When activists called Governor Cuomo "Governor 1%," he pushed to expand a form of the millionaire's tax. Even eviction could not slow the nascent movement. Post-eviction actions would target Goldman Sachs, the foreclosure crisis, and the need for public space where people can meet in the streets. And the dirty secret of income inequality in the United States was exposed for all to see, and even possibly do something about.

Many of the roots of Occupy began in places as diverse as Oaxaca, Mexico, and Madison, Wisconsin, and, notably, Cairo, Egypt. While there was an underground freedom movement among some Egyptians, an incident in which a fruit seller set himself on fire in protest in a neighboring country prompted a more widespread call for a movement toward democratization. The process began when a few organizers arranged meetings, using Facebook and other new social media to get out the word. Gradually, those involved started holding secret meetings in Cairo neighborhoods. To their surprise, large numbers came out and supported the idea of an "Egyptian Tunisia." Meetings turned to daily demonstrations in Cairo's central Tahrir Square (Arabic for "Liberation Square"), calling for President Hosni Mubarak to step down. Over

OWS individuals with signs.

Source: Photo by author

the next few weeks, protests swelled throughout the country: "To many people, the events in Egypt revealed a courage, a solidarity, an activism, and an intelligence that seemed to betray their very sense of what is possible," noted movement scholar Jeremy Brecher (2012, p. 3). The upheaval in Egypt electrified the Middle East, inspiring comparisons to the events in Eastern Europe in 1989. Commentators would dub this movement the "Arab Spring." In the United States, inspired by the uprising, trade unionists converged in Madison, Wisconsin, and around the country. Labor started feeling like a social movement again. "The events in Madison were as unanticipated as those in Egypt," noted Brecher. "Yet, from 1500 BC to today, history shows that nothing is as predictable as unpredictable popular upheavals" (p. 4).

Common Preservation

These movements were inspired by notions of sustainability and common preservation. "I use the phrase common preservation to denote a strategy in which people try to solve their problems by meeting each other's needs rather than exclusively their own," notes Brecher (p. 7). "I borrowed the phrase from the seventeenth century English Digger Gerrard Winstanley" (p. 7). The Diggers formed "self-governing work teams, occupied uncultivated lands, and began producing food for their own communities" (pp. 7–8). The action laid the foundation for models of mutual aid practiced by anarchists and many in the contemporary Occupy movements. In a world in which banks socialize losses and privatize gains as the rich accumulate, global warming increases, and nuclear power plants rust, common preservation offers an alternate route. This is a model of community development built on sustainability, interdependence, and recognition of linked destinies. Interdependence means we need each other. MLK preached about it; Walt Whitman wrote poetry about it. And Benjamin Barber begs us to build a polis in which the grammar of community is spelled around the notion of *we* not *me*. Here, democracy depends upon an awareness of the connection between self and other. From community gardens to bike lanes built into cities where people share space and common purpose, the seeds of common preservation are already very much a part of current movement practices (Shepard, 2012b).

The OWS Sustainability Committee

A prime example of a movement for common preservation took shape as the Occupy Wall Street (OWS) Sustainability Committee. The Sustainability Committee was born in

Peter, this author, and his daughters participating in a guerilla gardening action 2012. By the end of the day, the vacant lot had been transformed into a vibrant community garden dubbed Siempre Verde. Such efforts are part of a movement toward common preservation.

Source: Photo provided with permission by Barbara Ross

The author and his daughter at the garden action on Stanton Street. The community would back the effort. Today the garden enjoys widespread support.

Source: Photo provided with permission by Barbara Ross

Zuccotti Park in September of 2011 from a desire to prefigure a better world in the increasingly chaotic encampment taking shape in the park. It was also a response to a push by the New York Police Department. Several of the NYPD's actions seemed to backfire, noted OWS activist Brennan Cavanaugh. First, police pushed activists out of the city park they could control at Bowling Green into the publically owned private space known as Zuccotti Park, where Occupy activists stayed overnight starting September 17, and the police took the gas-powered generators out of the park on October 28, 2011, inspiring Times Up! to bring in peddle-powered generators. The movement's capacity to come up with innovative solutions to threats was a testimony to its resilience.

After his arrest on September 24, 2011, Cavanaugh jumped into involvement with a number of committees, including those on media and sustainability. "At that point, everything was just forming. The movement was one week old. It seemed like these working groups were just forming. People were coming in from all over the country."

Part of what made the space so vital was the image of mutual aid that took shape every day. On a Sunday afternoon in early October an African American boy passed out cookies, a man gave out sandwiches on a Tuesday morning—I rarely went by Occupy Wall Street without someone offering me something. The spirit of mutual aid, of sharing was very much a part of the dynamic in the space. It helped the movement develop and create its own meaning. "So many people are involved in so many different things," notes Cavanaugh. "But we've all been thinking the same things and talking about them, and reading the same things and going to the same lectures, just all separately. Now everyone who is down there is getting together there because they all know this is the time. This is the future. This is the way we can change the world. Just like being in jail. People are exchanging ideas and talking up ideas. And it's a very concentrated think tank."

"There is another group I helped form just out of necessity," notes Cavanaugh. "With the amount of food that was coming in and the donations and the amount of food being prepared, there was a lot of food waste. It was actually Catherine's idea to start creating compost buckets and start taking it out. Then it was my idea to start doing it on bicycles. With Time's Up! we have a lot of genius bicyclists. So we formed a bike brigade to remove compost."

Over time, bikes became a more and more integral part of the Sustainability Committee, transporting the waste to community gardens, such as El Jardin Del Paraiso, La Plaza, and Belinda M'Finda Kalunga Community Garden in the Lower East Side of Manhattan. "The garden is on an African burial ground," notes Cavanaugh. "And we also have the Lower East Side Ecology Center. And just yesterday, both gardens just offered me keys, so we can just go to their compost dumps directly."

In the following weeks, Time's Up! would organize several bike-related events in support of the movement, including the OWS Decompress Rides/dance parties held in early October. Such release would be part of the fun that would help sustain the movement, particularly as the cold started setting in.

October 29, 2011, witnessed an unseasonably early snow storm. The day before, the city had confiscated the heat generators used to warm the space. So, the movement was left to cope with the elements. On October 30, I rode down to the square and heard the drums once again. The sun was out and the space felt alive with energy. The snow storm felt like an anomaly. Members of Time's Up! were out with their bikes using peddle power to charge the generators that replaced the gas-powered generators confiscated by the police the previous Friday. Later that week, Time's Up! put out a call for support for the energy bikes. The video began with an image of a man standing outside Zuccotti Park. "My name is Keegan and I am with the Sustainability Committee of Occupy Wall Street," noted the Time's Up's volunteer and member of the OWS Sustainability Committee. "One of the first things we realized we had to do was to get everybody here off of fossil fuels. So we made an energy bike. And we can peddle to power a deep cycle battery. We brought it down here. We started powering some of the things this occupation needs like laptops, cell phones, and cameras. As soon as we plugged this in all the other committees approached us and said we need one too." The Time's Up! call for support asked for help:

1. Building more bike-powered generators for OWS and occupations in other cities

2. Buying cargo bikes for delivering compost to local farms and community gardens, and bringing local food back to OWS

3. Buying special cargo bikes for hauling water from local taps to OWS

4. Recycling, maintaining, and locking bike-share bikes for various OWS committees

Brennan and Catherine: both became active with the Sustainability Committee, bringing food and compost to and from Zuccotti Park by bike. Such gestures are part of a movement toward common preservation.

Source: Photo by Brennan Cavanaugh

While some have described this space as an image of a post-apocalyptic city, others imaged it as a vast generator of ideas. The dynamic element of the movement is that it is an experiment in democracy and ideas, thinking, creating, and trial and error. This feeling of trying to create something from new is both fascinating and vexing; it can be completely encouraging and frustrating, simultaneously. But this spirit of innovation is part of what is charging the movement. It is the light pushing this forward.

Keegan explained why he decided to collaborate with the Sustainability Committee to make the energy bikes. He had had one in his kitchen for a number of years prior.

The aim was to make the movement more sustainable. So we could create our own energy, not relying on the grid. We were not relying on gas generators. Not breaking laws. It made us more environmentally sustainable. The idea of sustainability is part of the movement. To be conscious of how we were using energy—to create an intentional community in which we consider our actions; we didn't want to fall back on old habits, didn't want to be using gas, a replicable society. A lot of people said we could not do it. But on a small scale we did it. All of us were involved in bringing bike power to Occupy Wall Street. The Sustainability Committee was formed by Laura Muniss and Brennan [Cavanaugh] and I supporting her. One of the first things we realized was we needed to get OWS off fossil fuels. If we were going to be reimagining what society should look like, we needed to get off those gas generators. I had the solution in my living room, this bike power generator. We proposed it to the General Assembly. We brought one bike in. Brennan and I rode it in.

Then other committees wanted one. The kitchen, media, library, they all asked for one. "George, who has been involved in the Sustainability Committee, did an energy map of the park." People immediately responded positively to the bike power generators. Everyone who rides seemed to appreciate the idea of doing this. The idea was attractive

Top left: Time's Up! OWS sustainability group speed bomb ride 2012. *Bottom and top right:* Free food, pedal power, mutual exchange, and energy bikes at ABC No Rio in the Lower East Side and the Times Up! space in Williamsburg, using the lessons of Occupy and local organizing for storm relief. Social organizing propelled the effort.

Source: Photos by Brennan Cavanaugh

for a number of reasons, primarily because it is replicable. "People can do this all over the world. We were running a huge media center on a bike generator. We need to get the bike generators fine-tuned so we can bring them into other occupations. It's about setting up an intentional community to create a new community that everyone can latch onto."

Not surprisingly, the bikes were confiscated during the raid in the early morning of November 15, and Keegan was arrested trying to get through the police lines to get to the bikes. Over the next two days, members of Time's Up! recovered 12 of the 14 stands and generators confiscated by police from the police precinct. Two days later, those deep cell batteries, just retrieved from NY Sanitation after the raid, helped project a movement signals off the Verizon building. By 2013, the NYPD would pay Time's Up! $8,500 for damages to the generators (Seifman, 2013).

Rejecting Scarcity in Favor of Economic Democracy

In the years before Occupy was born, many argued the expanding gap between the fate of the affluent 1% and the 99% was fundamentally unfair. In 2010, for example, 93% of the new income created in the United States went to the top 1% of taxpayers, an 11.6% increase from the previous year. That same year, 37% of additional earnings went to the top 0.01%, those super-rich holding an average $23.8 million. They saw their income increase by over 21.5%. The other 99% received an increase of $80.00 a year. Conversely, the top 1%, those with over a million in average income, enjoyed an 11.6% increase in income (Rattner, 2012). With income inequality expanding, critics suggested this system was built around a fundamentally flawed model of accumulation, noting that capitalist profit stems from the ability of those in control of the means of production to "extract surplus labor from workers" (Panayotakis, 2011, p. 18). "Allowing this disparity to continue is both bad economic policy and bad social policy," argues Steven Rattner (2012). "We owe those at the bottom a fairer shot at moving up."

Many others have challenged a politics of scarcity. Autonomous movements, such as the Zapatistas in Mexico, worked to create "liberated spaces and parallel institutions based on direct democracy and the rejection of both consumerism and the colonization of people's everyday life by the logic of capital," notes Costas Panayotakis, (2011, p. 135). For those involved, the revolution is already occurring in their experiments in living. In 2003, in Argentina, for example, workers transformed nearly 200 bankrupt factories, becoming stockholders and managers, sharing administrative responsibilities and profits. While critics remain skeptical of the viability of such models, those such as economist Elinor Ostrom, who won the 2009 Nobel Prize in Economics for her research on economic governance of the commons, suggest such models deserve serious consideration. Ostrom has demonstrated how common property can be successfully managed by user associations. Challenging the conventional wisdom that common property is poorly managed and should be either regulated by central authorities or privatized, Ostrom (1990, 1992) argues that such projects are creating innovative forms of social organization with successful outcomes.

Through economic democracy people gain voices over the way the economy works, what it produces, for whom, and for how much. Here, regular people help shape sustainable and humane models of post-capitalist living, "creat[ing] a different kind of human subject," Panayotakis (2011, p. 151) continues. The aim is to balance planning, policy, and markets, combining democratic governance and the benefits of public ownership of some means of production. Such models of economic democracy steer clear of the authoritarian failures of Stalinism. We already see them taking shape in places such as Brazil where citizens have been able to take control of the means of production of certain health-care services and medications, while making health care accessible to all. Such a system favors the needs of people rather than profits.

Struggles against scarcity take place at a time when activists the world over are discussing alternatives to the state response to political crisis. Here in New York, groups such as the Union of Radical Political Economists and even those in the socially

responsible business sector have come to embrace Occupy Wall Street (OWS) (Quick, 2011). In the early days of the movement, philosophers such as Judith Butler and Cornell West came to talk to organizers. Many recognized the fundamental unfairness of the attack on the working class taking place under the auspices of scarcity. Slovenian philosopher Slavoj Zizeck came, making the simple point that we can dream about the earth being destroyed all the time in movies, but rarely do we imagine living in worlds outside of capitalism. OWS offered fuel for that imagining.

The point is that, hopefully, community movements can help create more sustainable models of economic democracy that offer less collateral damage than our current, unsustainable system (Harvey, 2010). Such community building helps us reimagine what economic democracy might look like, reminding us there is another storyline for the politics of scarcity. Here, urban living involves models with nonpolluting transportation, community banks and gardens, local foods, less global warming, and by extension less-toxic models of capitalism. Struggles for economic fairness are tied to a common struggle for something better in the here and now. Humans have been in a slow dance toward suicide for thousands of years. But

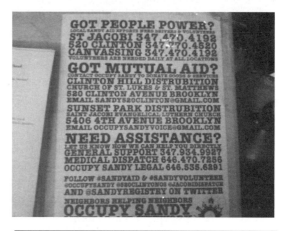

Occupy Wall Street morphed into Occupy Sandy after the storm.

Source: Photos by author

they have also done everything they can do to create communities and solutions that help build spaces for resistance, preservation, and pleasure. Eros versus Thanatos—it is a delicate dance (Shepard, 2009). Through common preservation we trace an alternate set of steps aimed toward a space where it's hoped we can all live together and create something more sustainable and humane (Brecher, 2012).

Zapatismo From Oaxaca to the Bronx

As the discussion of Occupy suggests, for decades activists have challenged the social and economic implications of neoliberalism. The race to the bottom, as capital chases the cheapest wages, goods, and services across borders and trade blocs, has robbed local communities of distinct characteristics, autonomous spaces, and sovereignty around the world. George Ritzer (1993) calls it the McDonaldization of the globe. Yet, activists the world over have come to offer a counter-narrative, a cry that another world is possible, heard from a convergence of movements and World Social Forums from Brazil to Barcelona. Many movements have found their identity within this open space, where ideas, counter-proposals, and narratives of resistance intermingle. Some of these include the Zapatistas' "one No and a thousand Yeses," and even the 1970s anti-IMF bread riots in Egypt over increases in the prices of bread. Many struggles intersect in this cry against the austerity programs of neoliberalism. "[I]t is primarily a political, social, and economic system characterized by the privatization of public services, deregulation of industry, lowering of trade barriers, and reduced public spending on social services," writes Heather Gautney (2010, p. 1). "Its underlying ethos reflects a view of human freedom as best realized through free market activity, unregulated competition, and private property rights protected by the neoliberal state" (p. 1). "Neoliberalism refers to an ideology that advocates expanding global free trade and competition and withdrawing the state from regulating economic activity; the result is the deregulation of basic living standards among the poor and working class," notes Immanuel Ness (2005, p. 2).

While neoliberal institutions, such as the World Bank, International Monetary Fund, and World Trade Organization have extended the system around the globe, the process has not been without bumps, tear gas, riots, street parties, protests, blockades, and literally billions spent to secure most every meeting of these institutions, while wiping away signs of dissent (Seifman, 2013). Opposition has expanded into a growing number of social forces and movements, taking on distinct and often unique forms. Perhaps the most influential of these groups is the Zapatistas from Chiapas, Mexico. As Naomi Klein writes, "the strategic victory of the Zapatistas was to insist that what was going on in Chiapas could not be written off as a narrow 'ethnic' or 'local' struggle—that it was universal. They did this by identifying their issue not only as the Mexican state but as 'neoliberalism.'" Others describe the Zapatistas as an "informational guerrilla movement" (Gautney, 2010 p. 40). Linking the power of the Internet with an iconic conflict, this group rescaled a local struggle in transnational terms, channeling the global sentiment to challenge neoliberalism into a movement of movements, linking activism across borders, between a vast cross-section of struggles (p. 40).

For San Francisco organizer David Solnit, Zapatismo helped him reimagine what activism could mean as a theory and practice. "I had done single-issue organizing from 1980 to the early 1990s, and had dropped out for a year. Partly I was just tired of single-issue organizing, even mass direct action organizing. And I believe in direct action." The challenge was simple: "We all knew that the problems were systemic." But the old tactics were not up to the task. "We also felt like our tactics and our forms of resistance and communication were very stale," he explains. With Zapatismo, he found a new model. "[I]t was qualitatively different from the Sandinistas and the FMLN," Solnit recalls. "[The Zapatistas] were talking about poetry. And they were not trying to take power. Their strategy was probably more theater than military strategy. A lot of us were quite inspired." Zapatismo was a breath of fresh air. Here was a way to open up lots of different storylines. "There was a merging of intelligence," Solnit explains. "People involved in social movements around the world were looking for new ways to change the world because the old ones weren't working." With the end of the Cold War, the old ways of organizing were wiped away, creating a new kind of movement story. "The final blow that kind of freed that space up was the collapse of the Soviet Union," he continues. "The miserably failed model of the left finally fell in on itself. And that freed a lot of us up." With Zapatismo, a different kind of a left story filled this void. "When Margaret Thatcher said 'there is no alternative,' the Zapatistas said 'Ya Basta.' Here's a story of a different way to change the world," Solnit explains.

The Zapatistas helped the world see there are alternatives (Gautney, 2010). And supporters the world over came to see the Zapatista struggle as a struggle for life and health for the poor (Farmer, 2005). They came to see these were people with stories and hopes. There are other ways to organize, tell stories, and live lives. During an interview at a film festival, Subcomandante Marcos was asked why the Zapatistas rebelled. He answered that he dreamed of a day where it would be possible to live a different cinema program every day. The Zapatistas rebelled because they had been forced to watch the

Zapatismo in New York, mural at 117th and 2nd.

Source: Photo by Craig Hughes

same film for the past five hundred years, to live an existence where mere survival trumped truly living (Shukaitis, 2009 p. 49).

While the struggle is anything but simple or easy, there is room for agency. Identifying simple issues and organizing around them, Occupy Movements and Zapatistas helped remind us that we are not passive spectators of history. There are other ways of living. It is up to us to re-create them. Everyone has a chance to take part in this story.

Postscript

Concluding Notes on Friendships, Social Networks, and Social Change

Through the three sections of this work, we have traced a story of direct action: from theory to practice in the first two sections, and praxis in the final section. Throughout these chapters we explored a seven-stage schema of organizing, moving from identification of an issue through research, mobilization, action, legal strategies, cultural activism, and efforts aimed at sustainability and fun. Part II outlined the workings and practice of this model, and the programs and movements profiled in Part III traced this schema through steps from direct action to direct practice. We witnessed ways different groups laid out an issue—housing or neoliberal economics—and organized around it. Some worked through the Internet. Others started organizations. Yet, everyone started organizing.

Cyclists celebrate a community of their own invention at Critical Mass Bike Summer 2003.

Source: Photo provided with permission by Peter Meitzler, Copyright © 2003–2014

Exploring best practices in organizing case studies, Part III also laid out a few basic questions about organizational development. Should groups form organizations that run the risk of becoming uncaring bureaucratic structures themselves, or should they follow a decentralized model of organizing without organizations, more dependent upon nodes than of formal structures (Shirky, 2008)? For some, organizing is most vital as a source of resistance culture, while others see resistance as a formal mechanism in need of clear goals and outcomes. Both are legitimate forms of community practice. They are both ways to organize to create a better world.

Most of the organizers who shared their stories in this text are friends of mine. They are people I have known from the streets, courts, and jails of New York and around the country. When we see each other, we share a smile or a recollection or insight about what is going on out there. Through our friendship, I have witnessed the gestures of kindness and mutual aid from direct action to direct services described throughout this book. It is through these networks of friends and comrades we come to see a world of interconnection between *we's*, not *me's*. Through them, we beat back alienation, survive, and thrive. If this text suggests anything, it is that caring actions—be it corking a street on a bike ride or sharing a smile, planting a garden with kids, a song or a meal with others—these gestures are the first step in building a better world in the here and now. These are also the first steps in exiting from individual to collective experience. These connections are born between individuals connecting with groups and communities.

Much of organizing begins through this process, between networks and relationships (Juris, 2007, 2008; Shirky, 2008). "I heard about it from a friend" is a consistent response to questions about how people got involved in organizing efforts (O'Donnell, Ferreira, Hurtado, & Floyd, 1998, p. 143). Friendships make us feel more comfortable about leaving our individual worlds and connecting with broader social worlds. It is easier for people to get started if, as a new participant, they "know someone at the meetings" (p. 143). Such contacts can also be positive outcomes in themselves: "I made good friends. I can say that. I made good friends here," one organizer explained (p. 147). At their core, these friendships involve the nexus between private and public spheres, between individual and community issues (Nardi, 1999). This is part of a long organizing tradition. In 1970, community organizer Si Kahn wrote, "In some ways, the organizer's main job in the community in the early stages of organizing is simply to make friends with the people there. That these friendships are also essential to the work of organizing the community does not mean that they are any less real" (Kahn, 1970, p. 26). Through such ties, activists transform the workings of everyday life (Boyd, 2003; Shepard, 2015).

Sunset on the world naked bike ride New York City 2013. Riders making their way through the evening sunset after a joyous day of social action and community building.

Source: Photo by author

These friendships are part and parcel of the resources necessary to challenge the system. "Also, if you do it right, it is a place where you actually intersect with another person and you can create space where you actually start to build friendships," notes Mark Andersen. "And hopefully reasonably equal friendships ultimately across these bounds, and that helps to advance the search for justice, the broader community empowerment and transformation. . . . People have to survive day to day. Without that they ain't there for any revolution." The history of social movements is full of stories of friendships propelling innovations. After all, changing the world should and can be a joyous endeavor (Kahn, 1970). This is what these stories are all about, as they propel a project understood as social organizing. Finishing this book, hopefully you can add your chapter to the history of community organizing.

References

Abramovitz, M. (1998). Social work and social reform: An arena of struggle. *Social Work, 43*(6), 501–509.

Abramovitz, M. (1999). *Regulating the lives of women*. Boston, MA: South End Press.

Abramovitz, M. (2000). *Under attack, fighting back*. New York, NY: Monthly Review Press.

Abron, J. M. (1998). "Serving the people": The survival programs of the Black Panther Party. In C. E. Jones (Ed.), *The Black Panther Party reconsidered*. Baltimore, MD: Black Classic Press. Retrieved from http://www.mindfully.org/Reform/BPP-Serving-The-People1998.htm

Abu-Lughod, J. (Ed.). (1994). *From urban village to East Village: The battle for New York's Lower East Side*. Cambridge, MA: Blackwell.

Ackelsberg, M. (2001). *Free women of Spain: Anarchism and the struggle for the emancipation of women*. Bloomington: Indiana University Press.

Ackerman, P., & DuVall, J. (2001). *A force more powerful: A century of non-violent conflict*. New York, NY: St. Martin's.

ACT UP civil disobedience manual. (n.d.). *ACT UP civil disobedience manual*. Retrieved from http://www.actupny.org/documents/CDdocuments/CDindex.html

Addams, J. (1910). *Twenty years at Hull-House*. Retrieved from http://digital.library.upenn.edu/women/addams/hullhouse/hullhouse.html

Adler, M. (2011). Young, gay and homeless: Fighting for resources. *NPR*. Retrieved from http://www.npr.org/2011/11/20/142364493/young-gay-and-homeless-fighting-for-resources

Adorno, T., Frenkel-Brunswik, E., Levinson, D. J., & Sanford, R. N. (1993). *The authoritarian personality* (Abridged ed.). New York, NY: W. W. Norton. (Original work published 1964)

Aidala, A., & Lee, G. (2000). *Housing services and housing stability among persons living with HIV/AIDS* (Community Health Advisory & Information Network Update Report No. 32). New York, NY: Columbia University School of Public Health.

Alerman, B., Collins, K. V., & Jewell, J. R. (2011, June 10). *Community organizing is NOT a radical practice but integrative practice!* A paper presented at the Social Welfare Action Alliance Meetings, Catholic University, Washington, DC.

Alexander, M. (2010). *The new Jim Crow: Mass incarceration in the era of colorblindness*. New York, NY: New Press.

Alinsky, S. (1969). *Rules for radicals*. New York, NY: Vintage Books.

amfAR. (2010). *amfAR annual report 2009*. Retrieved from http://ar.amfar.org/annualreport2009.pdf

Antebi, N., Dickey, C., & Herbst, R. (2007). *Failure! Experiments in aesthetic and social practices*. Los Angeles, CA; Journal of Aesthetics and Protest Press.

Arenson, K. W. (2003, June 10). From welfare to (course) work; students on benefits help write their own rights. *New York Times*. Retrieved from http://www.nytimes.com/2003/06/10/nyregion/from-welfare-to-course-work-students-on-benefits-help-write-their-own-rights.html

Aronowitz, S. (1992). *False promises.* Durham, NC: Duke University Press. (Original work published 1974)

Ayers, B. (2001). *Fugitive days.* Boston, MA: Beacon Press.

Bailey, R., & Brake, M. (1975). *Radical social work.* New York, NY: Pantheon.

Bakhtin, M. (1981). *The dialogic imagination: Four essays.* Austin: University of Texas Press.

Banks, S. (2003). The concept of community practice. In S. Banks, H. Butcher, P. Henderson, & J. Robertson (Eds.), *Managing community practice* (pp. 9–22). Bristol, UK: Policy Press.

Bennet, D. (2009, October 11). The upside of "down with" protesters' secret: They're out there because it makes them happier. *Boston Globe.* Retrieved from http://www.boston.com/bostonglobe/ideas/articles/2009/10/11/protesters_secret_theyre_out_there_because_it_makes_them_happier/

Bennett, J. (1981). *Oral history and delinquency.* Chicago, IL: University of Chicago Press.

Berkowitz, R. (2003). *Stayin' alive: The invention of safe sex, a personal history.* Boulder, CO: Westview Press/Perseus Books.

Berube, A. (2001). How gay stays White. In B. Rasmussen, I. Nexica, & E. Klingenberg (Eds.), *The making and unmaking of Whiteness* (pp. 234–265). Durham, NC: Duke University Press.

Bey, H. (2003). *Immediatism.* Retrieved from http://www.sterneck.net/musik/bey-immediatism/index.php

BikeBlogNYC. (2008, December 17). Time's Up demands end to police harassment [Web log post]. Retrieved from http://www.bikeblognyc.com/2008/12/times-up-demands-end-to-police-harassment/

BMP (BuildingMovementProject). (2006*). Social service and social change: A process guide.* Retrieved from http://www.buildingmovement.org/pdf/ProcessGuide.pdf

Bogad, L. M. (2003). Facial insufficiency: Political street performance in New York City and the selective enforcement of the 1845 mask law. *TDR: The Drama Review, 47*(4), 75–84.

Bogad, L. M. (2005). *Electoral guerrilla theatre: Radical ridicule and social movements.* New York, NY: Routledge.

Borden, W. (2009*). Contemporary psychoanalytic theory and practice.* Chicago, IL: Lyceum Books.

Bordowitz, B. (2002, December 17). Interview for ACT UP Oral History Project. Retrieved from http://www.actuporalhistory.org/interviews/interviews_01.html#bordowitz

Boyd, N. A. (2003). *Wide open town: A history of queer San Francisco.* Berkeley: University of California Press.

Braine, N. (Panelist). (2010, September 21). *Harm reduction, health care, and public health: Barriers and possibilities.* Panel conducted at City Tech/CUNY, New York, NY.

Brake, M., & Baily, R. (Eds.). (1980). *Radical social work practice.* London, UK: Arnold.

Bravo, B. (2007). *Solutionary women: Have fun do good.* Retrieved from http://havefundogood.blogspot.com/2007/06/solutionary-women-alli-chagi-starr.html

Brecher, J. (2012). *Save the humans: Common preservation in action.* Boulder, CO: Paradigm.

Brecher, J., Costello, T., & Smith, B. (2000). *Globalization from below: The power of solidarity.* Cambridge, MA: South End Press.

Bronski, M. (2009, June). STONEWALL was a riot. *The Guide.* Retrieved from http://theragblog.blogspot.com/2009/06/stonewall-was-riot-gay-liberation-and.html

Brooks, F. (2005). Resolving the dilemma between organizing and services: Los Angeles ACORN. *Social Work, 50*(3), 262–269.

Buber, M. (1970). *I and thou* (Trans. Walter Kauffman). New York, NY: Simon & Schuster.

Buffett, P. (2013, July 26). The charitable-industrial complex. *New York Times.* Retrieved from http://www.nytimes.com/2013/07/27/opinion/the-charitable-industrial-complex.html

Bulmer, M. (1986). *The Chicago school of sociology.* Chicago, IL: University of Chicago Press.

Burghardt, S. (1982). *The other side of organizing: Resolving personal dilemmas and political demands of daily practice.* Cambridge, MA: Schenkman.

Burns, J. F. (2011, August 11).British Prime Minister faces questioning in House of Commons over rioting. *New York Times,* p. A4. Retrieved from http://www.nytimes.com/2011/08/12/world/europe/12cameron.html?pagewanted=all&_r=0

California Newsreel (Producer). (2008). *Unnatural causes: Is inequality making us sick?* [DVD documentary series]. Retrieved from http://www.unnaturalcauses.org/

Carlson, C. (2008). *Nowtopia.* Oakland, CA: AK Press.

Carter, D. (2004). *Stonewall.* New York, NY: St. Martin's.

Castells, M. (2007). Communication, power and counter-power in the network society. *International Journal of Communication 1*(2007), 238–266. Retrieved from http://ijoc.org/index.php/ijoc/issue/view/1#more1

Centers for Disease Control. (2014). HIV among African Americans. http://www.cdc.gov/hiv/risk/racialethnic/aa/facts/index.html

Chambers, E. (2003). *Roots for radicals: Organizing for power, action, and justice.* New York, NY: Continuum.

Chayko, M. (2008). *Portable communities: The social dynamics of online and mobile connectedness.* Albany: State University Press of New York Press.

Chivers, C. J., & Forero, J. (2000, May 24). City to ask immediate suspension of bus line after fatality. *New York Times.* Retrieved from http://www.nytimes.com/2000/05/24/nyregion/city-to-ask-immediate-suspension-of-bus-line-after-fatality.html?pagewanted=print&src=pm

CIVICUS, AIVE, & UNV. (2008). Volunteering and social activism: Pathways for participation in human development. *World Volunteer Web.* Retrieved from http://www.worldvolunteerweb.org/resources/research-reports/global/doc/volunteering-and-social-activism.html

Clark, K. (1963). *Prejudice and your child* (2nd ed.). Boston, MA: Beacon Press.

Clear, A. (2009, January 17). Obama's fix: Syringe exchange is a major component. *Huffington Post.* Retrieved from http://www.huffingtonpost.com/allan-clear/obamas-hiv-fix-syringe-ex_b_158799.html

Clemens, E. (1993). Organizational repertoires and institutional change. *American Journal of Sociology, 98*(4), 755–798.

Clemens, E. (1997). *The people's lobby.* Chicago, IL: University of Chicago Press.

Clover, J. (2005, November 16–22). The mirror sage. *Village Voice,* p. 36.

Cloward, R., & Epstein, I. (1967). Private social welfare's disengagement from the poor: The case of family adjustment agencies. In G. Brager & F. Purcell (Eds.), *Community action against poverty* (pp. 40–63). New Haven, CT: College and University Press.

Cloward, R., & Piven, F. F. (1975). Notes toward a radical social work. In R. Bailey & M. Brake (Eds.), *Radical social work* (pp. vi–xvii). New York, NY: Pantheon.

Cloward, R., & Piven, F. F. (1977, January/February). The acquiescence of social work. *Society, 14*(2), 55–63.

Cohen, C. (1999). *The boundaries of Blackness.* Chicago, IL: University of Chicago Press.

Cohler, B. J. (2004). Saturday night at the tubs: Age cohort and the social life at the urban bath. In G. Herdt & B. de Vries (Eds.), *Gay and lesbian aging: Research and future directions.* New York, NY: Springer.

Colangelo, L. L., & Ingrassia, R. (2000, May 24). City votes bus shutdown, roadblock eyed after fatality. *New York Daily News.* Retrieved from http://articles.nydailynews.com/2000-05-24/news/18131381_1_bus-driver-license-new-york-apple-tours

Collins, C., Alagiri, P., & Summers, T. (2002). *Abstinence-only vs. comprehensive sex education: What are the arguments? What is the evidence?* San Francisco: University of California, AIDS Research Institute.

Cooper, M. (2002, May 18). What's the ostrich for? Politics; budget protests use street theater and star powers. *New York Times,* p. B1.

Couto, R. A. (1993). Narrative, free space and political leadership in social movements. *Journal of Politics, 55*(1), 57–79.

Cowger, C. (1994). Assessing client strengths: Clinical assessment for client empowerment. *Social Work, 39*(3), 262–268.

Crass, C. (2002). Tools for White guys who are working for social change. In M. Prokasch & L. Raymond (Eds.), *The global activist's manual* (pp. 96–97). New York, NY: Nation Books.

Critchley, S. (2007). *Infinitely demanding: Ethics of commitment, politics of resistance.* New York, NY: Verso.

Crimp, D. (2002). *Melancholia and moralism: Essays on AIDS and queer politics.* Cambridge, MA: MIT Press.

Crow, S. (2011). *Black flags and windmills: Hope, anarchy and the Common Ground Collective.* Oakland, CA: PM Press.

Cylar, K. (2002). Building a caring community from ACT UP to Housing Works: An interview with Keith Cylar by Benjamin Shepard. In B. Shepard & R. Hayduk (Eds.), *From ACT UP to the WTO: Urban protest and community building in the era of globalization.* New York, NY: Verso.

D'Ambrosio, A. (2004). *Let fury have the hour: The punk rock politics of Joe Strummer.* New York, NY. Nation Books.

Danto, E. (2005). *Freud's free clinics: Psychoanalysis and social justice.* New York, NY: Columbia University Press.

Davey, J. (1995). *The new social contract: America's journey from welfare state to police state.* Westport, CT: Praeger.

Davids, J. (2007, April 5). What Larry didn't tell you. *Gay City News.*

Davis, J. (2002). This is what bureaucracy looks like. In E. Yuen, G. Katsiaficas, & D. B. Rose (Eds.), *The battle of Seattle: The new challenge to capitalist globalization* (pp. 175–182). New York, NY: Soft Skull Press.

Davis, M. (1992). *City of quartz.* New York, NY: Vintage Books.

DeCarlo, P., Susser, E., & Peterson, T. J. (1996). What are homeless people's HIV prevention needs? *SpareSomeChange.com.* Retrieved from http://www.sparesomechange.com/search/engine/read-aloud.asp?id=697

Deegan, M. J. (1990). *Jane Addams and the men of the Chicago school, 1892–1918.* New Brunswick, NJ: Transaction Press.

Delgato, M. (1999). *Social work practice in nontraditional settings.* New York, NY: Oxford University Press.

D'Emilio, J. (1983). *Sexual politics, sexual communities: The making of a homosexual minority in the United States, 1940–1970.* Chicago, IL: University of Chicago Press.

D'Emilio, J. (2004). *The lost prophet.* Chicago, IL: University of Chicago Press.

Denning, P. (2004). *Practicing harm reduction psychotherapy: An alternative approach to addictions.* New York, NY: Guilford Press.

Des Jarlais, D., Marmor, M., Paone, D., Titus, S., Shi, Q., Perlis, T. . . . Friedman, S. R. (1996). HIV incidence among injection users in New York City syringe exchange programmes. *The Lancet, 348*(9033), 987–991.

Dolgan, C., & Baker, C. (2010). *Social problems: A service learning approach.* Thousand Oaks, CA: Pine Forge Press.

Dolgan, C., & Chayko, M. (2010). *Pioneers of public sociology: Thirty years of humanity and society.* Cornwall-on-Hudson, NY: Sloan Publishing.

Douglas, E. (2007, April 3). ACT UP's new urgency. *The Nation.* Retrieved from http://www.thenation.com/doc/20070416/douglas

Dreir, P., & Atlas, J. (2008, September 22). GOP mocks public service. *The Nation.* Retrieved from http://www.thenation.com/doc/20080922/dreier_atlas

Duncomebe, S. (n.d.). *Notes on punk.* Unpublished manuscript. New York University, Gallatin School.

Duncombe, S. (1997). *Notes from the underground: Zines and the politics of underground culture.* New York: Verso.

Duncombe, S. (2002a). *Cultural resistance: A reader.* New York: Verso.

Duncombe, S. (2002b). Stepping off the sidewalk. In B. Shepard & R. Hayduk, (Eds.), *From ACT UP to the WTO: Urban protest and community building in the era of globalization* (pp. 202–214). New York: Verso.

Duncombe, S. (2003). The poverty of theory: Anti-intellectualism and the value of action. *Radical Society, 30*(1), 11–17.

Duncombe, S. (2007). *Dream: Re-imagining progressive politics in an age of fantasy.* New York, NY: The New Press.

Duncombe, S., & Tremblay, M. (2011). *White riot: Punk rock and the politics of race.* New York, NY: Verso.

Dunier, M. (1993). *Slim's table.* Chicago, IL: University of Chicago Press.

Dwyer, J. (2005a, April 12). Videos challenge accounts of convention arrest. *New York Times.* Retrieved from http://www.nytimes.com/2005/04/12/nyregion/12video.html?_r=0

Dwyer, J. (2005b, May 27). City to pay AIDS group in settlement. *New York Times.* Retrieved from http://www.nytimes.com/2005/05/27/nyregion/27settlement.html

Dwyer, J. (2008a, July 30). When official truth collides with cheap digital technology. *New York Times.* Retrieved from http://www.nytimes.com/2008/07/30/nyregion/30about.html

Dwyer, J. (2008b, August 20). One protest, 52 arrests and a $2 million payout. *New York Times,* p. B1.

Echols, A. (1990). *Daring to be bad: Radical feminism in America, 1967–1975.* Minneapolis: University of Minnesota Press.

Edroso, R. (2010, January 5). 10 arrested at protest over detention of immigration reform advocate [Web log post]. *Village Voice Blog.* Retrieved from http://blogs.villagevoice.com/runninscared/archives/2010/01/10_arrested_at_1.php

Edsall, T. (2012). *How scarcity will remake American politics.* New York, NY: Doubleday.

Effrat, M. P. (1974). *The community approaches and applications.* New York, NY: Free Press.

Ehrenreich, B. (2007). *Dancing in the streets: A history or collective joy.* New York, NY: Metropolitan Books.

Ehrenreich, J. (1985). *The altruistic imagination: A history of social work and social policy in the United States.* Ithaca, NY: Cornell University Press.

Ehrlich, T. (2000). Civic engagement. *Measuring Up 2000: The state-by-state report card for higher education.* Retrieved from http://www.carnegiefoundation.org/elibrary/civic-engagement-measuring-2000-state-state-report-card-higher-education

Eigo, J. (2002). The city as body politic/the body as city unto itself. In B. Shepard & R Hayduk (Eds.), *From ACT UP to the WTO: Urban protest and community building in the era of globalization* (pp. 178–195). New York, NY: Verso.

Eigo, J. (2012). ACT UP alumni post [Facebook page]. Retrieved from https://www.facebook.com/groups/ACTUPNYAlumni/

Elgear, S., & Hutt, R. (1991). *Voices from the front.* San Francisco, CA: Frameline.

Eligon, J. (2010, April 29). Ex-officer convicted of lying about confrontation with cyclist. *New York Times.* Retrieved from http://www.nytimes.com/2010/04/30/nyregion/30pogan.html

Elliot, E. (1990). Afterword. In *The Jungle* by Upton Sinclair. New York, NY: New American Library.

Elovich, R. (n.d.). I'll hold your story, I'll be your mirror. *Symposium.* Retrieved from http://www.artistswithaids.org/artery/symposium/symposium_elovich.html

Elovich, R. (2002). *Harm reduction training.* New York, NY: Harm Reduction Coalition.

Elovich, R. (2007, May 14). Sarah Schulman interview with Richard Elovich. *ACT UP Oral History Project.* Retrieved from http://www.actuporalhistory.org/interviews/images/elovich.pdf

Elshtain, J. B. (2001). *Jane Addams and the dream of American democracy*. New York, NY: Basic Books.

Epstein, B. (1991). *Political protest and cultural revolution*. Berkeley: University of California Press.

Epstein, B. (2001). What happened to the women's movement? *Monthly Review, 53*(1).

Epstein, D., Lemire, J., & Becker, M. (2004, August 27). Nude and rude. We'll being seeing a lot (maybe not this much!) of protesters. *New York Daily News*, p. 1.

Epstein, I. (1975). The politics of behaviour therapy: The new cool-out casework? In H. Jones (Ed.), *Towards a new social work* (pp. 138–150). London, UK: Routledge & Kegan Paul.

Epstein, S. (1996). *Impure science: AIDS, activism, and the politics of knowledge*. Berkeley: University of California Press.

Errico Malatesta, Italian anarchist. (n.d.). In *The anarchist encyclopedia*. Retrieved from http://recollectionbooks.com/bleed/Encyclopedia/MalatestaErrico.htm

Fanon, F. (1984). *A dying colonialism*. New York, NY: Grove Press.

Farmer, P. (2005). *Pathologies of power: Health, human rights and the new war on the poor*. Berkeley: University of California Press.

Favaro, J. (Panelist). (2008, April 12). *Anti-authoritarian mutual aid and radical social work: From direct action to direct services*. Panel conducted at the New York City Anarchist Bookfair, New York, NY.

Favaro, J. (2010, September 9). WHCP in amfAR annual report. Email.

Feldman, A. (1998). Ethnographic evaluation of SRO harm reduction outreach of the Center for AIDS Outreach and Prevention. Manuscript prepared for the National Development and Research Institutes Inc., New York, NY.

Ferguson, I., & Woodward, R. (2009). *Radical social work in practice: Making a difference*. Bristol, UK: Policy Press.

Fernandez, L. (2008). *Policing dissent: Social control and the anti-globalization movement*. New Brunswick, NJ: Rutgers University Press.

Fernandez, L. (2009). On being there: Thoughts on anarchism and participatory observation. In R. Amster, A. DeLeon, L. Fernandez, A. J. Nocella II, & D. Shannon (Eds.), *Contemporary anarchist studies: An introductory anthology of anarchy in the academy* (pp. 93–192). New York, NY: Routledge.

Fernandez, L. (2012). Luis Fernandez, the "accidental criminologist." *Outcomes* [Researcher Profile at NAU]. Retrieved from https://www.research.nau.edu/newsletter/fall2010/fernandez.aspx

Ferrell, J. (2001). *Tearing down the streets*. New York, NY: Palgrave/St. Martin's.

Ferrell, J. (2006). *Empire of scourge*. New York, NY: New York University Press.

Fine, G. A. (1995). Public narration and group culture: Discerning discourse in social movements. In H. Johnson & B. Klandermans (Eds.), *Social movements and culture*. Minneapolis: University of Minnesota Press.

Finkelstein, M. (2005). *With no direction home: Homeless youth on the road and in the streets*. Belmont, CA: Wadsworth.

Fiscal Policy Institute. (2010). *Grow together or pull further apart: Income concentration trends in New York*. Retrieved from http://www.fiscalpolicy.org/FPI_GrowTogetherOrPullFurtherApart_20101213.pdf

Fish, J. H. (1973). *Black power/White control: The struggle of the Woodlawn Organization in Chicago*. Princeton, NJ: Princeton University Press.

Fish, J. H. (2005). The Woodlawn Organization. In *The encyclopedia of Chicago*. Accessed from http://www.encyclopedia.chicagohistory.org/pages/1377.html

Fisher, R. (1994). *Let the people decide*. New York, NY: Twayne Publishers.

Fitch, J. (1940, July). The nature of social action. *The Survey*, 28–220.

Flyvbjerg, B. (2001). *Making social science matter*. Cambridge, UK: Cambridge University Press.

Foucault, M. (1985). *The use of pleasure: History of sexuality* (Vol. 2). New York, NY: Random House.

Foucault, M. (2006). *History of madness.* New York, NY: Routledge.

Fraser, N. (1989). *Unruly practices: Power, discourse and gender in contemporary social theory.* Minneapolis: University of Minnesota Press.

Freeman, R. B. (1999). *The new inequality.* Boston, MA: Beacon Press.

Freeman, S. (2009, October 19). The Rev. Luis Barrios, Episcopal Minister: Civil disobedience practiced from the pulpit, the podium, and the jailhouse. *New York Times.* Retrieved from http://www.throughyourbody.com/the-rev-luis-barrios-episcopal-minister-civil-disobedience-practised-from-the-pulpit-the-podium-the-jailhouse/

Freire, P. (2000). *Pedagogy of the oppressed* (30th anniversary ed.). New York, NY: Continuum International Publishing.

Friedus, N., & McDowell, C. (n.d.). Narrative and community building [Class syllabus]. Retrieved from http://comm-org.wisc.edu/syllabi/freidus.htm

Gallagher, B., & Wilson, A. (2005). Sex and the politics of identity: An interview with Michel Foucault. In M. Thompson (Ed.), *Gay spirit: Myth and meaning.* Maple, NJ: Lethe Press. (Original work published 1987)

Galper, J. (1980). *Social work practice: A radical perspective.* Englewood Cliffs, NJ: Prentice Hall.

Garland, D. (2001). *The culture of control.* Chicago, IL: University of Chicago Press.

Gautney, H. (2010). *Protest and organization in the alternative globalization era: NGOs, social movements, and political parties.* New York, NY: Palgrave Macmillan.

Gay Shame. (n.d.). *How to start a non-hierarchical direct action group.* Retrieved March 17, 2014, from http://www.gayshamesf.org/index2.html

Gilbert, M. (Ed.). (2005a). *Anarchists in social work–Known to the authorities* (2nd ed.). Ulverston, UK: Author.

Gilbert, M. (2005b). *Known to the authorities: Anarchists in social work.* Retrieved from http://anarchistsinsocialwork.org.uk/index.php

Gitterman, A., & Schulman, L. (Eds.). (2005). *Mutual aid groups, vulnerable and resilient populations, and the life cycle.* New York, NY: Columbia University Press.

Glissen, S. (2000). *"Neither bedecked nor bebosomed": Lucy Randolph Mason, Ella Baker and women's leadership and organizing in the struggle for freedom* (Unpublished doctoral dissertation). College of William and Mary, Williamsburg, VA.

Goss, R. (1993). *Jesus ACT UP: A gay and lesbian manifesto.* San Francisco, CA: HarperSanFrancisco.

Governor Cuomo and Mayor de Blasio announce affordable housing protection for low-income New Yorkers living with HIV/AIDS [Press release]. (2014, February 13). Retrieved from http://www.governor.ny.gov/press/02132014-affordable-housing-protection

Graeber, D. (2009). *Direct action: An ethnography.* New York, NY: AK Press.

Gramsci, A. (1971). *Selections from the Prison Notebooks.* New York, NY: International Publishers.

Griffiths, J. (2013, March). The politics of play. *Orion Magazine.* Retrieved from http://www.orionmagazine.org/index.php/articles/article/7379/

Grineski, S. (2006). Local struggles for environmental justice: Activating knowledge for change. *Journal of Poverty, 10*(3), 25–49.

Grove, D. (1997). [Plenary speech]. New York City ACT UP 10 Year Anniversary AIDS Activist Conference March 22. Retrieved from http://www.actupny.org/diva/CBgrove.html

Groves, T. (2003). Direct action casework manual. *Ontario Coalition Against Poverty.* Retrieved from http://ocap.ca/node/322

Gusfield, J. R. (1986). *Symbolic crusade: Status politics and the American temperance movement* (2nd ed.). Urbana: University of Illinois Press.

Guy, A. (2004). Case advocacy and active citizenship. *BCASW Summer Newsletter.* Retrieved from http://www.vcn.bc.ca/seatosky/advocacy.pdf

Habermas, J. (1991). *The structural transformation of the public sphere.* Cambridge, MA: MIT Press. (Original work published 1962)

Hall, S., Critcher, C., Jefferson, T., Clarke, J., & Roberts, B., et al. (1978). *Policing the crisis.* New York, NY: Holmes and Meier Publishers.

Halperin, D. (1995). *St. Foucault.* New York, NY: Oxford University Press.

Hammett, J., & Hammett, K. (2007). *The suburbanization of New York.* Princeton, NJ: Princeton Architectural Press.

Hanna, M., & Robinson, B. (1994). *Strategies for community empowerment: Direct action and transformative approaches to social change practice.* Lewiston, NY: Edwin Mellon Press.

Harm reduction and steps toward change. (1999). *Training and resource book: Substance use counseling and education.* New York, NY: Gay Men's Health Crisis.

Harm Reduction Coalition. (n.d.). *Principles of harm reduction.* Retrieved from http://harmreduction .org/about-us/principles-of-harm-reduction/

Harvey, D. (2010, May). Organizing for the anti-capitalist transition. *Interface: A Journal For and About Social Movements, 2*(1), 243–261.

Hasenfeld, Y. (1987). Power in social work practice. *Social Service Review, 619*(3), 469–483.

Hasenfeld, Y., & Gidron, B. (2005). Understanding multi-purpose hybrid voluntary organizations: The contributions of theories on civil society, social movements, and non-profit organizations. *Journal of Civil Society, 1*(2), 97–112.

Hausman, B. (1995). *Changing sex.* Durham, NC: Duke University Press.

Haynes, K. S., & Mickelson, J. S. (2002). *Affecting change: Social workers in the political arena.* Boston, MA: Allyn and Bacon.

Heckerling, A. (1995). *Clueless: Memorable quotes.* Retrieved from http://www.imdb.com/title/ tt0112697/quotes

Heimer, R., Kaplan, E. H., & Cadman, E. (1992). Prevalence of HIV-infected syringes during a syringe-exchange program. *New England Journal of Medicine, 327*(26), 1883–1884.

Heller, D., McCoy, K., & Cunningham, C. (2004, January-February). An invisible barrier to integrating HIV primary care with harm reduction services: Philosophical clashes between the harm reduction and medical models. *Public Health Reports, 119*(1), 32–39.

Heller, D., & Shepard, B. (2001). *The CitiWide Harm Reduction HOME model of services.* [Position paper in a private collection].

Henderson, P. (2007). Introduction. In H. Butcher, P. Henderson, & J. Robertson (Eds.), *Critical community practice* (pp. 1–16). Bristol, UK: The Policy Press.

Hercules, B., & Orenstein, B. (1999). *The democratic promise: Saul Alinski and his legacy.* PBS. Retrieved from http://www.deepdyve.com/lp/sage/the-democratic-promise-saul-alins ki-and-his-legacy-media-process-6HTqfd1tsM

Hilmer, J. (2010). Anarchy: Past and present. *Anarchist Studies, 18*(1), 102–106.

History Matters. (n.d.). "To determine the destiny of our Black community": The Black Panther Party's 10-Point Platform and Program. Retrieved from http://historymatters.gmu .edu/d/6445/

Hollibaugh, A. (2000). Sexuality and the state: The defeat of the Briggs initiative. In *My dangerous desires.* Durham, NC: Duke University Press. (Original work published 1979)

Holtzman, B., Hughes, C., & Van Meter, K. (2004). Do it yourself . . . and the movement beyond capitalism. *Radical Society, 31*(1), 7–20.

Homan, M. S. (2008). *Promoting community change: Making it happen in the real world* (4th ed.). Pacific Grove, CA: Brooks/Cole.

Homan, M. S. (2011). *Promoting community change: Making it happen in the real world* (5th ed.). Pacific Grove, CA: Brooks/Cole.

Hooker, E. (1957). The adjustment of the male overt homosexual. *Journal of Projective Techniques, 21*, 18–31.

Horton, A. I. (1989). *The Highlander Folk School: A history of its major programs, 1932–1961* (Martin Luther King, Jr. and the Civil Rights Movement Series, Vol. 13). Brooklyn, NY: Carlson Publishing.

Horwitt, S. (n.d.). Alinsky: More important now than ever. Retrieved from http://comm-org .wisc.edu/papers97/horwitt.htm

HUD Office of HIV/AIDS Housing. (n.d.). *Housing opportunities for people with AIDS.* Retrieved from http://portal.hud.gov/hudportal/HUD?src=/program_offices/comm_planning/ aidshousing

Hudema, M. (2004). *An action a day keeps global capitalism away.* Toronto, Ontario, Canada: Between the Lines.

Icarus Project. (2006). Icarus Project mission statement. Retrieved from http://theicarusproject .net/about-us/icarus-project-mission-statement

Incite! Women of Color Against Violence. (2007). *The revolution will not be funded.* Cambridge, MA: South End Press.

Jacobs, R. (2002). *Race, media and the crisis of civil society.* New York, NY: Oxford University Press.

Jacoby, B., & Associates. (2009). *Civil engagement in higher education: Concepts and practices.* San Francisco, CA: Jossey-Bass.

Jagose, A. (1996). *Queer theory: An introduction.* New York: New York University Press.

Janis, I. L. (1971, November). Groupthink. *Psychology Today,* 43–46.

Jay, M. (1973). *The dialectical imagination: A history of the Frankfurt school and the Institute of Social Research, 1923–1950.* Boston, MA: Little, Brown.

Jimenez, J. (2010). *Social policy and social change.* Thousand Oaks, CA: Sage.

Johnson, A. (2001). Self emancipation and leadership: The case of MLK. In C. Barker, A. Johnson, & M. Lavalette (Eds.), *Leadership and social movements* (pp. 96–115). Manchester, UK: Manchester University Press.

Jones, C. (2001). *Stitching a revolution: The making of an activist.* San Francisco, CA: HarperOne.

Juris, J. (2007). Practicing militant ethnography. In S. Shukaitis & D. Graeber (Eds.), *Constituent imagination* (pp. 164–178). Oakland, CA: AK Press.

Juris, J. (2008). *Networking futures: The movements against corporate globalization.* Durham, NC: Duke University Press.

Kahn, S. (1970). *How people get power.* New York. NY: McGraw-Hill.

Kahn, S. (1995). Community organization. In R. L. Edwards & J. G. Hopps (Eds.), *Encyclopedia of social work* (19th ed.). Washington, DC: NASW Press.

Katsiaficas, G. (2004). Seattle was not the beginning. In E. Yuen, D. Burton-Rose, & G. Katsiaficas (Eds.), *Confronting capitalism: Dispatches from a global movement* (pp. 3–10). New York, NY: Soft Skull Press.

Kauffman, L. A. (2004). A short, personal history of the global justice movement. In E. Yuen, D. Burton-Rose, & G. Katsiaficas (Eds.), *Confronting capitalism: Dispatches from a global movement* (pp. 275–288). New York, NY: Soft Skull Press.

Kettner, P. M., Moroney, R., & Martin, L. L. (1999). *Designing and managing programs: An effectiveness-based approach* (2nd ed.). Thousand Oaks, CA: Sage.

Kifner, J. (1999, December 20). Giuliani's hunt for red menaces. *New York Times,* p. B3.

King, M. L., Jr. (1963). *Letter from Birmingham Jail.* Retrieved from http://web.cn.edu/kwheeler/ documents/Letter_Birmingham_Jail.pdf

Kingsbury, K. (2011, May 19). Subject: [HEALTHGAP] WMA/IFHHRO call for end to incarceration as treatment for drug users. Retrieved from https://lists.critpath.org/pipermail/ healthgap/2011-May/002632.html

Klar, M., & Kasser, T. (2009). Some benefits of being an activist: Measuring activism and its role in psychological well-being. *Political Psychology, 30*(5), 755–777.

Klein, N., & Levy, D. A. (2002). *Fences and windows: Dispatches from the front lines of the globalization debate.* New York, NY: Picador.

Knickmeyer, R. (1972, July). A Marxist approach to social work. *Social Work,* 58–65.

Kretzmann, J. P., & McKnight, J. (1993). *Building communities from the inside out: A path toward finding and mobilizing a community's assets.* Chicago, IL: ACTA Publications.

Kropotkin, P. (1902). Mutual aid: A factor of evolution. *Project Gutenberg.* Retrieved from http://www.gutenberg.org/etext/4341

Krugman, P. (2009, August 8). The town hall mob. *The Global Edition of the New York Times,* p. 7.

Kupfer, D. (2011). Pete Seeger on the power of songs: An interview. *People's World.* Retrieved from http://peoplesworld.org/pete-seeger-on-the-power-of-songs-an-interview/

Lantos, B. (1943). Work and the instincts. *International Journal of Psychoanalysis, 24,* 114–119.

Lasn, K. (1999). *Culture jam: How to reverse America's suicidal consumer binge–And why we must.* New York, NY: Harper Paperbacks.

Lease, M. E. (2004). Wall Street still owns the country. In H. Zinn & A. Arnove (Eds.), *Voices of a people's history of the United States* (p. 226). New York, NY: Seven Stories Press. (Original work published 1890)

Lee, A., & Ettinger, M. (2006, May/June). Lessons for the Left from the radical transgender movement. *Left Turn.* Retrieved from http://leftturn.org/backissue&tid=206

Lee, C. W. (2010, March 18). Bake-in! Lower Manhattan, 4 P.M. [Web log post]. *The New York Times Blog.* Retrieved from http://cityroom.blogs.nytimes.com/2010/03/18/bake-in/

Lefebvre, H. (2003). *The urban revolution.* Minneapolis: University of Minnesota Press.

Lens, V., & Gibelman, M. (2000). Advocacy be not forsaken. *Families in Society: The Journal of Contemporary Human Services, 81*(6), 611–619.

Lewis, J., Lewis, M., Daniels, J. A., & D'Andrea, M. (2011). *Community counseling: A multicultural-social justice perspective* (4th ed.). Belmont, CA: Brooks/Cole.

Lewis, M. (2011). Then and now: The importance of play. *Classroom to Capitol.* Retrieved from http://melindaklewis.com/2011/08/09/then-and-now-the-importance-of-play/#comments

Lichtblau, E. (2010, August 18). Killings of homeless rise to highest level in a decade. *New York Times.* Retrieved from http://www.nytimes.com/2010/08/19/us/19homeless.html?_r=1#

Lindhorst, D., & Eckert, A. (2003, June). Conditions for empowering people with severe mental illness. *Social Service Review,* 280–304.

Liukkonen, P. (2008). Authors' calendar. Upton Beall Sinclair (1878–1968). Retrieved from http://www.kirjasto.sci.fi/sinclair.htm

Lovell, J. (2009). *Crimes of dissent: Civil disobedience, criminal justice, and the politics of conscience.* New York: New York University Press.

Löwy, M. (2006, August 31). Marx, Weber and the critique of capitalism. *International Viewpoint.* Retrieved from http://www.internationalviewpoint.org/spip.php?article1106

Lyon, J. (2001, November). Back to the old neighborhood: The founder of a needle exchange dies from a dose. June/July 1996: Needle exchange renegade Brian Weil helped transform public health in New York. *CitiLimits.* Retrieved from http://www.citylimits.org/news/article_print.cfm?article_id=2561

Mail on Sunday Reporter. (2012). Wheelchair users chain themselves together and blocked central London over welfare cuts. *Daily Mail Online.* Retrieved from http://www.dailymail.co.uk/news/article-2093286/Wheelchair-users-chained-blocked-central-London-welfare-cuts.html

Mananzala, R., & Spade, D. (2008, March). The nonprofit industrial complex and trans resistance. *Sexuality Research & Social Policy, 5*(1), 53–71.

Marcuse, H. (1964). *One dimensional man: Studies in the ideology of advanced industrial society.* Boston, MA: Beacon Press.

Marcuse, H. (1978). *The aesthetic dimension.* Boston, MA: Beacon Press.

Margolin, L. (1997). *Under the cover of kindness: The invention of social work*. Charlottesville: University of Virginia Press.

Marina. (2004). [Movement dynamics letter]. Posted to Direct Action Network List Serve 8/10.

Marlatt, G. A. (2002). *Harm reduction: Pragmatic strategies for managing high risk behaviors*. New York, NY: Guilford Press.

Marx, K. (1845). *Theses on Feuerbach*. Retrieved from http://www.marxists.org/archive/marx/works/1845/theses/index.htm

Mary. (2010). Gay shame "department of mental security." *Indybay.org*. Retrieved from http://www.indybay.org/newsitems/2010/10/15/18661471.php

Mateik, T., & Gaberman, D. (2002). *Sylvia Rivera tribute tape* [Video]. New York, NY: Paper Tiger TV.

Mattilda, AKA Matt Bernstein Sycamore. (2004). *That's revolting: Queer strategies for resisting assimilation*. Brooklyn, NY: Soft Skull Press.

McAdam, D. (1996). The framing function of movement tactics: Strategic dramaturgy in the American civil rights movement. In D. McAdam, J. D. McCarthy, & M. N. Zald (Eds.), *Comparative perspectives on social movements*. Cambridge, UK: Cambridge University Press.

McAdam, D., McCarthy, J. D., Zald, M. N., & Mayer, N. (1988). Social movements. In N. J. Smelser (Ed.), *Handbook of sociology* (pp. 695–730). Newbury Park, CA. Sage.

McArdle, A., & Erzen, T. (Eds.). (2001). *Zero tolerance: Quality of life and the new police brutality in New York City*. New York, NY: New York University Press.

McCarthy, J., & Zald, M. N. (1973). *The trend of social movements in America: Professionalization and resource mobilization*. Morristown, NJ: General Learning Press.

McCracken, G. (1988). *The long interview*. Newbury Park, CA: Sage.

McKnight, J. (1987). Regenerating community. *Social Policy, 17*(3), 54–58.

McKnight, J. (1995). *The careless society: Community and its counterfeits*. New York, NY: Basic Books.

Mele, C. (2000). *Selling the Lower East Side*. Minneapolis: Minnesota University Press.

Melendez, M. (2003). *We took the streets: Fighting for Latino rights*. New York, NY: St. Martin's.

Merrifield, A. (2002). *Metromarxism: A Marxist tale of the city*. New York, NY: Routledge.

Merton, R. (1936). The unintended consequences of purposive social action. *American Sociological Review, 1*(6), 894–904.

Meyer, J. W., & Rowan, B. (1977). Institutional organizations: Formal structure as myth and ceremony. *American Journal of Sociology, 83*, 340–363.

Midwest Academy. (n.d.). Direct action organizing. Accessed October 1, 2007 from http://www.midwestacademy.com/direct_action_organizing.html

Milano, M. (2009, September 17). From: Mark M <marknyc@hotmail.com> To: Mark M <marknyc@hotmail.com> Subject: Health Care action on the 29th—a personal note from Mark Milano. Date: Sep 17, 2009 5:13 PM.

Miller, J. (2002). A narrative interview with Richard A. Cloward. *Reflections: Narratives of Professional Healing, 8*(1), 44–64.

Mills, C. W. (1959). *The sociological imagination*. Oxford, UK: Oxford University Press.

Minkoff, D. (2002). The emergence of hybrid organizational forms: Combining identity based service provision and political action. *Nonprofit and Voluntary Sector Quarterly, 31*(3), 377–401.

Mitchell, S. (1988). *Relational concepts in psychoanalysis: An integration*. Cambridge, MA: Harvard University Press.

Moch, M.. ((2009). A critical understanding of social work by Paolo Freire. *Journal of Progressive Human Services, 20*(1), 92–97.

Mohai, P. (2003). Dispelling myths: African American concern for the environment. *Environment, 45*(5), 11–21.

Montifiore Medical Center. (2001). SPNS outreach evaluation proposal. Project Title: Outreach and Intervention Program to Reach HIV Infected Persons Living in Bronx New York Single Room Occupancy Hotels. Project Director: Chinazo Cunningham, MD. Co-Project Director: Daliah Heller, MPH.

Moody, K. (2007). *From welfare state to real estate*. New York, NY: The New Press.

Moore, K., & Shepard, B. (2012). Direct action. In D. A. Snow, D. della Porta, B. Kinderman, & D. McAdam (Eds.), *The encyclopedia of social and political movements*. London, UK: Wiley-Blackwell.

Moore, K., & Young, M. (2002). *Organizing and organization in the new sociology of social movements*. Unpublished manuscript. Available from lead author at kmoore11@luc.edu.

Moore, P. (2004). *Beyond shame: Reclaiming the abandoned history of radical gay sexuality*. Boston, MA: Beacon Press.

Morgan, G. (2006). *Images of organization*. Thousand Oaks, CA: Sage.

Morone, J. A. (2003). *Hellfire nation: The politics of sin in American history*. New Haven, CT: Yale University Press.

Moynihan, C. (2012, January 6). Documenter Of Protests Has Run-In of His Own. *New York Times*, p. A23.

Mullaly, R. (1993). *Structural social work*. Toronto, Ontario, Canada: McClelland and Stewart.

Nachmanovitch, S. (1990). *Free play: Improvisation in life and art*. New York, NY: Tarcher and Putnam.

Nardi, P. (1999). *Gay men's friendships: Invincible communities*. Chicago, IL: University of Chicago Press.

NASW Foundation. (n.d.). *NASW social work pioneers. Bertha Capen Reynolds*. Retrieved from http://www.naswfoundation.org/pioneers/r/reynolds.htm

National Organization for Human Services. (1996). Council for standards in human service education adopted 1996. *National Organization for Human Services*. Retrieved from http://www.nationalhumanservices.org/mc/page.do?sitePageId=89927&orgId=nohs

Ness, I. (2005). *Immigrants, unions, and the new US labor market*. Philadelphia, PA: Temple University Press.

Netting, F. E., Kettner, P. M., & McMurtry, S. L. (2004). *Social work: Macro practice* (3rd ed.). Boston, MA: Pearson Education.

New Alternatives for LGBT Homeless Youth. (2011). Social Services. Retrieved from http://www.newalternativesnyc.org/services/

Niebuhr, R. (1932). *Moral man and immoral society: A study of ethics and politics*. New York, NY: Scribner's.

NY1 News. (2010). SoHo detention rally ends in 10 arrests. NY1 News. Retrieved January 5, 2010, from http://ny1.com/5-manhattan-news-content/top_stories/111547/soho-detention-rally-ends-in-10-arrests

Ochs, E., & Capps, L. (1996). Narrating the self. *Annual Review of Anthropology, 25*, 19–43.

O'Donnell, J., Ferreira, J., Hurtado, E. A., & Floyd, R. E. (1998). Partners for change: Community residents and agencies. *Journal of Sociology and Social Welfare, 25*(1), 133–151.

Ollman, B. (1977). *Alienation: Marx's conception of man in a capitalistic society*. Cambridge, UK: Cambridge University Press.

Ostrom, E. (1990). *Governing the commons: The evolution of institutions for collective action*. New York, NY: Cambridge University Press.

Ostrom, E. (1992). *Crafting institutions for self-governing irrigation systems*. San Francisco, CA: Institute for Contemporary Studies.

Otterman, S. (2010, February 23). No brownies at bake sales, but Doritos may be O.K [Web log post]. *New York Times Blog*. Retrieved from http://cityroom.blogs.nytimes.com/2010/02/23/no-brownies-at-bake-sales-but-doritos-may-be-o-k/

Panayotakis, C. (2011). *Remaking scarcity*. London, UK: Pluto Press.

Pappas, S. (2013). Bondage benefits. *Live Wire*. Retrieved from http://www.livescience .com/34832-bdsm-healthy-psychology.html

Patterson, C. (2012, January 5). Videotaping '88 park riot turned me into an activist. *The Villager*. Retrieved from http://www.thevillager.com/?p=1420

Patterson, C. (Ed.). (2006). *Resistance*. New York, NY: Seven Stories Press.

Patton, M. Q. (2001). *Qualitative research and evaluation methods*. Thousand Oaks, CA: Sage.

Payne, C. (1995). *I've got the light of freedom: The organizing tradition of the Mississippi civil rights movement*. Berkeley: University of California Press.

Pelofsky, J. (2009, July 10). U.S. House Democrats eye funding for needle exchanges. *Reuters*. Retrieved from http://www.reuters.com/article/2009/07/10/us-usa-budget-needles-idUS TRE5694WU20090710

Perez, R. (2000). A young lord remembers. *Boricua Tributes*. Retrieved from http://www .virtualboricua.org/Docs/perez_00.htm.

Phelan, S. (2010, June 28). SF human services agency occupied. *San Francisco Bay Guardian Online*. Retrieved from http://www.sfbg.com/politics/2010/06/28/sf-human-services -agency-occupied

Piven, F. F. (2006). *Challenging authority: How ordinary people change America*. Lanham, MD: Roman and Littlefield.

Piven, F. F., & Cloward, R. (1977). *Poor people's movements: Why they succeed, how they fail*. New York, NY: Vintage.

Piven, F. F., & Cloward, R. (1993). *Regulating the poor*. New York, NY: Vintage.

Plummer, K. (1995). *Telling sexual stories*. New York, NY: Routledge.

Polletta, F. (2006). *It was like a fever: Storytelling in protest and politics*. Chicago, IL: University of Chicago Press.

Prokosch, M., & Raymond, L. (2002). *The global activist's manual: Local ways to change the world*. New York, NY: Nation Books.

Putnam, R. D. (2000). *Bowling alone: The collapse and revival of American community*. New York, NY: Simon & Schuster.

Pyles, L. (2009). *Progressive community organizing: A critical approach for a globalizing world*. New York, NY: Routledge.

Quick, P. (2011, October 23). URPE supports Occupy Wall Street [Web log post]. URPE's Blog Hub. Retrieved from http://urpe.wordpress.com/2011/12/13/urpe-supports-occupy-wall-street/

Quilitch, R., & Risley, R. (1973). The effects of play materials on social play. *Journal of Applied Behavior Analysis, 6*, 573–578.

Ramirez, M. (2010). Pentecostal Bishop Arthur Brazier dies at 89. 22 October. Retrieved from http://archive.chicagobreakingnews.com/2010/10/pentecostal-bishop-arthur-brazier-dies -at-89.html

Ransby, B. (2003). *Ella Baker and the Black Freedom Movement: A Radical Democratic Vision*. Chapel Hill, NC: University of North Carolina Press.

Rattner, S. (2012, March 25). The rich get even richer. *New York Times*. Retrieved from http:// www.nytimes.com/2012/03/26/opinion/the-rich-get-even-richer.html?_r=0

Read, K. (2006). *Learning history by half-light*. Retrieved November 1, 2006, from http://www .kirkread.com/1998

Reason, P., & Bradbury, H. (2001). *Handbook of action research: Participative inquiry and practice*. Thousand Oaks, CA: Sage.

Reclaim the Streets. (n.d.). How to sort a street party. Retrieved from http://webcache.googleuser content.com/search?q=cache:xxHaKlsO2poJ:www.tacticalmediafiles.net/mmbase/attach ments/42264/Reclaim%2520the%2520Streets-%2520How%2520to%2520sort%2520a%2520 street%2520party.pdf+&cd=1&hl=en&ct=clnk&gl=us

Reed, T. V. (2005). *The art of protest: Culture and activism from the Civil Rights Movement to the streets of Seattle*. Minneapolis: University of Minnesota Press.

Reel, M. (2003, February 22). Seniors, peaceniks, punks set to share turf in Shaw Center targets groups' common ground. *Washington Post,* p. B01.

Reeser, L. C., & Epstein, I. (1990). *Professionalization and activism in social work: The sixties, the eighties, and the future.* New York. NY: Columbia University Press.

Reich, W. (1980). *The mass psychology of fascism.* New York, NY: Farrar, Straus & Giroux.

Reilly, M. (Ed.). (1974). *Play as exploratory learning.* Beverly Hills, CA: Sage.

Reisch, M. (1987). From cause to case and back again: The reemergence of advocacy in social work. *The Urban and Social Change Review, 19,* 20–24.

Reisch, M., & Andrews, J. (2002). *The road less taken: A history of radical social work in the United States.* New York: Brunner-Routledge.

Reynolds, B. C. (1963). *An unchartered journey.* New York, NY: Citadel Press.

Reynolds, P. (1984, Spring). Cultural animation: "Just plain folks" building culture—rather than just consuming it. Art and ceremony in sustainable culture. *Context Institute,* (IC#5), 32.

Ritzer, G. (1993). *The McDonaldization of society.* Newbury Park, CA: Sage.

Roberts, S. (2011, September 22). One in five New York City residents living in poverty. *New York Times.* Retrieved from http://www.nytimes.com/2011/09/22/nyregion/one-in-five-new-york-city-residents-living-in-poverty.html

Robinson, J. G. (1987). *The Montgomery bus boycott and the women who started it.* Knoxville: University of Tennessee Press.

Rofes, E. (1997, November 16). *The emerging sex panic targeting gay men.* Speech given at the National Gay and Lesbian Task Force's Creating Change Conference, San Diego, California.

Rorty, R. (1982). *The consequences of pragmatism.* Minneapolis: University of Minnesota Press.

Rosenberg, M. (2003). *Non-violent communication: A language of life.* New York, NY: Puddledancer Press.

Rothman, J. (1995). Approaches to community intervention (locality development, social planning, social action). In J. Rothman, J. L. Erlich, & J. E. Tropman (Eds.), *Strategies of community intervention* (5th ed.). Itasca, IL: F. E. Peacock.

Rubin, H. J., & Rubin, I. (2007). *Community organizing and development* (3rd ed.). Boston, MA: Allyn and Bacon.

Ruckus Society. (2011). *Check list for effective direct action media.* Retrieved from http://www.ruckus.org/article.php?id=107

Saini, A. N. (2009, September 14). Service providers question ability to meet needs: Nonprofit leaders wonder when "something is going to snap" in the city's social services due to funding cuts. *City Limits.* Retrieved from http://www.citylimits.org/news/article.cfm?article_id=3803

Saleeby, D. (1994). Culture, theory and narrative: The intersections of meanings in practice. *Social Work, 39*(4), 351–359.

Saleeby, D. (Ed.). (1996). *The strengths perspective in social work practice.* New York, NY: Longman.

Saul, M. (2005, August 31). 1 in 5 NYers live below the poverty line. *New York Daily News,* p. 12.

Sawyer, E. (2004). Oral history with Eric Sawyer. *ACT UP Oral History Project.* Retrieved from http://actuporalhistory.org/beta/interviews/images/sawyer.pdf

Schiavi, M. (2011). *Celluloid activist: The life and times of Vito Russo.* Madison: University of Wisconsin Press.

Schon, D. (1987). *Educating the reflective practitioner.* San Francisco, CA: Jossey-Bass.

Schram, S. (2002). *Praxis for the poor: Piven and Cloward and the future of social science and social welfare.* New York: New York University Press.

Schubert, G., & Hombs, M. E. (1995, November/December). Housing Works: Housing opportunities for homeless persons. *Clearinghouse Review,* pp. 740–751.

Schulman, S. (2008). Interview of Karen Ramspacher. *ACT UP Oral History Project.* Retrieved from http://actuporalhistory.org/interviews/images/ramspacher.pdf

Schulman, S. (2002). The reproductive rights movement. In B. Shepard & R. Hayduk (Eds.), *From ACT UP to the WTO: Urban protest and community building in the era of globalization* (pp. 133–140). New York, NY: Verso.

Scott, J. (1985). *Weapons of the weak: Everyday forms of peasant resistance.* New Haven, CT: Yale University Press.

Scott, J. (1990). *Domination and the arts of resistance: Hidden transcripts.* New Haven, CT: Yale University Press.

Seale, B. (1970). *Seize the time: The story of the Black Panther Party and Huey P. Newton.* New York, NY: Random House.

Sedgwick, E. (1991). *Epistemology of the closet.* Berkeley: University of California Press.

Seifman, D. (2013, April 9). City settles "Occupy" lawsuit for $3350K. *New York Post.* Retrieved from http://www.nypost.com/p/news/local/city_settles_occupy_lawsuit_for_UwR3B19 O3hSHd0Lo4DRpeO

Self, R. (2003). *American Babylon: Race and the struggle for postwar Oakland.* Princeton, NJ: Princeton University Press.

Sellers, J. (2004). Raising a ruckus. In T. Muertes (Ed.), *Movement of movements: Is another world really possible?* (pp. 175–191). New York, NY: Verso.

Semple, K. (2010, January 15). Demonstrators press for Haitian advocates release. *New York Times,* p. A22.

Sen, K. (2003). *Stir it up: Lessons in community organizing and advocacy.* San Francisco, CA: Jossey-Bass.

Sen, K., & Mamdouh, F. (2008). *The accidental American: Immigration and citizenship in the age of globalization.* San Francisco, CA: Berrett-Koehler.

Shaw, C. (1930). *The jack-roller: A delinquent boy's own story.* Chicago, IL: University of Chicago Press.

Shaw, C. (1939). *Chicago Area Project: An experimental neighborhood program for the prevention and treatment of juvenile delinquency and crime.* Chicago, IL: University of Chicago.

Shaw, R. (2001). *The activists' manual: A primer.* Berkeley: University of California Press.

Shdaimah, C. S., Stahl, R. W., & Schram, S. S. (2011). *Change research: A case study on collaboration between social workers and advocates.* New York, NY: Columbia University Press.

Shepard, B. (1997a). *In search of the community in community organizing: An oral history of the Chicago Area Project.* Unpublished manuscript. Completed as part of the Master's Program at the University of Chicago School of Social Services Administration.

Shepard, B. (1997b). *White nights and ascending shadows: An oral history of the San Francisco AIDS epidemic.* London, UK: Cassell Press.

Shepard, B. (2002a). Amanda Milan and the rebirth of the Street Trans Action Revolutionaries. In B. Shepard & R. Hayduk (Eds.), *From ACT UP to the WTO: Urban protest and community building in the era of globalization* (pp. 156–163). New York, NY: Routledge.

Shepard, B. (2002b). Building a healing community from ACT UP to Housing Works: An interview with Keith Cylar. In B. Shepard & R. Hayduk (Eds.), *From ACT UP to the WTO: Urban protest and community building in the era of globalization* (pp. 351–360). New York, NY: Verso.

Shepard, B. (2002c). The reproductive rights movement, ACT UP, and the Lesbian Avengers: An interview with Sarah Schulman. In B. Shepard & R. Hayduk(Eds.), *From ACT UP to the WTO: Urban protest and community building in the era of globalization.* New York, NY: Verso.

Shepard, B. (2003a). Absurd responses versus earnest politics. *The Journal of Aesthetics and Protest, 1*(2), 95–115.

Shepard, B. (2003b, February 18). Breaking through the panic: An afterward to February 15. *Counterpunch.* Retrieved from http://www.counterpunch.org/shepard02182003.html

Shepard, B. (2003c). From global justice to antiwar and back again: A personal chronicle of a season of "better to laugh than cry" antiwar activism. *Journal of Aesthetics and Protest,*

1(2 web special). Retrieved September 14, 2005, from http://www.journalofaestheticsand protest.org/1/shepard2/

Shepard, B. (2004). Sylvia and Sylvia's children. In Mattilda aka M. B. Sycamore (Ed.), *That's revolting: Queer strategies for resisting assimilation* (pp. 123–140). Brooklyn, NY: Soft Skull Press.

Shepard, B. (2005a). Play, creativity, and the new community organizing. *Journal of Progressive Human Services* (formerly *The Catalyst*), *16*(2), 47–69.

Shepard, B. (2005b). The use of joy as a community organizing strategy. *Peace and Change: A Journal of Peace Research, 30*(4), 435–468.

Shepard, B. (2006). Not quite queer. In Mattilda aka M. B. Sycamore (Ed.), *Nobody passes: Rejecting the rules of gender and conformity.* Emoryville, CA: Seal Press.

Shepard, B. (2007a). Harm reduction outreach services and engagement of chemically dependent homeless people living with HIV/AIDS: An analysis of service utilization data to evaluate program theory. *Einstein Journal of Biology and Medicine, 23*(1), 26–32.

Shepard, B. (2007b). Sex panic and the welfare state. *Journal of Sociology and Social Welfare, 34*(1), 155–172.

Shepard, B (2008a). Housing works, shelter kills: An oral history of Housing Works. *Reflections: Narratives of Professional Helping, 14*(1), 4–14.

Shepard, B. (2008b). On challenging authority: An oral history interview with Frances Fox Piven. *Reflections: Narratives of Professional Helping, 14*(2), 3–15.

Shepard, B. (2009). *Queer politics and political performance: Play, pleasure and social movement.* New York, NY: Routledge.

Shepard, B. (2010). Reviving the tribe: Friendship and social relations in the work and play of Eric Rofes theory in action. *Theory in Action, 3*(3), 21.

Shepard, B. (2011a, March 23). In defense of the silly. *Huffington Post.* Retrieved from http://www.huffingtonpost/benjamin-shepard/times-up-nyc-pies of march_b_839389.html

Shepard, B. (2011b). *Play, creativity, and social movements: If I can't dance, it's not my revolution.* New York, NY: Routledge.

Shepard, B. (2012a, October). From social movement to community organization: The Street Trans Action Revolutionaries to Sylvia Rivera Law Project. *Journal of Social Service Research,* 1–20.

Shepard, B. (2012b). Community gardens, creative community organizing and environmental activism. In M. Gray, J. Coates, & T. Hetherington (Eds.), *Environmental social work* (pp. 121–134). London, UK: Routledge.

Shepard, B. (2013). From flooded neighborhoods to sustainable urbanism: A New York diary. *Socialism and Democracy, 27*(2), 42–64.

Shepard, B. (2015). *Rebel friendships: "Outsider" networks and social movements.* New York, NY: Palgrave.

Shepard, B., & Hayduk, R. (Eds.). (2002). *From ACT UP to the WTO: Urban protest in the era of globalization.* New York, NY: Verso.

Shepard, B., & Smithsimon, G. (2011). *The beach beneath the streets: Exclusion, control and play in public space.* New York: State University Press of New York.

Shichor, D. (1997). Three strikes as a public policy. *Crime and Delinquency, 43*(4), 470.

Shirky, C. (2008). *Here comes everybody: The power of organizing without organizations.* New York, NY: Penguin.

Shukaitis, S. (2008). Dancing amidst the flames: Imagination and self organization in a minor key. *Organization, 15*(5), 743–764.

Shukaitis, S. (2009). *Imaginal machines: Autonomy and self-organization in the revolutions of everyday life.* New York, NY: Minor Compositions.

Siplon, P. (2002). *AIDS and the policy struggle in the United States.* Washington, DC: Georgetown University Press.

Sites, W. (2003). *Remaking New York: Primitive globalization and the politics of urban community.* Minneapolis: University of Minnesota Press.

Smith, A. (2006, May/June). Beyond inclusion: Recentering feminism. *Left Turn, 20*(4).

Smith, N. (1996). *The new urban frontier.* New York, NY: Routledge.

Smith, R. (1996, February 8). Brian Weil, 41, photographer who founded needle exchange. *New York Times.* Retrieved from http://www.nytimes.com/1996/02/08/nyregion/brian-weil-41-photographer-who-founded-needle-exchange.html?pagewanted=print

Smith, R. A., & Siplon, T. (2006). *Drugs into bodies: Global treatment activism.* Westport, CT: Praeger.

Solnit, D. (2004). Introduction: Globalize liberation. In D. Solnit (Ed.), *Globalize liberation* (pp. xi-xxiv). San Francisco, CA: City Lights Press.

Solnit, R. (2005). *Hope in the dark: Untold histories, wild possibilities.* New York, NY: Nation Books.

Sonnie, A., & Tracy, J. (2011). *Hillbilly nationalists, urban race rebels, and Black power.* New York. NY: Mellville Press.

Spade, D. (2004). Fighting to win. In Mattilda aka M. B. Sycamore (Ed.), *That's revolting* (pp. 31–38). Brooklyn, NY: Soft Skull Press.

Spade, D. (2006). For lovers and fighters. In M. Berger (Ed.), *We don't want another wave* (pp. 28–39). Oakland, CA: AK Press.

Spade, D. (2011). *Normal life: Administrative violence, critical trans politics, and the limits of law.* Brooklyn, NY: South End Press.

Specht, H., & Courtney, M. (1994). *Unfaithful angels: How social work has abandoned its mission.* New York, NY: The Free Press.

Spencer, A. (2005). *DIY: The rise of low-fi culture.* London, UK: Marion Boyars Publishers.

Spitzer, E. (2002). Memorandum of agreement between Attorney General and community gardeners. Retrieved May 23, 2004, from http://www.oag.state.ny.us/environment/community_gardens_agreement.pdf

Springer, E. (1991). Effective AIDS prevention with active drug users: The harm reduction model. In M. Shernoff (Ed.), *Counseling chemically dependent people with HIV/AIDS* (pp. 141–158). Binghamton, NY: Haworth Press.

Springer, E. (n.d.). Intermediate harm reduction. In *Skill building for behavior change.* New York, NY: Harm Reduction Training Institute.

Starhawk. (2000, Summer). Spirals: How to conjure justice. *Reclaiming Quarterly,* 59 Retrieved from http://www.reclaimingquarterly.org/web/starhawk/RQ79-32-Starhawk-SpiralsWTO.pdf

Starhawk. (2004). A feminist view of global justice. In D. Solnit (Ed.), *Globalize liberation* (pp. 45–50). San Francisco, CA: City Lights Press.

Stebner, E. (1997). *The women of Hull House: A study in spirituality, vocation, and friendship.* Albany: State University press of New York.

Stedile, J. P. (2003). Brazil's landless battalions. In T. Mertes (Ed.), *A movement of movements: Is another world really possible?* (pp. 17–48). New York, NY: Verso.

Steinberg, D. M. (2004). *The mutual-aid approach to working with groups: Helping people help one another.* New York, NY: Hayworth.

Stoecker, R. (1994). *Defending community: The struggle for alternative redevelopment in Cedar-Riverside.* Philadelphia, PA: Temple University Press.

Stoecker, R. (1996). *The community development corporation model of urban redevelopment: A political economy critique and an alternative.* Retrieved from http://comm-org.utoledo.edu/papers96/cdc.html

Stoecker, R. (2005). *Research methods for community change.* Thousand Oaks, CA: Sage.

Stoller, N. (1998). Lesbian involvement in the AIDS epidemic. In P. Nardi & B. Schneider (Eds.), *Social perspectives in lesbian and gay studies.* New York, NY: Routledge.

Story, L., et al. (2010, January 14). Wall Street helped to mask debts shaking Europe, nations skirted rules, complex deals allowed Greece to overspend fueling a crisis. *New York Times,* p. A1.

Stringer, E. T. (1999). *Action research* (2nd ed.). Thousand Oaks, CA: Sage.

Stryker, S., & Kuskirk, J. V. (1996). *Gay by the Bay.* San Francisco, CA: Chronicle Books.

Stumpe, J., & Davey, M. (2009, May 31). Abortion doctor shot to death in Kansas church. *New York Times.* Retrieved from http://www.nytimes.com/2009/06/01/us/01tiller.html?page wanted=all&_r=0

Sullivan, H. S. (1954). *The psychiatric interview.* New York, NY: W. W. Norton.

Talen, B. (2003). *What happens if Reverend Billy enters my store?* New York, NY: The New Press.

Tatarsky, A. (2002). Harm reduction psychotherapy. In A. Tatarsky (Ed.), *Harm reduction psychotherapy: A new treatment for drugs and alcohol problems* (pp. 16–49). Northvale, NJ: Jason Aronson.

Taylor, F. (1911). *The principles of scientific management.* New York, NY: Harper.

Taylor, M. (2005). *Religion, politics and the Christian Right.* Minneapolis, MN: Augsburg Fortress Publishers.

Teal, D. (1995). *The gay militants.* New York: St. Martin's. (Original work published 1971)

Team Colors (Craig Hughes, Stevie Peace, Kevin Van Meter). (2010). *In the middle of a whirlwind: Movement, movements, and contemporary radical currents in the United States.* Oakland, CA: AK Press.

Tedlock, B. (1991). From participant observation to observation of participation: The emergence of narrative ethnography. *Journal of Anthropological Research, 47,* 69–94.

Thoreau, H. D. (n.d.) On the duty of civil disobedience. Retrieved from http://www.constitution .org/civ/civildis.htm (Originally published 1849 as Resistance to civil government)

Thyer, B. (2011, March). Harmful effects of federal research grants. *Social Work Research, 35,* 3–7.

Tirrant, S. (Ed.). (2007). *Men speak out.* New York, NY: Routledge.

Tobocman, S. (2000). *War in the neighborhood.* New York, NY: Autonomedia.

Tompson, N. (2002). Social movements, social justice and social work. *British Journal of Social Work, 32*(6), 711–722.

Totten, V. (2008, April 5). Re-framing the problems of poverty and homelessness: Paradigm shift. Mid-Atlantic Consortium for Human Services. 5 April.

Treatment Action Campaign. (2001). The Medicines and Related Substances Control Amendment Act 90 of 1997—A step toward ending apartheid in health care.

Tsoi-A-Fatt, R. (2011, September 14). Why the new poverty numbers should be a wake-up call [Opinion]. *The Grio.* Retrieved from http://thegrio.com/2011/09/14/why-new-poverty -numbers-should-be-a-wake-up-call/

Turner, V. (1969). *The ritual process: Structure and anti-structure.* Chicago, IL: Aldine.

Van Kleunen, A. (1994). The squatters: A chorus of voices . . . But is anyone listening? In J. Abu-Lughod (Ed.), *From urban village to East Village: The battle for New York's Lower East Side* (pp. 285–312). Oxford, UK: Blackwell.

Van Rooyen, C. A. J., & Gray, M. M. A. (1995). Participatory research and its compatibility to social work. *Social Work Practitioner-Researcher, 8*(3), 87–93.

Vitale, A. (2008). *City of disorder.* New York: New York University Press.

Vitale, A., & McHenry, K. (1994, September). Food not bombs. *Z Magazine,* 19–21.

VOCAL/NYCAHN. (2009). *Stuck in the system.* Retrieved from http://www.vocal-ny.org/ wp-content/uploads/2013/07/VOCAL-Stuck-in-the-System-Report-Final.pdf

VOCAL/NYCAHN. (n.d.). NYCAHN model. Retrieved from http://www.vocal-ny.org/

Wagner, D. (1989, June). Radical movements in the social services: Toward a theoretical framework. *Social Service Review, 63*(2), 264–284.

Wagner, D. (1990). *The quest for a radical profession: Social service careers and political ideology.* Lanham, MD: University Press of America.

Wagner, D. (1993). *Checkerboard Square: Culture and resistance in a homeless community.* Boulder, CO: Westview Press.

Wagner, D. (2009). Radical social work as conceit. *Journal of Progressive Human Services, 20*(2), 104–106.

Weber, M. (1992). *The Protestant ethic and the spirit of capitalism.* New York, NY: Routledge. (Original work published 1930)

Weissman, H. (1969). *Community development in the mobilization for youth experience.* New York, NY: Association Press.

Weissman, H. (1990). *Serious play: Creativity and innovation in social work.* Silver Spring, MD: National Association of Social Workers Press.

Wenner, M. (2009, January 28). The serious need for play. *The Scientific American.* Retrieved from http://www.sciam.com/article.cfm?id=the-serious-need-for-play

West, C. (2011, August 25). Dr. King weeps from his grave. *New York Times.* http://www.nytimes.com/2011/08/26/opinion/martin-luther-king-jr-would-want-a-revolution-not-a-memorial.html?_r=1

Wettergren, A. (2009). Fun and laughter: Culture jamming and the emotional regime of late capitalism. *Social Movement Studies, 8*(1), 1–15.

Wilder, C. (2001). *A covenant with dolor: Race and social power in Brooklyn.* New York, NY: Columbia University Press.

Wilson, W. J. (1997). *When work disappears: The world of the new urban poor.* New York, NY: Viking.

Winter, R. (2010). Plutocracy reborn: U.S. wealth inequality gap largest since 1928. *Eco Localizer.* Retrieved from http://ecolocalizer.com/2010/04/12/plutocracy-reborn-wealth-inequality-gap-largest-since-1928/

Wolfe, M. (1990). AIDS and politics. In ACT UP/NY and Women AIDS Book Group (Eds.). *Women, AIDS, & activism* (pp. 233–237). Boston, MA: South End Press.

Wood, L. J., & Moore, K. (2002). Target practice–Community activism in a global era. In B. Shepard & R. Hayduk (Eds.), *From ACT UP to the WTO: Urban protest and community building in the era of globalization* (pp. 21–34). New York, NY: Verso.

Wright, S. (2010). Second national survey of violence and discrimination against sexual minorities. *National Coalition for Sexual Freedom.* Retrieved from https://ncsfreedom.org/home-main-menu-1.html

Writers for the 99%. (2011). *Occupying Wall Street: The inside story of the action that changed America.* New York, NY: OR Books.

Yin, R. (1994). *Case study research.* Thousand Oaks, CA: Sage.

Yuen, E., Katsiaficas, G., & Burton Rose, D. (2004). *Confronting capitalism: Dispatches from a global movement.* Brooklyn, NY: Soft Skull Press.

Zald, M., Morrill, C., & Rao, H. (2005). The impact of social movements on organizations: Environmental responses. In G. F. Davis, D. McAdam, W. R. Scott, & M. N. Zald (Eds.), *Social movements and organization theory* (pp. 249–253). Cambridge, UK: Cambridge University Press.

Zinn, H. (1970). The problem is civil disobedience. *Democratic Underground.* Retrieved from http://www.democraticunderground.com/discuss/duboard.php?az=view_all&address=132x3598598

Zinn, H. (2002). *You can't be neutral on a moving train: A personal history of our times.* Boston, MA: Beacon Press.

Zinn, J. (n.d.). John Brown's last speech. *Zinn education project: Teaching a people's history.* Retrieved from http://zinnedproject.org/posts/7671

Index

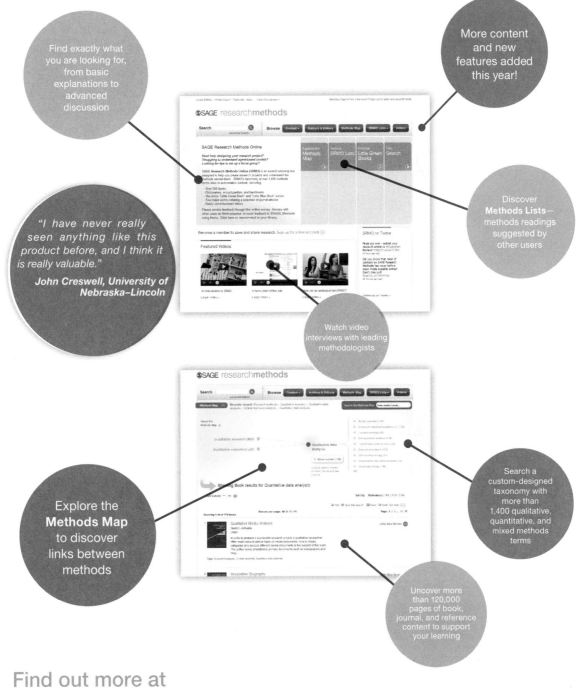